Scholastic Visual Sports Encyclopedia

ISBN 0-439-85933-6

12 11 10 9 8 7 6 5 4 3 2 1   6 7 8 9 10 11/0

Printed in the U.S.A.   66

First Scholastic paperback printing, March 2006

Note: Sports may involve risk of injury. Always use proper safety equipment and participate in sports under appropriate adult/professional supervision.

Scholastic Visual Sports Encyclopedia was created and produced by:

QA International
329, rue de la commune Ouest 3e étage
Montréal (Québec) H2Y 2E1 Canada
T 514.499.3000   F 514.499.3010
www.qa-international.com

Managing editor	Caroline Fortin
Writers	Donna Vekteris Francis Magnenot Martine Podesto
Copyeditor	Ross Peterson
Project manager	Carla Menza Guylaine Houle
Production technician	Sophie Pellerin
Researchers	Gilles Vezina Kathleen Wynd
Content consultant	George Sullivan
Graphic designer	Sylvie Darêche Anne Tremblay
Layout	Véronique Boisvert Geneviève Théroux Béliveau Pascal Goyette
Art director	Jean-Yves Ahern
Assistant art director	Claude Thivierge
Computer-graphics supervisors	Jocelyn Gardner Rielle Lévesque Michel Rouleau
Illustrators	Yan Bohler Mélanie Boivin Charles Campeau Mivil Deschênes Martin Desrosiers Jonathan Jacques Danièle Lemay Alain Lemire Martin Lortie Raymond Martin Annie Maurice Nicolas Oroc Frédérick Simard Yan Tremblay Mathieu Blouin Sébastien Dallaire Hoang Khanh Le Anne-Marie Ouellette Pierre Savoie Mamadou Togol

Scholastic Visual Sports Encyclopedia

SCHOLASTIC REFERENCE

An imprint of
SCHOLASTIC INC.
New York Toronto London Auckland Sydney
Mexico City New Delhi Hong Kong Buenos Aires

Contents

Measurements   6

Introduction   7

Sports and the Human Body   8

The Olympic Games   14

1. Track and Field   17

Introduction   18
100 Meter   20
200 and 400 Meters   21
800, 1,500, 5,000,
   and 10,000 Meters   22
Relays   23
Hurdles   24
Discus and Hammer   25
Javelin   26
Shot Put   27
High Jump   28
Pole Vault   29
Long Jump and Triple Jump   30
Racewalking   31
Marathon   32
Cross-country   33
Heptathlon and Decathlon   34

2. Cycling   35

Road Racing   36
Track Racing   38
BMX   40
Mountain Biking   44

3. Gymnastics   47

Artistic Gymnastics   48
Rhythmic Gymnastics   54
Trampoline   56

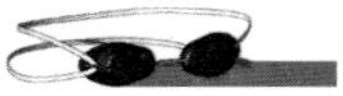

4. Aquatic Sports   57

Swimming   58
Synchronized Swimming   63
Water Polo   66
Diving   68

5. Nautical Sports   71

Ocean Surfing   72
Waterskiing   74
Rowing   76
Canoeing and Kayaking   78
Sailboarding   80
Sailing   82

6. Equestrian Sports   85

The Horse   86
Tack   87
Dressage   88
Jumping   90
Combined Eventing   92
Polo   93

7. Precision and Accuracy 95

Archery   96
Curling   97
Bowling   98
Golf   99

8. Ice and Snow Sports   103

Hockey	104
Figure Skating	108
Speed Skating	112
Luge, Skeleton, Bobsledding	116
Alpine Skiing	118
Freestyle Skiing	122
Speed Skiing	125
Ski Jumping	126
Cross-country	127
Snowboarding	128

9. Ball Sports   131

Baseball	132
Softball	136
Lacrosse	138
Cricket	140
Field Hockey	142
Soccer	144
Australian-Rules Football	148
Handball	149
Team Handball	150
Basketball	152
Football	156
Rugby	160
Netball	164
Volleyball	166
Beach Volleyball	168

10. Racket Sports   169

Tennis	170
Badminton	174
Table Tennis	176
Squash	178
Raquetball	180

11. Combat Sports   181

Karate	182
Judo	185
Tae Kwon Do	188
Fencing	190
Wrestling	193
Boxing	196

12. Sports on Wheels   199

Skateboarding	200
In-line Skating	202
Roller Hockey	204

13. Motor Sports   205

Automobile Racing	206
Formula 1	208
Formula 3000	211
Indy Car Racing	212
Motorcycling	214
Rallying and Off-road Rallying	216

14. Multi Sports   217

Triathlon	218
Pentathlon	219
Orienteering	220

Glossary	221
Index	222
Acknowledgments	224
Photo credits	224

Measurements

Measurements

Most measurements in this book are written in abbreviated (shortened) form. Below you will find a key that explains what these abbreviations mean.

If you do not understand a metric measurement that you encounter in the book, look it up in the conversion chart below to see what it means in U.S. measurements. If you want to know what 300 m is in feet, for example, look up 100 m, which is 328.08 ft, and multiply it by 3: 328.08 X 3 = 984.25 ft.

Key to Abbreviations	
cm =	centimeter
m =	meter
km =	kilometer
yd =	yard
ft =	feet
in. =	inch
mph =	miles per hour
lb =	pound
sec =	second

Conversion Chart

Metric		U.S.
1 cm	=	0.4 in.
1 m	=	3.28 ft
1 km	=	0.62 mile
50 m	=	164.04 ft
100 m	=	328.08 ft
500 m	=	1640.4 ft
800 m	=	2624.64 ft
1000 m	=	3280.8 ft
5 km	=	3.11 miles
10 km	=	6.21 miles
20 km	=	12.43 miles
100 km	=	62.14 miles

Introduction

The *Scholastic Visual Sports Encyclopedia* is an illustrated guide to more than 100 different sports. Whether you're a player or a spectator, you'll find all the basic facts you need to know about most of the sports practiced in the world today. This book describes in detail how each sport is played, what the rules are, what skills are needed, and what kind of equipment is used. It explains the roles of the players on a team and the responsibilities of the officials who supervise each sport.

Along with the text are detailed, computer-generated images of the playing fields, courts, or courses where each sport is practiced. The images of athletes in action are based on actual photographs. This gives them a realistic look and allows certain features to be shown in greater detail. For example, a platform dive is broken down into a series of separate images. This helps you see the many complicated movements that make up the athlete's performance.

How to use this book

The contents page at the beginning of the book lists the 14 chapters and their contents. Each chapter is color-coded and features a group of sports that are related to one another.

The glossary on page 221 lists alphabetically some words used in the book that you may not know. You will find, for example, the words *intercept* and *tactic* along with explanations of what each means and how these words are used in certain sports. The index on pages 222–223 is an alphabetical listing of important words used in the book. Next to each word is the page number(s) on which the word appears.

Many sports use metric measurements, such as meters and kilometers, terms with which you may not be familiar. The conversion chart on page 6 lists metric measurements and shows their equivalents in U.S. measurements. Both the rules and the measurements referred to in this book are those used in Olympic competition, unless otherwise stated. These rules and measurements may at times differ from those used in professional, college, or high school sports.

Enjoy the book.

Sports and the Human Body

The human body is an amazing machine. Even simple activities like walking, running, or throwing a ball are complex processes that use the entire body. Going beyond everyday movements, the body is also capable of extraordinary athletic achievements. From discus throwing to long jumping to running hurdles, the performances of top athletes show the body's incredible range and power. And yet strength alone does not make a winner. Top athletes know that self-confidence, teamwork, and a positive attitude are as important as physical training in helping them to achieve their goals.

The amazing human machine

The bones, the muscles, the brain, and the heart all play active roles during sports activities. They are grouped in four main systems that perform specific functions.

The motor system
The motor system is made up of bones, muscles, and joints. Together, they drive the body's movements.

The nervous system
The nervous system is made up of the brain and the spinal cord. The nervous system directs the body during sports activities. It receives information from senses such as sight, touch, and hearing. It is because of the nervous system that an athlete can estimate how much force is needed to throw a basketball into a basket.

The circulatory system
The circulatory system is made up of arteries, veins, and the heart. The heart pumps five to six quarts of blood every minute. If the blood vessels in the body were laid end to end, they would form a line so long that it could circle the earth about 10 times!

The respiratory system
The respiratory system is basically composed of the right and left lungs. The respiratory system's job is to transport air to the lungs and to eliminate carbon dioxide from the body. Carbon dioxide is the waste produced by the body's cells during the breathing process.

Sports and the Human Body

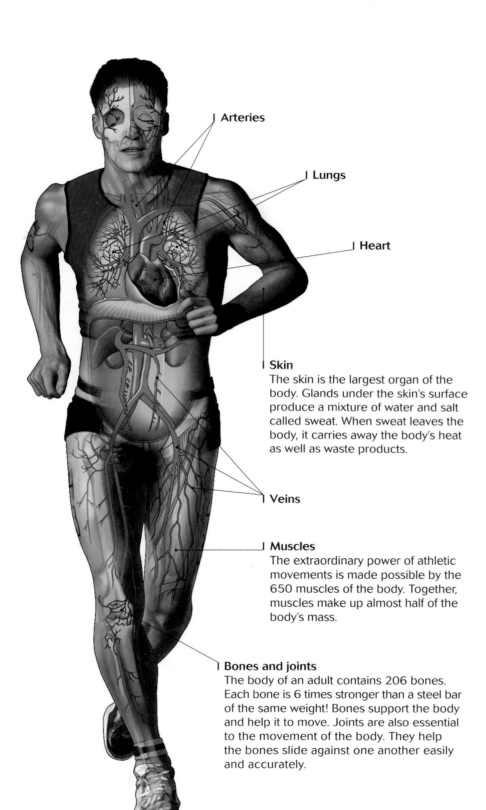

Arteries

Lungs

Heart

Skin
The skin is the largest organ of the body. Glands under the skin's surface produce a mixture of water and salt called sweat. When sweat leaves the body, it carries away the body's heat as well as waste products.

Veins

Muscles
The extraordinary power of athletic movements is made possible by the 650 muscles of the body. Together, muscles make up almost half of the body's mass.

Bones and joints
The body of an adult contains 206 bones. Each bone is 6 times stronger than a steel bar of the same weight! Bones support the body and help it to move. Joints are also essential to the movement of the body. They help the bones slide against one another easily and accurately.

Glossary:

Arteries
The arteries transport blood out of the heart. Their walls, which are made of muscular and elastic fibers, contract as well as expand.

Arterioles
The arterioles are smaller arteries.

Capillaries
Capillaries are tiny, thin-walled blood vessels that allow the exchange of gases and nutrients between cells and the blood.

Cell
The cell is the smallest living unit in the human body. The body contains billions of cells, all of which specialize in performing specific tasks.

Gland
A gland is an organ, a tissue, or a cell that produces a special chemical substance that the body needs to function.

Organ
The organs, such as the heart, lungs, and stomach, are parts of the body that specialize in performing precise functions.

Senses
The senses are functions that allow us to perceive what is going on outside our bodies. The 5 senses are sight, touch, smell, hearing, and taste.

Veins
Veins are blood vessels with much thinner walls than arteries. They transport the blood to the heart.

Venules
Venules are small veins that collect blood from the capillaries and send it flowing into the veins.

✱ Sports and the physically challenged

For more than 40 years, athletes with physical disabilities have been participating in their very own games, called the Paralympics. Today, more than 5,000 athletes compete in some 15 events, including basketball, fencing, swimming, and judo. Special Olympics for the mentally challenged have been held since 1968.

Sports and the Human Body

Muscles: the body's hard workers

Muscles are like small motors that help the body perform precise movements by contracting and relaxing. Muscles can be divided into three groups: the smooth muscles, which are found in the walls of the arteries as well as in the walls of some of the body's organs; the cardiac (heart) muscles; and, finally, the skeletal muscles, which participate in the body's movements. While the first two groups of muscles perform their work without our being aware of them, the skeletal muscles wait to receive orders from the brain before they can contract. Like all motors, muscles need fuel to be able to do their work. That fuel is called ATP (adenosine triphosphate). ATP exists in small quantities in the muscles in the form of reserves. Cells in the body make ATP using sugars found in the foods we eat.

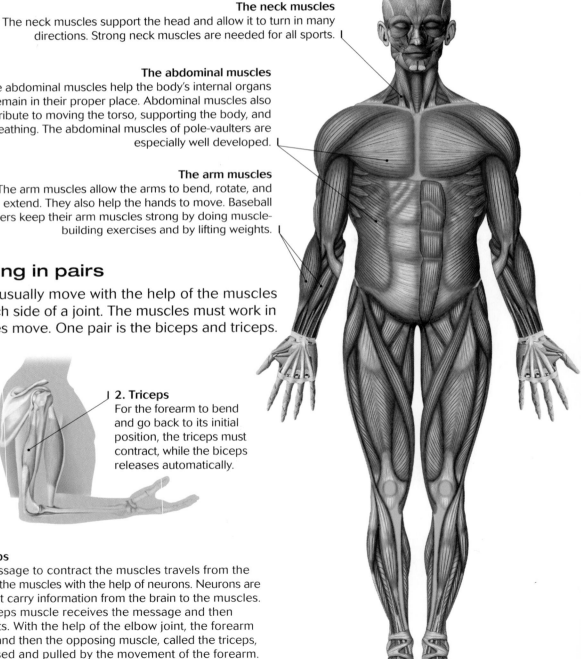

Front

The neck muscles
The neck muscles support the head and allow it to turn in many directions. Strong neck muscles are needed for all sports.

The abdominal muscles
The abdominal muscles help the body's internal organs remain in their proper place. Abdominal muscles also contribute to moving the torso, supporting the body, and breathing. The abdominal muscles of pole-vaulters are especially well developed.

The arm muscles
The arm muscles allow the arms to bend, rotate, and extend. They also help the hands to move. Baseball players keep their arm muscles strong by doing muscle-building exercises and by lifting weights.

Muscles: working in pairs

Bones in the skeleton usually move with the help of the muscles that are located on each side of a joint. The muscles must work in pairs to make the bones move. One pair is the biceps and triceps.

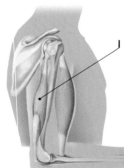

2. Triceps
For the forearm to bend and go back to its initial position, the triceps must contract, while the biceps releases automatically.

1. Biceps
The message to contract the muscles travels from the brain to the muscles with the help of neurons. Neurons are cells that carry information from the brain to the muscles. The biceps muscle receives the message and then contracts. With the help of the elbow joint, the forearm bends, and then the opposing muscle, called the triceps, is released and pulled by the movement of the forearm.

Sports and the Human Body

The muscles' specialties

The muscles of the body work in groups. From the head down, these groups include the neck muscles; the muscles of the shoulders, arms, and back; the abdominal muscles; the buttock muscles; and the muscles of the legs and the feet.

✳ An amazing chemical laboratory

During intense physical activity, the body manufactures a large quantity of hormones. Hormones are special chemical substances the body needs to function properly. Some of these hormones, such as adrenaline, help the muscles work better and help the body withstand pain more easily. Adrenaline also reduces the amount of water lost by the body in the process of sweating.

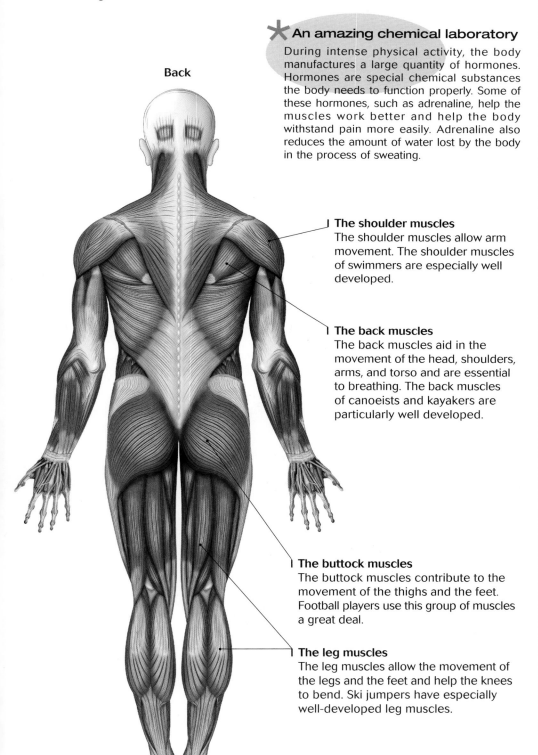

Back

The shoulder muscles
The shoulder muscles allow arm movement. The shoulder muscles of swimmers are especially well developed.

The back muscles
The back muscles aid in the movement of the head, shoulders, arms, and torso and are essential to breathing. The back muscles of canoeists and kayakers are particularly well developed.

The buttock muscles
The buttock muscles contribute to the movement of the thighs and the feet. Football players use this group of muscles a great deal.

The leg muscles
The leg muscles allow the movement of the legs and the feet and help the knees to bend. Ski jumpers have especially well-developed leg muscles.

Energy and kilocalories

The energy that is burned or used up by the body, as well as the energy supplied by foods, is measured in calories (cal). Between the ages of 9 and 12, girls and boys need about 2,000 calories per day. However, an athlete competing in a long-distance bicycle race may need 5 times as many calories!

Energy burned by 9–12 year olds per hour of activity

Activities	Approximate Energy Burned (cal)
Sleeping	30
Working at a computer	50
Playing guitar	90
Taking a shower	120
Playing golf	140
Playing badminton	230
Playing beach volleyball	260
Riding a BMX bicycle	280
Doing judo	320

Approximate energy values of foods

Foods	Approximate Amount of Energy Supplied (cal)
1 teaspoon of sugar	20
3.5 oz of green beans	40
2 oranges	40
1 teaspoon of butter	47
1 slice of white bread	65
1 medium-size apple	80
1 glass of grape juice	106
1 banana	110
1 tablespoon of oil	135
3.5 oz of salmon	175
1 cup of chocolate milk	200
3.5 oz of roast pork	240
3.5 oz of steak	260
7 oz of pasta	280
3.5 oz of chicken	300
1 serving of lasagna	446
3.5 oz of peanuts	600

Sports and the Human Body

An effective distribution network

Even if well supplied with sugar, muscles cannot function without their most important partner: oxygen. This gas is present in the air we breathe. Oxygen enters the body through the lungs and is transported in the blood by some 25 trillion tiny cells, called red blood cells. The circulatory system is responsible for sending oxygen to all the parts of the body. Each minute, about five quarts of blood travel through the veins and arteries of the circulatory system, delivering oxygen to the entire body. In addition to transporting oxygen, minerals, sugar, and vitamins, blood also helps the cells of the body to discharge their waste. The waste is then carried out of the body through the exhaling lungs as well as through sweat and urine.

The respiratory system

Air passes through the trachea and into the lungs through the bronchial tubes and bronchia. At the ends of the delicate bronchia are pulmonary alveoli, which are very thin, small sacs of membranes. Oxygen from the air passes through the thin walls of the alveoli and into the bloodstream. At rest, we breathe about five quarts of air per minute. During a sports activity, this may increase to 50 or even 100 quarts per minute! The more intense the activity, the more air our lungs take in, and the more oxygen we breathe.

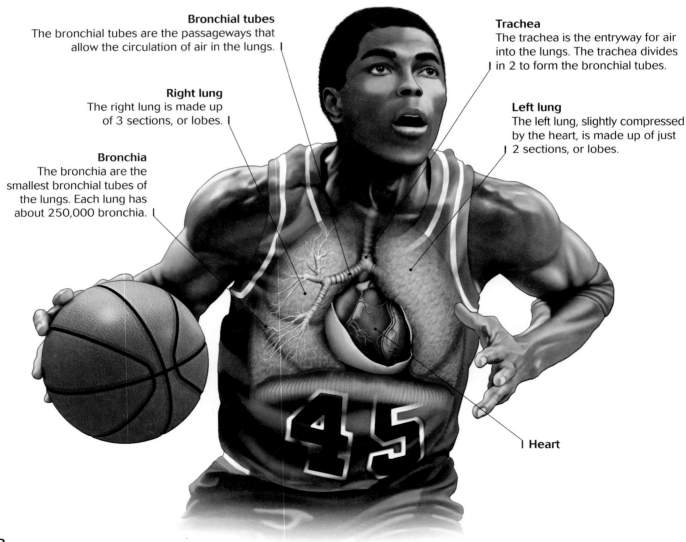

Bronchial tubes
The bronchial tubes are the passageways that allow the circulation of air in the lungs.

Right lung
The right lung is made up of 3 sections, or lobes.

Bronchia
The bronchia are the smallest bronchial tubes of the lungs. Each lung has about 250,000 bronchia.

Trachea
The trachea is the entryway for air into the lungs. The trachea divides in 2 to form the bronchial tubes.

Left lung
The left lung, slightly compressed by the heart, is made up of just 2 sections, or lobes.

Heart

Sports and the Human Body

The central pump

Despite its small size, the heart is the most active organ in the body. During its lifetime, the heart contracts continuously, pumping blood throughout the body. This impressive machine pumps more than two and a half million quarts of blood each year, sending it through the arteries, arterioles, capillaries, venules, and veins. In an adult at rest, the heart beats from 70 to 80 times a minute. This number of heartbeats is called the pulse rate. Pulse rates are much higher in newborn babies and lower in older people. Like all the muscles of the body, the heart gets stronger with regular sports activity. Following an endurance exercise program makes the heart's contractions more powerful and increases its capacity to pump blood. This allows blood to circulate more effectively in the body during strenuous activity. Some athletes' hearts are so powerful that they only need to beat 40 to 50 times per minute.

Aorta
The aorta is the largest blood vessel in the body. It transports oxygenated blood to the upper parts of the body, such as the arms and the head.

Superior vena cava
The superior vena cava transports blood from the upper body to the right atrium of the heart. The blood circulating in this area contains carbon dioxide waste.

Right pulmonary artery
The right pulmonary artery transports blood containing carbon dioxide to the right lung.

Right pulmonary veins
The right pulmonary veins transport oxygenated blood from the right lung to the left atrium.

Right atrium
The right atrium receives blood, which has been circulated throughout the body. This blood contains carbon dioxide waste.

✳ Sports make the world seem sunnier!
It has been proven that practicing sports increases our self-confidence and also has a positive effect on our mood. During intense physical activity, the body releases hormones called endorphins. Endorphins act on our brains and make us see the world in a sunnier light!

Pulmonary trunk
The pulmonary trunk transports blood containing carbon dioxide to the lungs.

Left pulmonary veins
The left pulmonary veins transport blood, which has been oxygenated by the lungs, to the left atrium.

Left atrium
The left atrium receives oxygenated blood from the lungs.

Left ventricle
The left ventricle propels oxygenated blood to the aorta.

Right ventricle
The right ventricle propels blood containing carbon dioxide toward the lungs through the pulmonary trunk.

Inferior vena cava
The inferior vena cava transports blood from the lower parts of the body to the right atrium. The blood circulating in this area contains carbon dioxide waste.

Thoracic aorta
The thoracic aorta distributes oxygenated blood to the lower parts of the body, such as the torso and the legs.

The Olympic Games

In the year 884 B.C., war was raging among the states of ancient Greece. Hoping for peace, one of the rulers of the states, King Iphitos of Elis, proposed that games be held that would please the gods and therefore bring peace to the land. The games he referred to are what we know today as the Olympic games. It is hard to know when the very first games were held. It is believed that they might have taken place as early as the year 1500 B.C. The games that King Iphitos revived in 884 B.C. were held in the city of Olympia every four years for another 1,000 years. The games were stopped in A.D. 392 by Roman emperor Theodose the Great. He banned the games by claiming they went against the teachings of Christianity. Another 1,500 years would pass before the Olympic flame would burn again. In 1892, Baron Pierre de Coubertin, a wealthy French educator, had the idea of reviving the Olympic games of ancient Greece. His dream became reality four years later when the first modern Olympic games were held in Athens, Greece. De Coubertin died in 1937 at the age of 74. His final wish was that his heart be buried in Greece, in the city of Olympia.

The Olympic symbols

The rings
The symbol of the Olympic games is a series of 5 rings of different colors. The rings are linked together from left to right. This symbol represents the union of the 5 continents and the joining together of athletes from around the world.

The flame
During the ancient Olympic games, a sacred flame was set to burn continuously on the altar of Zeus in Olympia. Since 1936, the flame has been relit each time the games are held. Carrying torches, athletes run in relays to transport the sacred flame from Olympia to the city hosting the games.

The motto
The Olympic motto "citius, altius, fortius" is a Latin saying that means "swifter, higher, stronger."

An unfortunate finish for the first marathon runner

The marathon, a 26-mile race, was first held as an Olympic event at the Athens games in 1896. The marathon commemorates the famous run of an ancient-Greek soldier, Philippides, who in 490 B.C. ran 26 miles from the city of Marathon to the city of Athens. Philippides died of exhaustion after delivering the news that the Greeks had won a battle with the Persians.

The Olympic movement
The Olympic movement brings together various groups of people who supervise the organization and operation of the Olympic games.

IOC
The IOC (International Olympic Committee) is the head organization of the Olympic movement. The IOC is the protector of official symbols such as the Olympic flag, the Olympic motto, and the Olympic anthem. In addition to supervising and organizing the games, the IOC's job is to promote a healthy and positive image of sports.

IFs
There are 35 IFs (International Federations), each responsible for a different Olympic sport. Each IF works to ensure that the rules of its sport are respected in international competition. The IFs set up trials in which athletes compete to qualify for participation in the Olympics. The IFs also select the referees, judges, and other officials needed to supervise their respective sports.

NOCs
Each country participating in the Olympic games has its own NOC (National Olympic Committee). NOCs are responsible for the well-being of their athletes. They provide training facilities for athletes and obtain the necessary funding to help them participate in the games.

OCOGs
The OCOG (Organizing Committee for the Olympic Games) works with the city that is hosting the games. It sets up the competition sites and the housing for athletes. It also organizes transportation to the competition sites for the athletes as well as the spectators.

Events and athletes

The first Olympics of ancient Greece featured only one event: a running race around the Olympic stadium. Several years later another race, which consisted of two turns around the stadium, was added. This was followed by the addition of the pentathlon, which included a running race, discus throw, javelin throw, jumping, and wrestling as well as chariot races. When the first modern Olympic games were held in 1896, the athletes numbered 245. The games consisted of nine events: track and field, cycling, fencing, gymnastics, weightlifting, wrestling, swimming, tennis, and archery. Today, more than 100 years later, athletes competing in the Olympics now number more than 10,000! New events continue to be added to the existing list of sports. There are now approximately 30 different sports on the calendar of Olympic events.

The performances of champions

Much time has passed since the Greek Koroibos of Elis was awarded the first prize for running around the Olympic stadium back in 776 B.C. Since then, hundreds of athletes have brought honor to their countries by performing athletic feats worthy of the ancient Greek gods. Here are just a few:

A challenge for women

No woman was permitted to take part in the Athens Olympics in 1896. Four years later, at the Olympic games in Paris, 19 women gained entry to compete in tennis and golf. Since then, the extraordinary performances of women in sports continue to be recognized, and more and more events are being created for women. A hundred years after the first modern games, there are more than 3,000 women competing in the Olympics.

Carl Lewis

This American athlete is the champion of the 100-meter sprint. Carl Lewis has won 17 gold medals in his 17-year career in international competition.

Bonnie Blair

This athlete is the only American woman to win 5 gold medals at the Olympic winter games. Champion in the 500 m and 1,000 m in 1992 and in 1994, she also won the 500 m in 1998.

Mark Spitz

Olympic champion in 1968 and star of the 1972 Olympics, this American swimmer broke 26 individual world records and 35 American records between 1967 and 1972.

Michael Jordan

As part of a team, this American athlete was an NBA (National Basketball Association) champion from 1991 to 1993 and from 1996 to 1998. As part of the Dream Team, one of the first Olympic teams made up of professional players, he was also an Olympic champion in 1984 and 1992. Michael Jordan is considered by many to be the greatest basketball player of all time.

Nadia Comaneci

This Romanian athlete was the first to have a perfect score in the history of women's gymnastics. She went on to obtain an additional 6 perfect scores in the 1976 Montreal Olympic Games. Nadia Comaneci's record has never been broken.

Muhammad Ali

This American athlete was a heavyweight boxing world champion from 1964 to 1967 and again in 1974 and 1978. Muhammad Ali was also an Olympic boxing champion in the middleweight category in 1960.

The Olympic Games

When they were first introduced in 1896, the modern Olympics featured only Summer Games. Convinced of the importance of bringing together athletes from the various winter sports, the IOC held the first Olympic Winter Games in 1928. For more than 60 years, the Summer Games as well as the Winter Games were held in the same year, once every four years. Since 1994, the Summer and Winter Games have been held separately, alternating every two years.

 The Canadian snow wagon event

The most important element of the Winter Olympics is snow. Unfortunately, snow does not always arrive when it should. In February 1928 in St. Moritz, Switzerland, following a large snowfall, the temperature soared to about 78° F. The warm temperatures caused the snow to melt and made it difficult to hold the skating and cross-country skiing events. Four years later, fearing a shortage of snow at the Winter Games in Lake Placid, New York, the Americans ordered wagonloads of snow to be driven to Lake Placid all the way from Canada!

The Olympics and the host cities

The IOC has the difficult task of selecting the city that will host the Olympic games. The IOC votes on the winning city 7 years in advance! Many cities dream of hosting the Olympics. To be awarded this honor, a city must prove that it can safely accommodate the thousands of athletes and visitors who come from around the world.

Host Cities Summer Olympic Games	
1896	Athens (Greece)
1900	Paris (France)
1904	St. Louis, Missouri (USA)
1908	London (UK)
1912	Stockholm (Sweden)
1920	Antwerp (Belgium)
1924	Paris (France)
1928	Amsterdam (Netherlands)
1932	Los Angeles, California (USA)
1936	Berlin (Germany)
1948	London (UK)
1952	Helsinki (Finland)
1956	Melbourne (Australia)
1960	Rome (Italy)
1964	Tokyo (Japan)
1968	Mexico City (Mexico)
1972	Munich (Germany)
1976	Montreal (Canada)
1980	Moscow (USSR)
1984	Los Angeles, California (USA)
1988	Seoul (South Korea)
1992	Barcelona (Spain)
1996	Atlanta, Georgia (USA)
2000	Sydney (Australia)
2004	Athens (Greece)
2008	Beijing (China)

Host Cities Winter Olympic Games	
1924	Chamonix (France)
1928	St. Moritz (Switzerland)
1932	Lake Placid, New York (USA)
1936	Garmisch-Partenkirchen (Germany)
1948	St. Moritz (Switzerland)
1952	Oslo (Norway)
1956	Cortina d'Ampezzo (Italy)
1960	Squaw Valley, California (USA)
1964	Innsbruck (Austria)
1968	Grenoble (France)
1972	Sapporo (Japan)
1976	Innsbruck (Austria)
1980	Lake Placid, New York (USA)
1984	Sarajevo (Yugoslavia)
1988	Calgary (Canada)
1992	Albertville (France)
1994	Lillehammer (Norway)
1998	Nagano (Japan)
2002	Salt Lake City, Utah (USA)
2006	Turin (Italy)

Track and Field

Introduction
100 Meter
200 and 400 Meters
800, 1,500, 5,000, and 10,000 Meters
Relays
Hurdles
Discus and Hammer
Javelin
Shot Put
High Jump
Pole Vault
Long Jump and Triple Jump
Racewalking
Marathon
Cross-country
Heptathlon and Decathlon

Introduction

Track and field is a group of sports that includes three basic types of activities: running, jumping, and throwing. Running is a track event. Jumping and throwing are field events. These sports focus on an athlete's natural strength, speed, and endurance, using very little equipment and no artificial assistance. Men and women athletes participate in events as individuals, not as teams. In the Olympic Games, there are close to 30 track-and-field events.

Stadium

To host an official competition, a stadium must have a 400 m track divided into six or eight lanes, areas for the jumping and throwing events, and a water jump for the steeplechase event. Races are always run counterclockwise, with the runners' left arms toward the inside of the track.

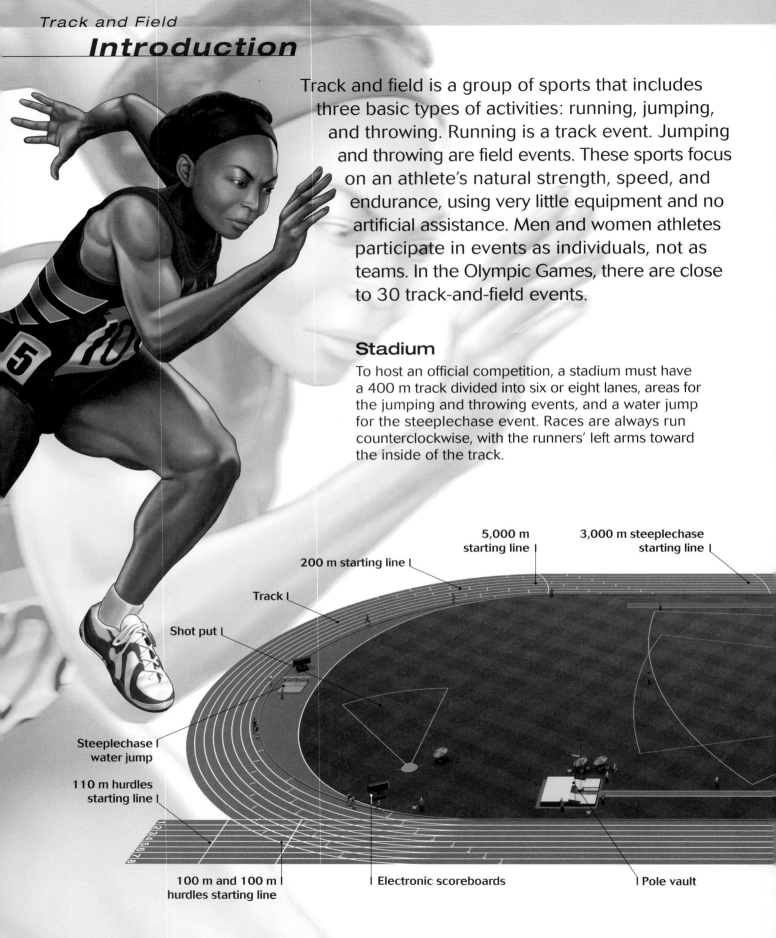

200 m starting line

Track

Shot put

Steeplechase water jump

110 m hurdles starting line

100 m and 100 m hurdles starting line

5,000 m starting line

3,000 m steeplechase starting line

Electronic scoreboards

Pole vault

Introduction

Timing and measurements

In every event, there must be a winner. A camera films the runners as they cross the finish line, and an electronic timer times them in hundredths of seconds. This helps to determine if any new records have been set. In the long jump, triple jump, and throwing events, the judges measure distances in meters and centimeters with the help of a steel measuring tape. High jumps are calculated using the measurements already marked on the supports holding the bar.

Camera
A camera films the runners as they cross the finish line. It is connected to an electronic timer.

Timing
Officials use an electronic timer, which is set off by a starter pistol or other start device. Stopwatches are also used to time races and determine records.

Starting blocks
These metal devices help athletes push off at the start of a race and keep their feet from slipping. The blocks are also used to detect if an athlete starts before the gun goes off.

Anemometer
This device measures and records the speed of the wind. It is used in races under 200 m, and in the long jump and triple jump. For a record to be approved, a tailwind must be less than 6.6 ft per second. A tailwind can push an athlete from behind, giving an unfair advantage.

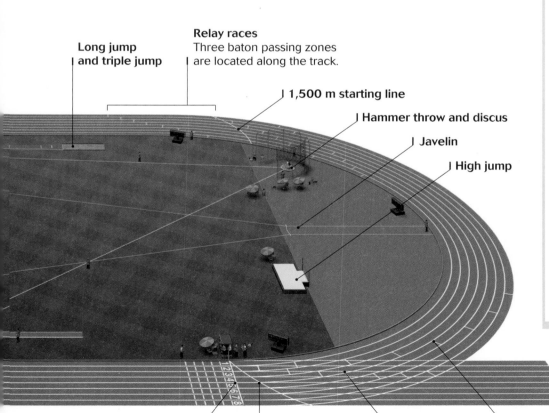

Long jump and triple jump

Relay races
Three baton passing zones are located along the track.

1,500 m starting line

Hammer throw and discus

Javelin

High jump

Finish line for all races

10,000 m and 4 x 400 m relay starting line

800 m starting line

400 m, 400 m hurdles, and 4 x 100 m relay starting line

100 Meter

The 100 meter event is a test of pure speed over a straight distance. It takes years of training to prepare for this race, which lasts less than 10 seconds. The eight runners with the best times in the qualifying heats (preliminary races) run in the final event. The fastest athletes get to run in the center lanes. The 100 meter has become the star event of the Olympics, with the winners of the men's and women's races recognized as the fastest human beings in the world.

Shoes
The shoes are lightweight, with up to 11 cleats on the front of the sole to help grip the track. The soles do not have heels, because the runners' heels never touch the ground; doing so would slow them down.

Technique

1. Set
The runner concentrates deeply and holds his breath, waiting for the start signal.

2. Start
When the starter's pistol fires, the runner "explodes" toward the finish line, leaning far forward to help him accelerate faster.

3. Acceleration
The sprinter reaches his running position between the fifth and eighth strides. He runs on his toes, so his heels never touch the track.

A complete stride may be 7.9 ft long.

4. Maximum speed
The sprinter may hit 5 strides per second and reach a speed of 25 mph. That is roughly as fast as you can ride a bicycle.

5. Maintaining speed
At the 60 m mark, the length of the runner's stride is at its maximum.

6. Finish line
Even if the runner reaches out toward the finish line with his arm or leg, the timer is stopped only when his chest crosses the finish line.

200 and 400 Meters

Shoes
The shoes are identical for the 200 m and 400 m. The soles have cleats but no heels.

Both the 200 meter and 400 meter events are classified as long sprints. Both male and female athletes start out fast and use long strides. In the 400 meter, the runners must never run at more than 90% of their maximum speed; if they do, they will run out of energy before the end of the race. Runners start in staggered positions along the track, with those toward the inside lanes starting farther back. This ensures that the distance is equal for all runners. During the race, runners must remain in their assigned lanes.

The race

The 200 m and 400 m require more strength and agility than the 100 m. Because the races start on the curved part of the track, runners are forced into a leaning position. This increases the risk of injury. It is impossible for athletes to maintain their maximum speed all the way to the finish line. They must concentrate on keeping their speed constant.

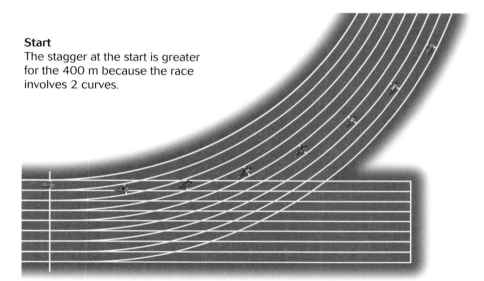

Start
The stagger at the start is greater for the 400 m because the race involves 2 curves.

The curves
Curves can cause athletes to slip, even though they have cleats on their shoes. Tighter curves also have a slowing effect. This means that a runner in the outside lane has a slight advantage over a runner in the inside lane who has a tighter curve to run.

800, 1,500, 5,000, and 10,000 Meters

These are endurance races that test the athletes' strength. The 800 and 1,500 meter events are called middle-distance races. The 5,000 and 10,000 meter events are long-distance races. Male and female runners begin in a standing position. Starting blocks are not used in these races. After the first curve, runners can leave their lanes, and move toward the inside so they have less distance to run. Running in a pack, athletes sometimes use their elbows to protect themselves from other runners. They must also watch out for runners who may trip and fall in front of them.

Shoes
The shoes are equipped with heels for running events that are 1,500 m or longer. The athletes need to run on their heels in these races. The soles have a maximum of 11 cleats.

Distances
800 m (0.5 mile) = 2 laps
1,500 m (0.9 mile) = 4 laps minus 1 curve
5,000 m (3.1 miles) = 12.5 laps
10,000 m (6.2 miles) = 25 laps

Technique

In the 800 and 1,500 m events, some athletes try to stay in front during the entire race, while others save their energy for the finish. In the 5,000 and 10,000 m events, runners use other strategies, speeding up at different times and forcing other runners to break their rhythm and tire themselves out.

Relay teams are made up of four athletes, who each take a turn running as quickly as possible while carrying a baton. Eight teams compete in the final event. In a relay race it is the baton, and not the runner, which is timed. The baton must be passed quickly and carefully; if it is dropped, the runner must pick it up before continuing. There are two kinds of events: the 4 x 100 meter and the 4 x 400 meter relays.

Baton
The baton is about the same length as a standard school ruler. It is a rigid tube made out of wood or metal, weighing at least 1.8 oz.

Technique

In both relays, the first runner is usually known for his quick start, while the athlete known for a strong finish is the last runner. In the 4 x 100 m, team members must remain in their lanes so they don't get in the way of the other runners. In the 4 x 400 m, the speed is slower and passing the baton less risky. Only the first lap and the first turn of the second lap are run in lanes.

| Passing zone

4 x 100 m relay

In the run-up zone, the receiver takes 6 to 8 strides, beginning when the passer has crossed the marker placed 6 to 9 m before the run-up zone.

In the passing zone, the passer shouts to the receiver that he is about to pass the baton to him, then puts it into his hand.

The receiver continues running without looking at the baton or changing stride. This is called a "blind pass."

Passing the baton

French grip
The baton is put into the open hand of the receiver in an upward motion. If both runners are not perfectly coordinated, they risk dropping the baton.

American grip
The baton is passed in a downward motion when the runners are almost side by side. This type of pass is easier to do, but takes more time.

4 x 400 m relay
In this race, the teammates watch each other during the exchange of the baton. Because this is a longer event, the passer is more tired and his speed may vary. This makes a "blind pass" too risky.

Hurdles

The 100 meter (for women), 110 meter, and 400 meter hurdle events are races in which athletes alternate between sprinting and jumping obstacles, called hurdles. There are 10 hurdles in a race. Runners can touch or knock down hurdles accidentally without penalty, but are disqualified if they deliberately knock one down or put a leg or foot outside the hurdle area.

Shoes
Shoes worn for hurdles look like sprinters' shoes, but the cleats in the front are shorter so that they don't get caught on the hurdle. The heels are reinforced to absorb the shock of landing.

Hurdles
The hurdle is made of metal and wood. A counterweight at the base keeps it from falling over too easily. The men's hurdles are slightly higher than the women's.

Technique

In the 110 m, the hurdles are placed close together. Runners must take three strides between each jump. When they jump, they barely clear the hurdle, maintaining their stride so they won't lose time. In the 400 m, hurdles are lower and placed farther apart (35 m), so the runner must take 13 to 17 strides between jumps.

1. Start and takeoff
The runner starts the race like a 100 m sprinter but must accelerate sooner in order to get ready to jump the first hurdle.

2. Flight
To stay balanced while in the air, the runner reaches out with one arm and tips her body forward.

3. Landing
In order to minimize the loss of speed when she hits the ground, the runner keeps her body leaning forward and her leg straight.

Run between hurdles
In the 110 m race, where the hurdles are placed closer together, the athlete takes an equal number of strides between hurdles, usually 3.

Final sprint
In the final sprint, the runner speeds toward the finish line the same way runners do in a 100 m sprint.

Steeplechase
The 3,000 m steeplechase is a spectacular race, featuring 28 hurdles and 7 water jumps. Athletes are not penalized for touching the hurdles with their hands or feet or for putting their feet in the water.

Discus and Hammer

Discus and hammer events are performed in the same area. Men and women athletes use a spinning approach to throw the discus or the hammer as far as possible. The winner is the one who makes the longest throw without stepping outside of the circle before the discus or hammer lands.

Shoes
Made of suede or leather, the shoes have flexible soles with rounded edges and no cleats. This gives the shoes a better grip on the cement surface of the throwing circle, and the rounded edges make spinning easier.

Technique

Discus
The athlete moves the discus back and forth in an arc, and then does a 1½ turn rotation. Pushing off one leg, he whips his arm around and releases the discus.

Hammer
The athlete swings the hammer back and forth like a pendulum, then rotates it 2 or 3 times. He spins himself around 3 or 4 times, then releases the hammer. Athletes need to spot a reference point for themselves while spinning so they can keep their balance and know where they are throwing.

Hammer grip
The athlete uses a leather glove with thick fingers to ensure a solid grip.

Discus grip
The hand is placed flat on the discus, with the fingers slightly spread and gripping the edge. There is no need to "hold" the discus because, as the athlete spins around, centrifugal force keeps the discus in his hand.

Equipment

Discus
It is made of wood or another suitable material, rimmed with iron, and inlaid with circular metal plates in the center of both sides.

Hammer
The head, linked to a handle by a steel wire, is made of brass or of another solid, dense material and covered with a thin layer of metal.

Throwing area
Since throws can be dangerous, the throwing circle is partly enclosed in a protective cage made of cord or wire, and the angle for throws does not exceed 40°. A discus can be thrown approximately 246 ft, a hammer approximately 279 ft.

Javelin

In this event, men and women athletes throw the javelin as far as possible into a landing area, called a fan. There is no target. The throw counts when the javelin touches the ground tip-first, but the javelin does not have to stick in the ground. The top eight athletes compete in the final event, with the best of their three throws determining the winner.

Shoes
Shoes worn for javelin are made of light leather or nylon. The cleats under the heel help the athlete to stop quickly at the point of throwing the javelin.

Technique

In order to run and throw at the right spot every time, the athlete places markers on the track. From the starting marker, he begins the run-up, taking 10 to 12 very quick strides and accelerating to about 23 ft per second.

Javelin grip

At the midway marker, the athlete takes about seven steps, moving into a throwing position. As he reaches the stopboard, which is a line at the end of the run-up zone, he stops running and releases the javelin in an explosive movement of the shoulder. He must not lose his balance or leave the track before the javelin lands.

| Shaft | Cord grip | Tip |

Javelin grips
There are 3 main grip techniques. In all of them, 2 fingers are placed behind the cord grip. This ensures that the athlete has a firm hold on the javelin.

Javelin
The javelin may be made of metal or wood. It must not have any moving parts that would change its center of gravity and make it easier to throw. Javelins fly at a distance of more than 325 ft at a speed of more than 60 mph.

The goal is to throw a heavy ball, called a shot, as far as possible. Each thrower has three tries. The shot must land in the landing area, called the fan. During the attempt, the athlete must not leave the circle, and his or her foot must not touch the top of the stopboard.

Stopboard

Shot put fan

Circle

Gripping the shot
The shot is held in an open hand, resting at the base of the fingers, which are bent and slightly spread.

Techniques

Champions have invented two throwing techniques.

O'Brien technique
The athlete starts with his back to the fan and turns toward it. This extra quarter-turn increases the flight speed of the shot. When American athlete Parry O'Brien started using the technique in 1952, it helped to increase his throwing distance by more than 3.3 ft.

Baryshnikov technique
In 1972, Russian athlete Alexsandr Baryshnikov added a spin to O'Brien's technique, a movement similar to that used by discus throwers. The rotation increases the flight speed of the shot. It is the most popular technique used today.

Equipment

The women's shot weighs about 9 lb.
The men's shot weighs more than 15 lb.

Shot
It has a smooth surface and can be made of bronze, copper, or a similar metal, or another material covered with a thin layer of metal.

High Jump

In the high jump, the athlete must jump over, or clear, a horizontal bar without knocking it down, using only the strength of her own body. To start, event organizers set a minimum height, which the athlete must clear in order to qualify. The bar is then raised progressively. Athletes are eliminated from competition if they fail to clear the bar three times in a row. Champions can clear a height of more than eight feet.

Technique

In the most popular technique, the athlete leaps up while at the same time turning his or her back toward the pole. In this position the athlete's center of gravity is closer to the bar, allowing a higher jump.

1. Approach
The jumper takes about 12 running steps. She needs to achieve speed and to arrive at the bar in the proper position for the jump.

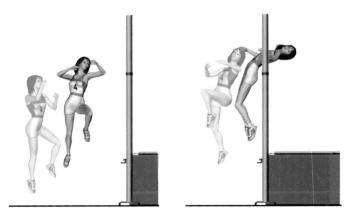

2. Takeoff
The jumper pushes off with the takeoff leg and rotates in the air. Then she lifts her other leg and gets into a horizontal position with her back to the crossbar.

3. Arch and landing
The jumper tips her shoulders back, bringing her heels up under her thighs while arching her body. When her hips have passed the bar, she flexes them, which raises her chest and legs, allowing her to clear the bar.

Pole Vault

Shoes
There are cleats under the ball of the foot and heel. The thickness of the sole must not exceed 0.5 in. This prevents an unfair height advantage.

In the pole vault, the athlete uses a flexible pole to clear a bar set as high as possible. The same rules as the high jump apply here. The difference is that the athlete jumps almost three times higher with the help of the pole.

Technique

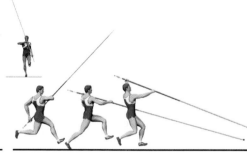

1. Approach
An athlete must run at least 130 ft in order to gain enough speed for the jump. The faster the athlete runs, the higher he can jump. It is difficult to run carrying the pole.

2. Takeoff
As the athlete nears the bar, he plants the pole in the pole box, which is placed between the 2 uprights holding up the bar. The force of the athlete's body makes the pole bend and propels him into the air.

3. Flight
The flight is very acrobatic. To lift his body as high as possible, the athlete pushes upward on the pole. At the last moment he turns to face the bar as he clears it.

Jumping area
Competitors may place markers beside the track, as long as the markers are not on the track itself.

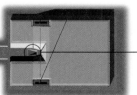

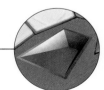

Pole
Poles are usually made of fiberglass or carbon fiber, but any smooth-surfaced material can be used. Jumpers choose the pole's length and diameter according to their own physical characteristics. Athletes usually bring 3 poles to competitions in case 2 break.

Pole box
The pole box measures only 7 in. x 31.5 in., and is set 8 in. below ground level. The pole box is difficult to aim for when the athlete is running fast and carrying a pole that is more than 16 ft long.

Long Jump and Triple Jump

In the long jump and the triple jump, men and women athletes need all their power to jump as far as possible. The long jump is a high-speed sprint, followed by a jump. The triple jump is a sprint, followed by a hop, a step, and a jump.

Shoes
The shoes are designed to give the feet firm support and prevent twisting during takeoff and landing.

Technique

Long jump

1. Run-up
The athlete accelerates. His body is relaxed and he takes long strides. As he reaches the takeoff board, he pushes off with one foot.

2. Jump
The athlete's movements while in the air do not change his direction or speed but keep him from losing his balance.

3. Landing
The athlete throws his legs and arms forward in order to land as far as possible from the takeoff board.

Triple jump

Jump
In the triple jump, the athlete tries to maintain his speed all the way through the 3 jumps.

Landing area
The landing area is filled with sand, and is raked after each jump to maintain the same height as the runway. In both the long jump and triple jump, distances are measured from the front edge of the takeoff board to the closest imprint made in the sand. Top athletes can jump almost 30 ft in the long jump, and more than 60 ft in the combined triple jumps.

Takeoff board

The jumper's foot must not touch the band of soft plastic placed in front of the board. Officials check to make sure that the jumper has left no mark on it.

Facilities

long jump takeoff board |

triple jump takeoff board |

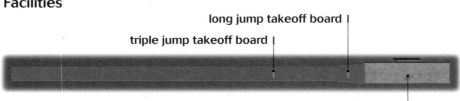

landing area |

Racewalking

In racewalking, the athlete uses a very difficult walking technique to move forward as rapidly as possible without running. Races are 10, 20, or 50 kilometers long. Athletes need great strength and ability to avoid the fatigue caused by these awkward movements.

Shoes
Racewalking shoes are light and the soles are thin to reduce friction with the ground.

Rules
The difference between walking and running is that in walking, one foot must always be on the ground. Walkers must follow this rule throughout the race; judges follow the athletes and check their steps. If three judges see an infraction, the athlete is disqualified.

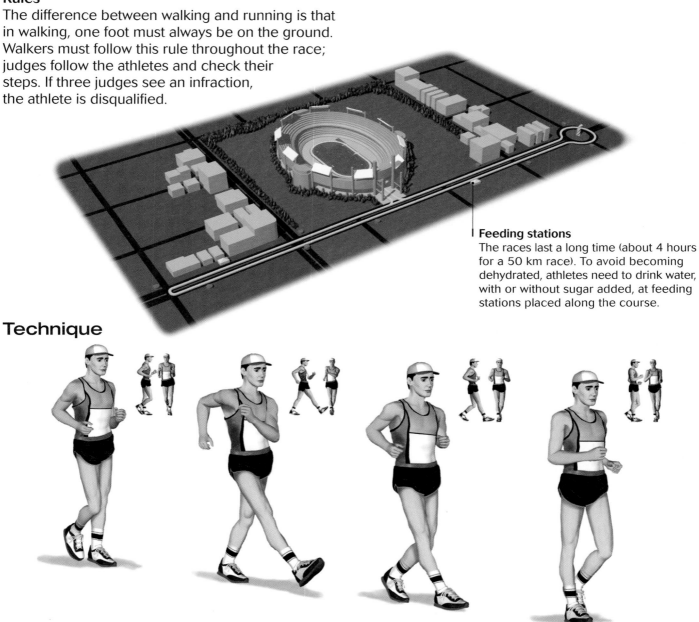

Feeding stations
The races last a long time (about 4 hours for a 50 km race). To avoid becoming dehydrated, athletes need to drink water, with or without sugar added, at feeding stations placed along the course.

Technique

The athlete pushes off with his back leg and stretches the other forward with a swing of the hip. Energetic arm movements add to the length of his stride and maintain his balance.

Before his back foot leaves the ground, the athlete puts his other foot on the ground. Placing one foot in front of the other in a straight line, he then uses his front leg to pull himself forward. The average speed of a racewalker is 9 mph.

Marathon

The marathon is the ultimate endurance test: 26.2 miles! The race usually begins in a stadium and then continues on a road course. Heat, wind, rain, and a challenging course (hills, for example) can add to the difficulty of the race. A marathon is one of the few events in which amateurs compete at the same time as the top champions.

Tactics and techniques

The athletes face two main challenges: physical and mental exhaustion. The first runner finishes the race in about two hours. Runners must conserve their energy and drink water. Some runners form groups that move at the same pace, while others try to outrun the competition at the slightest sign of weakness.

Feeding stations
Feeding stations are very important, because runners cannot store enough energy in their bodies to run at great speeds for the full distance. Athletes can lose up to 6 pints of water through perspiration in just 1 hour.

Shoes
Marathon running shoes are lightweight and provide foot stability and shock absorption.

Cross-country

Cross-country is a long-distance race usually run on trails with rough terrain. The combination of hills, natural obstacles, and bad weather can add to the challenge. Sometimes the race is held on an artificial course in a stadium. The world championship has races of 4 kilometers for men and women combined, plus 8 kilometers for women, and 12 kilometers for men. The number of participants can vary from 100 to as many as 35,000, with competitors running as individuals or in teams of four.

Shoes
The shoes are usually made of nylon, with a maximum of 11 rubber cleats to provide a good grip in muddy terrain.

Facilities

The racecourse is generally two to eight miles long. The start and finish lines are usually in the same place, and the course is a loop. For financial and practical reasons, official cross-country organizations are increasingly abandoning the countryside in favor of stadiums.

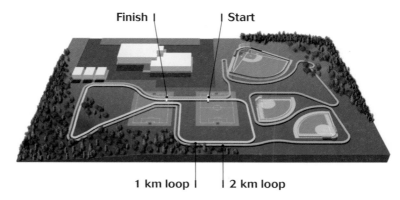

Finish | Start

1 km loop | 2 km loop

Outdoor race

Although rain, snow, and wind can add to the difficulty of the race, the pace is still very fast: 7.5 miles in 40 minutes!

Heptathlon and Decathlon

In these events, all-around athletes compete in 7 or 10 different events that are difficult even when practiced individually. Men compete in the decathlon (10 events) and women in the heptathlon (7 events). The competitions run 8 to 10 hours over two days. Athletes win points according to their results in each event. The winner is the athlete who accumulates the most points overall.

Heptathlon

Day 1

1. 100 m hurdles

2. High jump

Day 2

3. Shot put

4. 200 m

5. Long jump

6. Javelin

7. 800 m

Decathlon

Day 1

1. 100 m

2. Long jump

3. Shot put

4. High jump

Day 2

5. 400 m

6. 100 m hurdles

7. Discus

8. Pole vault

9. Javelin

10. 1,500 m

Cycling

Road Racing
Track Racing
BMX
Mountain Biking

Road Racing

In road racing, the goal is to pedal faster than the competition over a given distance. Men and women cyclists usually compete in teams of 6 to 10, but are scored individually. As a team, cyclists work together to help their best racer to win. They protect his or her position, and try to prevent breakaways by opponents.

Cups and championships

Classic race
The cyclists all start at the same time. They race from one city to the next in one day. The 25 fastest riders are awarded points: from 100 points for first place, down to one point for 25th place. The rider who earns the most points in a season wins the World Cup.

Circuit race
The cyclists ride a set number of laps on a road course. The fastest cyclist wins. The world championship is a circuit race; it is held at a different location every year.

Time trial
Each cyclist races against the clock, starting at set intervals (every minute or two) to try for the fastest time on the same course.

Stage race
Cyclists race a course over a period of 2 to 22 days; each stage lasts one day, but cannot be longer than 161.5 miles. The winner is the racer who covers the entire distance in the least time. The *Tour de France* and the Tour of Italy (the *Giro*) are stage races. Each is almost 2,500 miles long!

Bicycles

Road-racing bicycle
The road-racing bicycle usually has 18 gears, making it easier to ride on different kinds of terrain. The frame is strong and lightweight, and can be made of aluminium, carbon-fiber, or titanium. This bike is custom-made to fit the cyclist. It must allow him to ride in the correct position, with elbows bent to absorb bumps and chest relaxed for easier breathing.

Time-trial bicycle
This bicycle is designed for maximum aerodynamics. The tires are narrower and lighter than those on a classic racing bike, and the back wheel is a solid disk. The disk allows for higher speeds, because it creates less air resistance as it rotates forward than a wheel with spokes. The front wheel has spokes, however, because a solid disk might be pushed by side winds that could cause the bicycle to tip.

Road Racing

Aerodynamics

When a cyclist pedals, the force of air pushes against him, which slows him down. To counter this effect, he adopts a body position that allows him to cut through the air more easily. This position is called aerodynamic. Racing bicycles, which are built to offer less resistance to the wind, are also aerodynamic. Having an aerodynamic body position and an aerodynamic bicycle helps to increase the cyclist's speed.

Descent

Looking for speed, racers try to minimize their wind resistance by staying low and horizontal. They put their hands in the hollow of the handlebars and keep their upper legs close to their bodies. In this position, good racers can reach speeds of more than 55 mph.

Climbing

When the hill is very steep, racers stand on the pedals, using their weight to help push the pedals down.

Team car

Each team has several cars, for its coach, trainers, mechanics, and replacement bikes.

Lead motorcycle

The lead motorcycle always rides ahead of the lead racer. It announces to spectators that the racers will soon be passing through and ensures that the course is clear for them.

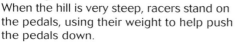

Lead racer

Peloton

Depending on the race, the peloton (which means "pack") may contain more than 150 cyclists who are forced to ride very close to one another. They must be careful to avoid falls.

Track Racing

In track racing there are two goals: to catch up to the other competitors, and to record the fastest time. In a sprint event, cyclists need to reach their maximum speed and maintain it. In an endurance event, cyclists must pedal at a steady speed over a long distance. Racing on a sloped track in a pack of cyclists requires precision and control: the bicycles can reach high speeds on the steep, banked turns, but do not have gears or brakes to slow them down.

Endurance events

Team and individual pursuit
Pursuit means chase. In the individual pursuit, two cyclists begin the race from start lines on opposite sides of the track. Their goal is to chase and catch up to their opponent, and to complete the 4 km course (3 km for women) in the shortest time. The team pursuit is a similar event for men, but with four cyclists taking turns leading their teammates around the track.

Olympic sprint
Two teams of three cyclists start in the same positions as in a pursuit event, at opposite sides of the track. Riders must take turns leading their team for one complete lap around the track. The race lasts for three laps. The clock stops once the third racer crosses the finish line at the end of the third lap.

Madison (paired) race
This is the longest race, lasting 20 to 60 km. It also features the most cyclists on the track at one time, with as many as 18 teams of two relay riders each. One cyclist races while her teammate pedals more slowly. Each rider's turn lasts until she catches up to her teammate —usually 1½ laps. The goal is to make as many laps as possible within the time limit set.

Track Racing

Sprint events

Time trial

In this 1,000 m race (500 m for women), there is only one cyclist on the track at a time. From the start signal to the finish, the rider races against the clock, trying to cover the distance in the shortest time possible.

Match sprint

Two cyclists race for three laps, but only the last 200 m is timed. The riders watch each other, switch positions, and sometimes come to a complete standstill before sprinting to the finish line.

Outgoing |

Incoming |

Relay technique

In order to transfer his speed and give momentum to a teammate entering the relay, the outgoing racer grabs some part of his teammate's bicycle, or his hand, and pushes him forward. This relay move requires a lot of practice.

Pursuit line
Indicates the start and finish lines for each cyclist in a pursuit event. |

Jury platform
Ten judges keep track of the race and announce the results from this viewing area.

Finish line
This is the finish line for all races except the pursuits. |

The track

Tracks are oval, with lengths of from 250 m to 400 m. The slope of the track can be quite steep on the turns; on a track that is 9 m wide, the outside edge may be as high as a two-story building!

| **Pursuit line**

| **200 m line**
In sprint events, the clock starts when a racer reaches this line.

Racers' area |
This is where racers rest and are cared for and where mechanics check and repair their bicycles.

BMX

BMX (bicycle motocross) is a spectacular sport, combining the physical skills of cycling with acrobatics. Men and women athletes are constantly pushing the sport to new limits. Today, bikers often spend more time in the air than on the ground! There are several kinds of BMX events. Track races and dirt competitions take place on clay courses, while freestyle or acrobatic events take place on flatland, street, and half pipe courses.

Equipment

Helmet with chin guard
The helmet is required for track racing and is widely used in dirt competitions and half pipe races.

Elbow pads

Shin guards

Knee pads

BMX

Track race

Cyclists ride a clay course of bumps and obstacles as quickly as they can. They never stop pedaling and try to stay on the ground as much as possible in spite of the bumps. The race lasts only 30 to 45 seconds. Eight cyclists compete at a time; the four slowest riders are eliminated.

Tactics

The cyclist who reaches the first curve in first place has a good chance of holding this position for the rest of the race. At this point, she has two advantages: no other cyclists in her way, and control over the pace of the race.

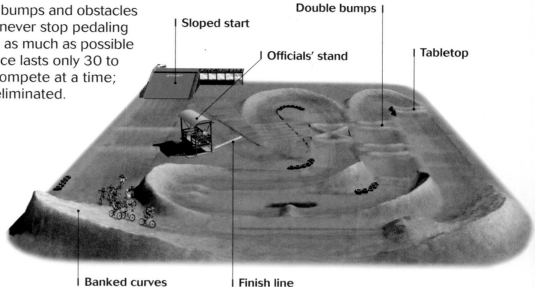

Sloped start

Double bumps

Officials' stand

Tabletop

Banked curves

Finish line

Dirt competition

Riders are allowed three attempts to make acrobatic jumps between two bumps. Four judges mark the jumps according to how difficult they are and how well they are performed. The winner of the event is the rider with the most points after three jumps.

Tail whip

1. The cyclist gains enough speed to make a high jump.

2. With his right foot, he pushes on the back wheel to spin the frame around.

3. He stops the rotation by putting his left foot down on the pedal and using his right foot to stabilize the bike.

4. Throughout the entire movement, the cyclist never takes his eyes off the point where he must land.

BMX

Flatland

This specialty requires constant training. On a flat area, cyclists perform a series of acrobatic maneuvers, or moves, which are set to music. They are penalized every time a foot touches the ground. Each competitor makes two qualifying passes. A pass usually lasts 2½ minutes. The 20 highest-ranked competitors go to the finals. Four judges rate the performances and give an overall mark out of 100 points. The cyclists are evaluated on the technical difficulty of their moves, their choreography, and the originality of the moves.

Decade

1. With his feet on the back foot pegs, the cyclist brakes hard on the back brake and lifts his front wheel.

3. With his weight resting completely on the handlebars, he makes a 360° rotation.

5. The figure is complete when he puts both feet back down on the pedals.

2. He puts his right foot on the frame of the bicycle to start the rotation.

4. At the end of the rotation, he puts his left foot on the frame and lowers the front wheel.

Half pipe

Riders have 1½ minutes to perform aerial moves to music on a U-shaped ramp called a half pipe. There are two kinds of figures: aerials, which are jumps above the half pipe, and lip tricks, which are performed on the top edges (copings) of the half pipe. Four judges give an overall mark out of 100 for height, technical difficulty, and smoothness of performance.

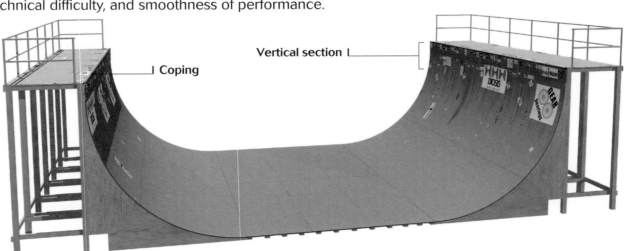

Coping

Vertical section

Street

The course is a series of obstacles you might encounter on a city street, such as stairs, benches, and walls. For 1½ minutes, cyclists perform acrobatics using these obstacles. Judges rate performances on the difficulty and originality of the maneuvers, which fall into two categories: jumps and grinds, which consist of sliding the bicycle on its foot pegs.

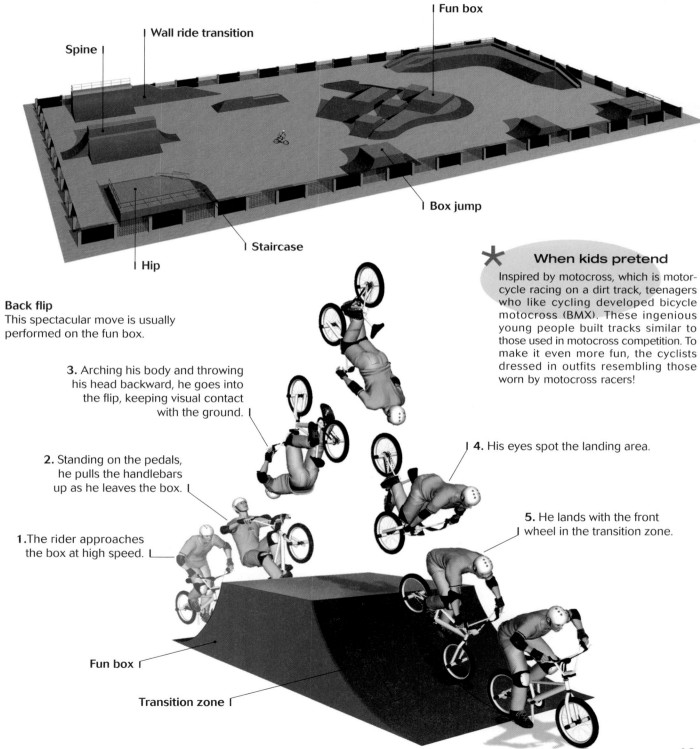

Fun box

Wall ride transition

Spine

Box jump

Staircase

Hip

Back flip
This spectacular move is usually performed on the fun box.

3. Arching his body and throwing his head backward, he goes into the flip, keeping visual contact with the ground.

2. Standing on the pedals, he pulls the handlebars up as he leaves the box.

1. The rider approaches the box at high speed.

Fun box

Transition zone

4. His eyes spot the landing area.

5. He lands with the front wheel in the transition zone.

✱ **When kids pretend**
Inspired by motocross, which is motorcycle racing on a dirt track, teenagers who like cycling developed bicycle motocross (BMX). These ingenious young people built tracks similar to those used in motocross competition. To make it even more fun, the cyclists dressed in outfits resembling those worn by motocross racers!

Mountain Biking

Mountain biking is practiced on courses that feature steep trails and difficult obstacles. The bikes are equipped with heavy-duty suspension systems. This helps to make the ride springy in spite of the bumps on the course. Athletes need good balance, quick reflexes, and endurance for this sport. Men and women compete in two types of events: cross-country and downhill.

Cross-country

The course is between 15 and 25 miles long and the race lasts about two hours. A cyclist must try to be the fastest throughout the race to finish first. There are many unexpected obstacles, and rain can quickly turn the track into deep mud. In addition, cyclists are not allowed any outside assistance, even if they have a flat tire or a mechanical breakdown. They need to carry their own tools and do their own repairs on the spot.

The bike
The bike is very light and solid, with wide, notched tires. It is equipped with 18 to 27 gears, to handle all kinds of terrain, as well as a container of compressed carbon dioxide for reinflating repaired tires.

Mountain Biking

Obstacles

The cyclist must anticipate what type of terrain surrounds the obstacle she is about to encounter. Knowing whether the ground is slippery, soft, or hard will determine her approach to the obstacle.

Ground obstacles
The cyclist pedals right up until the last moment so as not to lose speed. Once her front wheel crosses the obstacle, the cyclist brings her weight forward to help get the back wheel over the obstacle.

Climbs
During short climbs, the cyclist may stand on the pedals. If she leans too far forward, however, she can lose traction in the back wheel, causing the bike to slip or slide.

Mountain Biking

Downhill competition

This is a speed competition on a steep hill with many obstacles. Cyclists race against the clock, one by one, down a 2 to 5 km slope, and can reach speeds of more than 60 mph! Before the race, cyclists inspect the course to check out the obstacles they might encounter; they will have only tenths of seconds to avoid them during the race.

Turn
At high speed, the cyclist sticks out her foot to increase her stability and to support herself if the bike slips.

Equipment

Because of the risk of falls, racers wear back, shoulder, and chest protection, goggles, and a full-face helmet with chin guard.

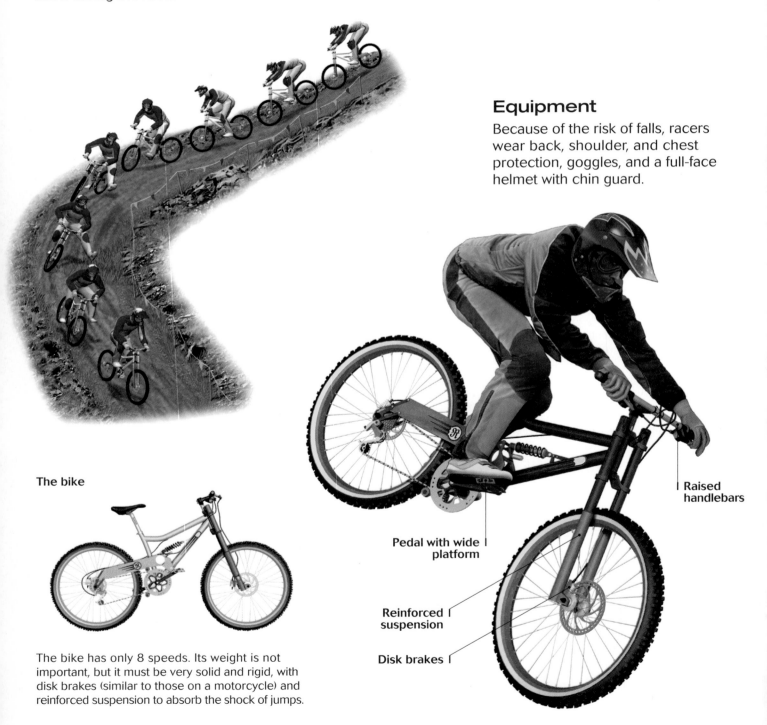

The bike

The bike has only 8 speeds. Its weight is not important, but it must be very solid and rigid, with disk brakes (similar to those on a motorcycle) and reinforced suspension to absorb the shock of jumps.

Raised handlebars

Pedal with wide platform

Reinforced suspension

Disk brakes

Gymnastics

Artistic Gymnastics
Rhythmic Gymnastics
Trampoline

Artistic Gymnastics

The artistic gymnast is always working to achieve perfection, while trying to make it look easy. Athletes must display confidence and flawless technique as they perform in a series of events using a variety of apparatuses. To reach the winners' podium, artistic gymnasts need muscular strength, balance, flexibility, and total concentration.

The competition

In teams of four to seven, gymnasts take turns performing routines that must include at least 10 acrobatic moves. The floor exercises and balance beam events are timed. There are six events for men, and four for women. Competitions start off as team events; the athletes who score the highest go on to compete individually.

Equipment

Hand protectors
Hand protectors give the gymnast a stronger grip on the apparatus with less effort. They also protect against burns and blisters.

Shoes
Gymnasts have a choice of wearing shoes or going barefoot in their routines.

Reverse double salto
The reverse double salto can be performed as part of the floor exercise. It is a back flip requiring 2 complete turns in the air before landing. The gymnast gains the needed momentum by doing a back handspring followed by a powerful upward spring.

Artistic Gymnastics

Scoring

Gymnasts are evaluated by judges, who mark their routines according to the level of difficulty and how well they are performed. Before competing, gymnasts give the judges a list of the elements in their program. For every mistake a gymnast makes, judges deduct several tenths of a point. Judges are very critical, and a perfect score of 10 is rarely awarded!

Women's events

Artistic expression is as important as acrobatic skill in the women's events. In international competition, the gymnasts perform in vault, uneven parallel bars, balance beam, and floor exercises.

Women's floor exercise

Gymnasts present a routine that is set to music and runs from 70 to 90 seconds. They must use as much of the floor area as possible while staying in bounds. The routine consists of a series of jumps and flips, and should demonstrate muscular strength, agility, and originality.

Double Schuschunova
Usually performed as the finale for a series of moves, it serves more as an artistic element than a display of technical skill.

✱ **Perfect score**
Nadia Comaneci of Romania was the first gymnast in the history of the sport to earn a perfect score of 10, at the 1976 Olympics in Montreal. She followed this feat with 6 more perfect scores. Her record has never been broken!

Apparatus
Apparatus refers to the bars or other equipment used in all gymnastic events except the floor exercise.

Dismount
Coming at the end of a routine, the dismount allows the gymnast to leave the apparatus with an acrobatic move. It is usually difficult and is designed to impress the judges. Unless the dismount is performed perfectly, the gymnast will not gain any extra points for it.

Magnesium
This is the white powder that we see on the hands and feet of the gymnasts. It makes surfaces less slippery and gives athletes a better grip on the apparatus.

Routine
A routine is a series of movements that gymnasts perform in front of the judges during a competition.

Salto
A salto is a difficult backward or forward flip. It can be performed in the tuck position (*see* reverse double salto, men's floor exercise), in the pike position (*see* reverse double salto, women's floor exercise), or in the layout position (*see* full-twisting layout Tsukahara, men's vault).

Artistic Gymnastics

Women's vault

Speed and precision are needed in this event. The athlete has two turns. Her final score is the average of the two attempts. After running to gain speed and momentum, the gymnast often performs a series of acrobatic jumps using the springboard and vault. She must control her speed in order to maintain her balance when landing.

Women's vault
The vault is placed widthwise across the track. It is covered in leather or synthetic material.

Yurchenko
The gymnast performs a roundoff before taking off from the springboard. This gives her the height she needs to do a double back flip.

Uneven parallel bars

The gymnast is expected to demonstrate acrobatic skill and athletic power in this event. The routine consists of a series of continuous, balanced movements, including rotations, flips, and changes in grip on the bars. The uneven bars provide an opportunity for the gymnast to end the program with a dramatic dismount.

Uneven parallel bars
The height and position of the bars must be adjusted for each gymnast. The bars are made of fiberglass or steel-reinforced wood, mounted on steel posts.

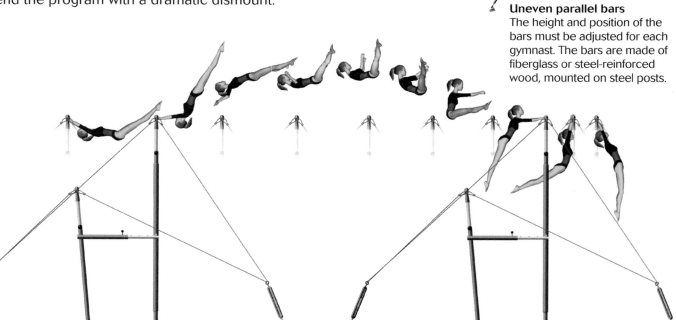

Tchatchev splits
The gymnast must be in a perfect position to properly grasp the high bar. A fall in the middle of the routine can cost several points.

Artistic Gymnastics

Balance beam

The balance beam is very narrow—barely wider than your foot! Performing on this surface requires precision, control, and a good sense of balance. The gymnast uses the entire length of the beam to execute a series of jumps and acrobatic moves. The program ends with the dismount.

Balance beam
The beam is 4 in. wide and is made of aluminum covered with a nonslip elastic material.

Rufolva
Getting enough momentum to do the back spring is the most difficult part. To properly land, the gymnast must regain sight of the beam as early as possible.

Men's events

The events for male gymnasts require power, coordination, and flexibility. Athletes compete in the following events: floor exercise, pommel horse, rings, vault, parallel bars, and horizontal bar.

Men's vault

Power and speed are essential in this exercise. Each athlete has only one turn on the vault. The jump must be long enough and high enough to allow for multiple turns in the air. No matter how difficult the jump, the landing must be perfectly controlled or the athlete will be penalized.

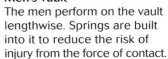

Men's vault
The men perform on the vault lengthwise. Springs are built into it to reduce the risk of injury from the force of contact.

Full-twisting layout Tsukahara
This move requires a fast run to the springboard to gain enough momentum for the jump. Horizontal speed is needed, but makes the landing harder to control.

Artistic Gymnastics

Rings

The rings are suspended more than 8 ft above the floor. Gymnasts are helped up by their coaches, but from then on must use their own power. They are expected to display both muscular strength and perfect balance while executing a series of demanding still positions and swinging moves. The program ends with a rapid dismount.

Rings

Rings are made of wood or plastic and are suspended on leather straps.

Inverted cross

To get into this position without swinging requires complete concentration and extraordinary muscle power. The position must be held for several seconds to be considered successful.

Parallel bars

In a routine that must span the full length of the bars, the gymnast is required to display acrobatic skill and athletic power. Aided by the elasticity of the bars, the athlete performs saltos, leaps, and balanced poses.

Parallel bars

The parallel bars are made of wood reinforced with fiberglass. The steel posts can be adjusted for the height of the gymnast.

Diamidov

After a complete turn on one arm, the gymnast regains his balance and remains standing on both extended arms for several seconds.

Artistic Gymnastics

Pommel horse

Resting only on his hands, the gymnast swings his legs above the pommel horse, never allowing the rest of his body to come into contact with it. His routine, which spans the entire length of the horse, involves a series of continuous swinging and kicking movements. Performing with hands and feet moving independently requires perfect coordination and muscles of steel.

Pommel horse
Made of wood or steel, it is covered in leather or synthetic material. The handles are made of wood or plastic.

Thomas flair
The gymnast can see the pommels (handles) only when his legs are behind the horse. He must spread his legs as far apart as possible.

Men's floor exercise

The men's floor exercise is a demonstration of strength, flexibility, and agility. The gymnast appears to bounce off the floor with little effort as he performs a series of acrobatic jumps and flips. The athlete must use as much of the floor area as he can, and should show variety and originality in his choice of movements.

Reverse double salto in the tuck position
The gymnast gets his momentum from a back handspring. Just before taking off, he focuses on a distant spot, and must not lose sight of it while he flips over.

Horizontal bar

Forward and backward rotations, abrupt changes in direction, leaps in the air, and balanced poses make up the gymnast's routine on the horizontal bar. His movements must be smooth and continuous. The athlete gains momentum in his rotations, which helps him perform a spectacular dismount at the end.

Dislocation
The gymnast moves his straight legs between his arms and stretches his body, pivoting around his shoulders. He finishes the move with a backward swing.

Horizontal bar
The bar is made of stainless steel and is supported by adjustable steel posts.

Rhythmic Gymnastics

In this series of five different events exclusively for women, dance and artistic expression are as important as the gymnastic moves. Athletes score additional points by demonstrating personality and originality in their routines. It also takes a talented performer to combine graceful dancing with the body control necessary for success in acrobatic exercises.

The competition

Accompanied by the music she selects, the gymnast performs dance and gymnastic movements while manipulating one of five kinds of apparatus: ball, hoop, rope, ribbon, or clubs. Even while throwing, catching, or rolling the equipment, she must be in motion at all times. The judges mark the gymnast's routine on its technical and artistic merits. In each competition, athletes are awarded points for individual as well as for team performance. There is also a group program, in which five gymnasts perform the same routine simultaneously.

Techniques

The various apparatuses, such as the ball and rope, are used differently. However, all routines feature some of the same four basic movements: spin, layback, balance, and jump.

Slippers
The slippers do not have heels and serve only to make turns and landings easier.

Hair
Hair is always tied back to keep it from interfering with the gymnast's sight or movements.

Spin   **Layback**   **Balance**   **Jump**

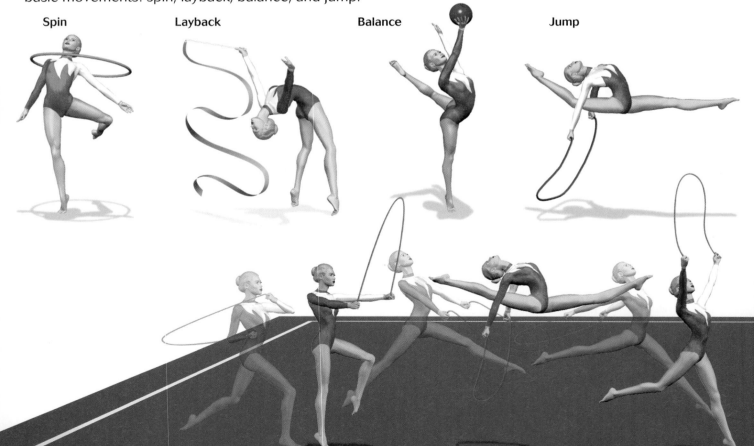

Rhythmic Gymnastics

Equipment

Gymnasts always try to demonstrate the ability to move independently while the apparatus stays in motion.

Hoop
The gymnast can throw the hoop, make it turn or roll, or pass it under her body.

Clubs
The gymnast twirls and throws the clubs in various ways that highlight rhythm and dance moves.

Rope
The rope is the most physically demanding apparatus. The gymnast needs both strength and stamina to keep the rope in constant motion.

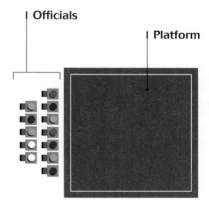

Officials

Platform

Ribbon
The ribbon must be in constant motion. The gymnast focuses on creating patterns such as circles and spirals.

Ball
Thrown with force and caught with delicacy, the ball allows the gymnast to express different talents.

Officials
Many judges share the task of evaluating a gymnast's performance: one group judges technical aspects, a second group judges artistic merit, and a third group notes the qualities and faults in the program. A head judge collects their notes and gives the final score.

Platform
The platform is carpeted, and there must be more than 26 ft between it and the ceiling, to allow gymnasts to throw their apparatuses high in the air.

Trampoline

With the aid of the trampoline, men and women gymnasts can bounce more than 25 ft in the air—almost the height of a two-story building! This gives the athletes time to perform complicated acrobatic moves. Trampolinists must know their exact position while in the air. They must take care to control their bounces and landings.

The competition

Athletes perform 3 routines of 10 acrobatic maneuvers each. The jumps are a combination of forward and backward somersaults and twists. The most difficult jump combines three somersaults and three twists. Gymnasts are not allowed to perform the same move twice in a row, and must always land in the designated square on the trampoline. Judges mark the routines according to how difficult they are and how well they are performed. The routines are so complicated that two judges are assigned to count the somersaults and twists.

Frame protector

Spotters
In case the trampolinist loses control, the spotters are there to catch him and break his fall.

Techniques

As in gymnastics, jumps can be executed in three positions: layout, pike, and tuck.

Layout

Pike

Tuck

Double mini-trampoline

This event was developed by gymnasts who use the mini-trampoline in their training; it has now become an international event. The gymnast takes a running jump, and then performs a series of acrobatic moves in the air, using the two trampolines. It requires great precision and control to land in a still position within the designated area.

Aquatic Sports

Swimming
Synchronized Swimming
Water Polo
Diving

Swimming

The goal of the competitive swimmer is to glide through the water faster and with less effort. Men and women athletes train constantly to achieve perfect technique. Champion swimmers are those who get the most power from their strokes through the least tiring movements. Athletes race against the clock and against other swimmers, competing as individuals or in relay teams. Races consist of swimming laps, or pool lengths, in distances of 50 to 1,500 meters. Some athletes train full time to be specialists in one of the four standard strokes: crawl, breaststroke, backstroke, or butterfly. Others specialize in medley events, which require them to swim using all four strokes in one race. In major events like the Olympic Games and the world championships, swimmers compete in stages: heats, quarterfinals, and semifinals. The final event brings together the eight fastest athletes.

Backstroke starting grips

Starting block
There is a starting block for each lane. The diving surface is between 19 and 29 inches above the water. The block is covered with a nonslip material.

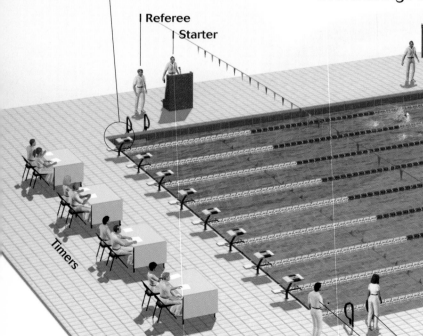

Referee

Starter

Timers

Stroke judges (4)
They check that each swimmer is performing the stroke legally.

Timekeepers and chief timer
Timekeepers watch and note the swimmers' times in case the electronic timing equipment fails. The chief timer verifies both the electronically recorded times and those of the timekeepers.

Finish judge
This judge records and reports the order in which the swimmers finish.

Swimming

Starts

At the starter's first signal, the swimmers take their positions on their starting blocks. At the second signal, they dive into the pool. For the backstroke event, swimmers start in the pool holding their backstroke grips. If any swimmer starts too soon, that swimmer is automatically disqualified from the race.

Backward start
The swimmers are in the pool, holding on to the starting grips. Their feet are underwater and braced against the wall. At the signal, they let go of the grips and push off with their feet, arching their bodies above the water to get a longer start.

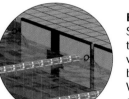

Electronic touch pads
Swimmers often finish a race very close together. To accurately determine the winners, electronic touch pads have been installed at the end of each lane. When a swimmer touches the pad the clock is stopped.

Forward start
The swimmers hold their breath as they wait for the signal. When the signal is sounded, the swimmers push off the blocks strongly with their legs, stretching their bodies out fully in the air before they hit the water.

Turn judges
They make sure that the turns are legal.

Backstroke flags

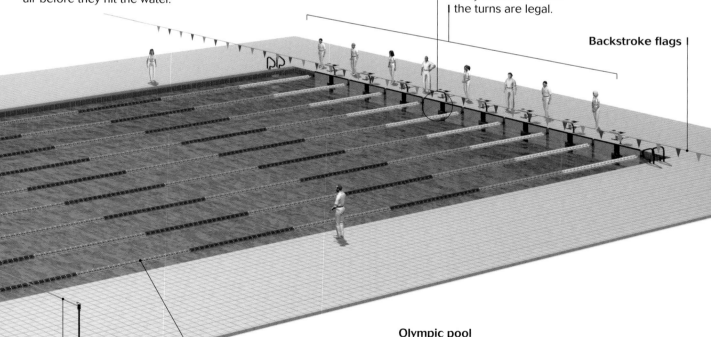

Floating lane dividers

False start recall rope
It is placed 15 m from the start wall. When a false start is called, a signal identical to that for the start indicates to swimmers that they must return to the blocks. At the same time, the rope falls into the water.

Olympic pool
An Olympic pool measures 50 m in length. It is divided into 8 lanes, which are separated by floating dividers of different colors. Lines painted on the bottom of the pool help to guide the swimmers and to keep them within their lanes. In the Olympic Games, the pool must be 5.9 ft deep, and the water temperature must be kept at 75° F.

Swimming

Crawl

The crawl is the fastest of the four standard strokes. It is the stroke swimmers always use in the freestyle events, even though they are allowed to use any stroke they wish. The 50 meter freestyle event is such a fast race that many swimmers do not take the time to take in air every third stroke as they normally would.

Olympic freestyle events
100 m freestyle
200 m freestyle
400 m freestyle
800 m freestyle (women)
1,500 m freestyle

Starting to swim
After diving under the water, swimmers return to the surface kicking their legs. They may not use their arms until they reach the surface.

Technique
To propel themselves forward, the swimmers perform flutter kicks with their legs while they alternate lifting their arms forward and pulling them through the water. Swimmers must face sideways to take in air every few strokes.

Backstroke

Performing the backstroke, swimmers are facing upward and therefore cannot see the lane markings. For that reason, flags are hung over the pool to guide them and to indicate when they are 5 m (16.4 ft) from the wall.

Olympic backstroke events
100 m backstroke
200 m backstroke

Starting to swim
After the backward start, swimmers stay underwater to maintain their momentum as long as possible. They can kick their legs separately or together. They must surface before they reach the 15 m mark.

Technique
In the backstroke, swimmers use a technique similar to the crawl but swim on their backs. In order to stay in the correct extended position, swimmers keep their heads tilted slightly backward.

Swimming

Breaststroke

The breaststroke is the slowest as well as the most demanding of the four swimming styles. Swimmers use their arms and legs to "push" the water away from their bodies. If they do not extend their arms and legs in unison, they are disqualified for swimming "freestyle."

Olympic breaststroke events
100 m breaststroke
200 m breaststroke

Starting to swim
After diving off the block, swimmers are allowed only one complete stroke and one kick of the legs underwater before surfacing.

Technique
The swimmer's stroke combines three movements: The arms are pushed away from the body, pulled downward toward the pool bottom, and then pulled inward toward the body. The swimmer's legs bend in unison, propelling the swimmer forward with a kick that provides more power than other leg movements.

Butterfly

The butterfly is the only stroke in which both of the swimmer's arms enter and exit the water together. The legs also work in unison.

Olympic butterfly events
100 m butterfly
200 m butterfly

Starting to swim
In order to keep their momentum going after the forward dive, swimmers perform a rolling movement with their bodies underwater, keeping their legs and feet together.

Technique
The swimmer's arms lift forward out of the water, and then pull backward together under the water. The legs move in unison in a dolphin kick, completing the wavelike movement begun by the arms. Swimmers take a breath every few strokes, while their arms are over their heads.

Swimming

Turn

A well-performed turn can improve a swimmer's time. In the crawl and in the backstroke, swimmers do an underwater somersault just before the wall, and then push off the wall with a powerful leg thrust. In the breaststroke and butterfly, swimmers must touch the wall with both hands before turning around and pushing off. Referees check to make sure the turns are performed correctly.

Goggles
Goggles are designed to fit perfectly. They must be watertight and streamlined to reduce water resistance.

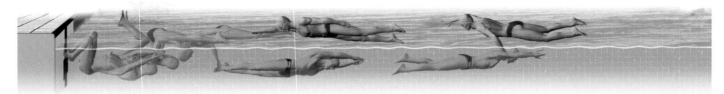

Flip turn
Swimmers bend their bodies and dive downward toward the bottom of the pool to perform a somersault.

★ Every second counts
Swimmers shave their bodies before major competitions. Shaving helps the athletes feel the water against their skin, making them more aware of their movements in the water. This helps swimmers move more efficiently, thereby saving valuable time.

Open turn
Swimmers must be in a horizontal position before their feet lose contact with the wall.

Medley and relay events

In a medley event, swimmers are required to use a combination of the breaststroke, backstroke, butterfly, and a freestyle stroke. Athletes must swim a minimum of one pool length (50 m) in each style. In a freestyle relay, each of four swimmers per team takes a turn swimming 100 or 200 m. In a medley relay, each swimmer on the team is required to use a different stroke.

Olympic medley and relay events
400 m individual medley
4 X 100 m medley relay
4 X 100 m freestyle relay (women)
4 X 200 m freestyle relay (men)

Relay
In a relay race, the swimmer waits on the starting block until his or her teammate has completed swimming the lap. When the teammate touches the electronic pad, the waiting swimmer dives off the starting block.

Synchronized Swimming

Synchronized swimming is an artistic sport that combines swimming, dancing, and gymnastics. Synchronized swimming is practiced exclusively by women, as a solo, duet, or team event. Accompanied by music, athletes perform acrobatic routines in the swimming pool, both above and under water. The sport is called synchronized swimming because the participants must perform their routines in perfect time with the music and with one another. Athletes spend many years perfecting their choreography, which is the series of movements that make up their programs.

The competition

The competition is divided into two sections: the technical routine and the free routine. Swimmers are judged on their technical ability and artistic presentation. The marks for the two routines are added together, giving a maximum score of 10 points. Swimmers are penalized if they touch the bottom of the pool or support themselves on the edge.

Technical routine

In the first part of the event, the swimmers demonstrate a set number of figures. Athletes must perform the figures in a specified order within the time limit. Solo swimmers have two minutes to perform six figures, duets have 2:20 minutes to perform seven figures, and teams have 2:50 minutes to perform eight figures. The marks for technique are more important than the marks for artistic performance. The technical routine counts for 35% of the final mark in the competition.

Technical routine		
	Duration	No. of figures
Solo	2:00	6
Duet	2:20	7
Team	2:50	8

Free routine

In this second part of the event, athletes present the personal and artistic elements of their programs. Performing programs that they have chosen themselves, the swimmers usually begin their routines beside the pool. They have up to 10 seconds before they must enter the water. The marks for artistic performance are more important than the marks for technique. The free routine counts for 65% of the final mark in the competition.

Free routine		
	Duration	No. of figures
Solo	3:30	no limit
Duet	4:00	no limit
Team	4:50	no limit

Synchronized Swimming

Basic positions and figures

There are approximately 20 basic positions in synchronized swimming. The figures performed in the free routines as well as in the technical routines are all based on these 20 positions. The two figures below demonstrate some of the basic positions.

Front walkover
This figure starts with the swimmer in a vertical position with her head underwater and her legs extended horizontally on the surface. The swimmer raises one leg in the air in the "castle" position. She then lowers her leg and raises her body to the surface until she is in a horizontal position on her back.

Nose clip
The nose clip is vital because it prevents water from entering the nasal cavity during the upside-down movements. Some swimmers keep a second clip attached to their swimsuit in case the first one is lost during the performance.

Barracuda
The Barracuda ends with the swimmer in a vertical position, head down and legs extended in the air. The swimmer's ankles, hips, and head must be perfectly aligned.

Routine

Synchronized swimmers create routines by performing a series of basic positions that are connected to form figures. During their programs, the swimmers use creative transitions to move from one part of the pool to the next. The transitions also give the athletes a chance to catch their breath after performing underwater figures.

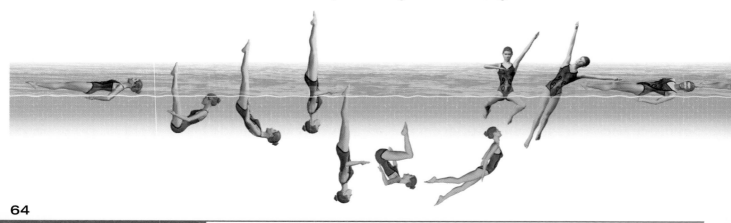

Synchronized Swimming

Team competition

In the free routine, the eight team members must stay perfectly in sync with one another, even if they are not all performing identical figures at the same time. Coordinating the movements of so many swimmers is difficult and requires long hours of training.

Platform

Without touching the bottom of the pool, the athletes group themselves underwater to make a "platform" on which to support one of the swimmers. At the end of the figure, the platform may sink or the swimmer may dive off.

Duet

Performing as a duet requires excellent coordination between the two swimmers, as well as perfect synchronization with the music. In the free routine, the swimmers are not required to perform the same figures at the same time, but their movements must still be coordinated in an artistic way.

Water Polo

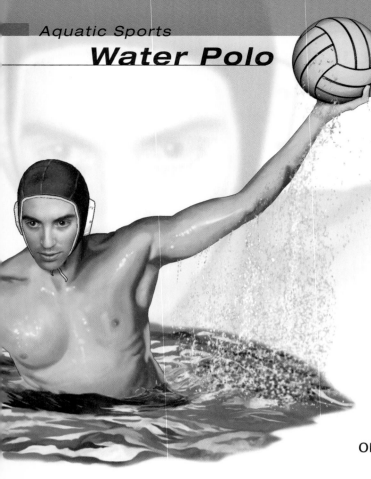

Water polo is a ball sport played between two teams in a swimming pool. The object is to score points by throwing the ball into the opponents' goal. Both men and women compete in this sport. Waterpolo demands strong swimming skills as well as the endurance to stay in motion in the water for long periods. Each team has 13 players, but only 7 of them are in the pool at the same time. Players are not allowed to touch the bottom of the pool or support themselves in any way. The goalkeeper is the only player allowed to hit the ball with his or her fists or to hold it with both hands.

Equipment

Cap
Each team wears numbered caps in different colors: white for one team, blue for the other team, and red for the two goalkeepers. The caps are equipped with soft plastic ear protectors.

The pool
The ideal pool is about 6 ft deep and measures 20 m by 30 m. Floating markers in different colors help to indicate the various play zones.

Ball
The ball is waterproof. It is about the size of a soccer ball and weighs a little less than a pound.

Referee

Goal judge

Goal line

Water Polo

The game

The game is played in four periods of seven minutes each. At the beginning of each period, the players line up on their respective goal lines. The referee throws the ball into the middle of the pool and the players race to take possession of it. The team holding the ball has only 35 seconds to throw it at the opposing goal. Timekeepers keep track of how long a team has held the ball and the referee calls an ordinary foul if this rule is broken. An ordinary foul entitles the opposing team to a free throw. The free throw must be taken from where the offense occurred. The player who has the free throw may throw the ball to another player or drop the ball in the water and dribble it before passing it. The referee calls a major foul if a player interferes with a free throw or purposely holds or hits another player. A major foul entitles the opposing team to a free throw or penalty shot. A penalty shot is a direct throw at a goal from a short distance of 4 m.

Dribbling
Players swim with their arms open, pushing the ball with the waves they create in front of them. They use their bodies to screen the ball from the other players. They are only allowed to touch the ball with one hand at a time.

Goalkeeper technique
Goalkeepers play in a forward-leaning position, staying close to the surface of the water. This makes it easier for them to straighten up quickly and to reach out to catch the ball.

Goal judges
They signal when goals have been scored and when balls are out of bounds.

Goals
The goals are held in the water by cables attached to the side of the pool or attached to the wall. They are made of fiberglass or plastic.

Penalty zone
Players given penalties by the referee must go to the penalty zone closest to their team's goal. They generaly wait there until signaled back into the game.

Referee
Referees on both sides of the pool watch the half of the pool to their right. They signal fouls by blowing a whistle and use their arms to point where the ball should be put back into play.

Diving

In competition diving, athletes jump from a platform or springboard and perform acrobatic movements before landing in the water. The goal is to perform perfect figures and enter the water with as little splash as possible. In the Olympic Games, men and women compete in individual and synchronized diving off the 10 meter platform and the 3 meter springboard. The world championships feature 1 meter springboard diving as well as the usual Olympic events. Judges award marks for technical ability and smooth movement.

Platform
The platform is 10 m high.

The competition

Olympic competitions consist of three phases:

Preliminaries: Women divers perform 5 dives (men perform 6) from the 10 m platform and from the 3 m springboard. The top 18 divers advance to the next round.

Semifinals: Divers perform 4 dives from the 10 m platform and 5 from the 3 m springboard. The scores are added to the results from the preliminaries. The 12 best divers go on to the finals.

Finals: The results from the preliminaries are eliminated. Athletes perform the same number of dives as in the preliminaries. The points they earn here are added to those from the semifinals to obtain the final score.

Scoring

Each dive can earn up to 40 points. Once all the points are awarded, the highest and lowest scores are dropped. The remaining scores are totaled and multiplied by their "difficulty factor." This corresponds to a number of points that judges award to each type of dive. The more difficult a dive is, the more points it earns.

Springboards
Olympic springboards are 3 m high.

Diving

Technique

There are 91 platform dives and 70 types of 3 m springboard dives. These dives fall into six groups. In each group, dives are identified by form (straight, pike, tuck, or free), by the movements presented (such as the number of somersaults), and by the type of entry into the water (headfirst or feetfirst).

Dive groups

Forward

Backward

Reverse

Inward

Arm stand

Twist

Water entry

Feetfirst
The body must be perfectly extended, with no flexing of the ankles, knees, hips, or shoulders.

Headfirst
The hands must be crossed and pressed tightly together. When entering the pool, the diver "opens up" the water with a quick movement of the hands, wrists, and arms. This reduces the amount of splash.

Body positions

Whatever type of dive is selected, the athlete's body must be in 1 of the 3 positions authorized by the regulations. The diver must master each position and be able to perform the dive smoothly.

Straight
Arms are stretched above the head or held alongside the body. There is no flexing of the knees or hips. Feet are together, with the legs straight and the toes pointed.

Pike
The body is bent at the hips and the legs are straight, with feet together and toes pointed. Arms may be stretched toward the toes, held out at the diver's side, or placed under the thighs or calves.

Tuck
Hips and knees are flexed, and the knees are tucked tightly under the body in line with the feet. The hands are on the legs and the toes are pointed.

Diving

Reverse dive with a twist
At the beginning of the rotation, the diver lowers one arm to set her body into a spin.

Forward somersault with a twist
After springing up, the diver brakes for a moment and then slowly guides her body into a rotation.

Forward three-and-a-half somersault in the tuck position
The takeoff from the platform must be high enough to ensure that the diver has the time to perform 3 complete turns before straightening out to enter the water.

Nautical Sports

Ocean Surfing
Waterskiing
Rowing
Canoeing and Kayaking
Sailboarding
Sailing

Ocean Surfing

Demonstrating their acrobatic skills, surfers balance on their boards and ride the ocean waves at impressive speeds. In competitive surfing, athletes must remain in motion as long as possible without falling into the water. Surfers have good balance and quick reflexes. They are also excellent swimmers. Thanks to their knowledge of the ocean, surfers are able to choose the waves that will give them their best rides. In surfing, men and women compete together as well as separately.

The competition

Athletes have 20 minutes to demonstrate their skills. The judges and the competition director evaluate the surfers on their best three or four waves. Athletes are awarded points for the difficulty of the waves chosen, their positions on the waves, the quality of their moves, and the length of time they are able to ride the waves.

Equipment

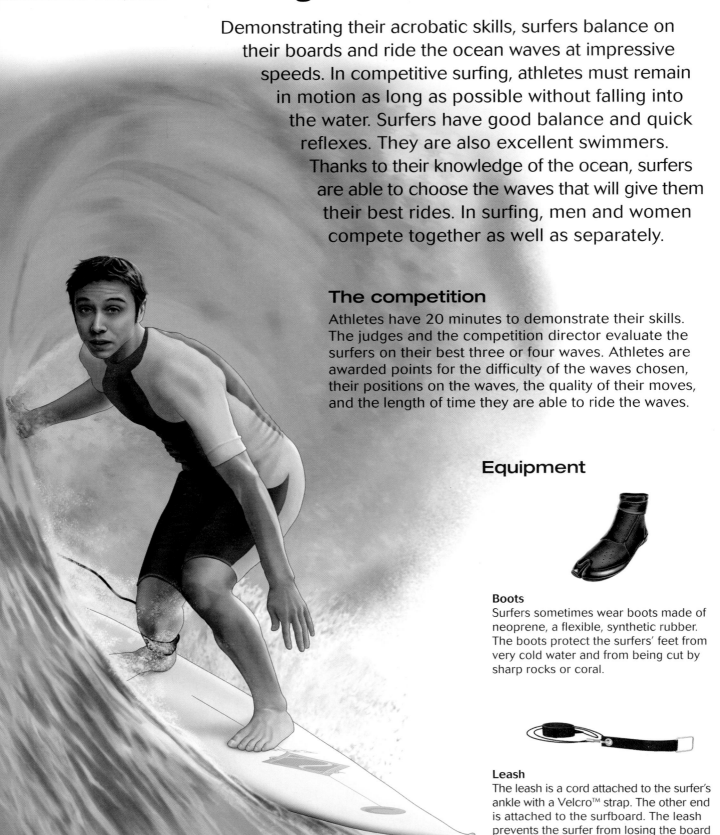

Boots
Surfers sometimes wear boots made of neoprene, a flexible, synthetic rubber. The boots protect the surfers' feet from very cold water and from being cut by sharp rocks or coral.

Leash
The leash is a cord attached to the surfer's ankle with a Velcro™ strap. The other end is attached to the surfboard. The leash prevents the surfer from losing the board if he or she falls into the water.

Ocean Surfing

Techniques

Every wave is different. A surfer must figure out how waves perform, and then ride them in ways that will most impress the judges.

Takeoff
The surfer lies on his stomach on the board, and then uses his arms to help him get to a standing position. He balances by keeping his knees bent and arms out.

Floater
The surfer rides up the front side, or "face," of the wave and over the "lip," which is where the wave breaks. He then rides along the "crest," or top, of the wave as far as he can before dropping back down the face of the wave.

Cut-back
The surfer rides the face of the wave. By shifting his weight to his heels, he turns the board in the opposite direction, toward the breaking curl of the wave.

Boards

Boards today are usually made of polyurethane foam covered with fiberglass. The way they perform in the water is determined by their shape and their weight.

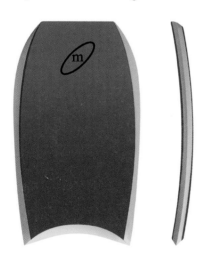

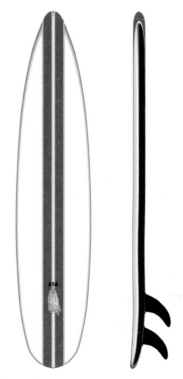

Bodyboard
The bodyboard is the shortest of the 3 boards, about 3½ ft long. Bodyboarders surf lying down. They sometimes wear diving fins on their feet.

Shortboard
The shortboard is very popular with all levels of surfers. It is about 6 ft long and is lightweight and streamlined to allow rapid maneuvers and turns.

Longboard
The longboard is heavy, very stable, and difficult to turn. It measures about 9 ft in length. In competition, it is mainly the choice of beginners.

Waterskiing

Waterskiing is a combination of surfing and skiing. It is a high-speed sport that demands quick reflexes and good balance. Athletes ski across the water using a towline attached to a powerful motorboat. Traveling at over 30 miles per hour, skiers perform spectacular maneuvers on one or two skis. There are four types of waterskiing competitions for men and women: slalom, figures, wakeboard, and jumping.

Slalom competition

The slalom competition is a high-speed race. The boat travels down the center of the course towing the skier on a single ski. The athlete must ski around six buoys in a zigzag pattern without falling down. The athlete skis the course first in one direction and then in the other. To make the race more difficult, the speed of the boat is gradually increased until it reaches about 35 mph. In addition, the towline on the boat is gradually shortened. This makes it harder for the skier, who has less time and room to ski around the buoys.

Slalom technique
Pulling against the towline with one hand, the skier leans into the turn and cuts across the water at right angles to the boat. This move increases her speed and enables her to jump over the wake, which is the wave formed by the speeding boat. After crossing the wake, the skier prepares for the next turn.

Equipment

Towline
The maximum length of the towline varies according to the event. The towline in the slalom is about 60 ft long at the start of the race, then gradually is shortened. The line is about 75 ft long for the jumping competition, 59 ft for wakeboard, and about 42 ft for figures.

Boat
The same motorboat tows all skiers. The boat is equipped with speedometers and 2 large rearview mirrors. This helps the judge, who rides on board, to check on the skiers and the speed of the boat.

Waterskiing

Figures competition

In the figures competition, the skier rides on a single ski and performs as many acrobatic figures and combinations as possible during a set period. Five judges evaluate the athlete's technical abilities. Before the event begins, the skier must submit a "routines sheet" to the jury, indicating the figures he intends to perform, as well as their order. The skier is not allowed to perform the same figure twice.

Wakeboard competition

In the wakeboard event, the skier must execute a combination of five figures in two passes lasting 25 seconds each. She may add a sixth figure at the end of the routine to impress the judges. The winner is the skier who demonstrates the best style while performing the most difficult figures.

Back roll
The skier begins the turn a good distance from the wake of the boat. This gives her time to build up her speed for the maneuver. When the skier hits the crest of the wave, she launches the board upward and goes into a roll. She looks toward the boat while regaining her balance upon landing.

Jumping competition

In the jumping event, skiers have three attempts to jump the greatest distance possible from a floating ramp. In addition to the distance they jump, skiers are rated according to their speed at the time of the jump, their body position while in the air, and their landing. Women athletes can jump more than 140 ft, and men more than 200 ft—longer than an Olympic-size swimming pool!

Types of skis

Slalom ski
The slalom ski is narrow with the skier's feet held one directly in front of the other. It has sharp edges to allow the athlete to cut through the water in sharp turns.

Figure ski
The figure ski has a smooth underside and edges cut at an angle, allowing the skier to turn more easily.

Wakeboard
The skier stands sideways on the wakeboard. The grooves on the board's underside make it "stick" to the water better.

Jump skis
Jump skis are wide and strong. They are made of fiberglass and aluminum.

Rowing

Seated in a long, narrow boat, called a shell, the athletes on a rowing team work as one, coordinating their movements to propel the boat smoothly. The object is to cross the finish line ahead of their opponents. Even though the rowers are seated, they need just as much strength and endurance for their sport as cross-country skiers or speed skaters. Athletes compete as singles or in teams of two to eight. Rowers sit facing backward and may be guided by buoys, referees' signals, or a fellow crew member called the coxswain. Races are usually held on lakes or lagoons, on a one to two kilometer course. There are also river courses of four to six kilometers.

Shell types

In sweep boats, each rower has only one oar; in sculls, each rower has two oars. Shells carry one, two, four, or eight rowers, with or without a coxswain.

Collar   **Sleeve**

Rubber handgrip   **Blade**

Oars
The oars are made of carbon fiber. The longest, called sweep oars, are 12.5 ft long. The end that goes into the water is called the blade. The blades are usually painted in the colors of the team's national flag or of their rowing club.

Skiff
The skiff is a racing shell built for a single rower. Skiffs are approximately 26 ft long and less than 1 ft wide. They can weigh as little as 30 lb.

Coxless double

Coxed eight

Straight four

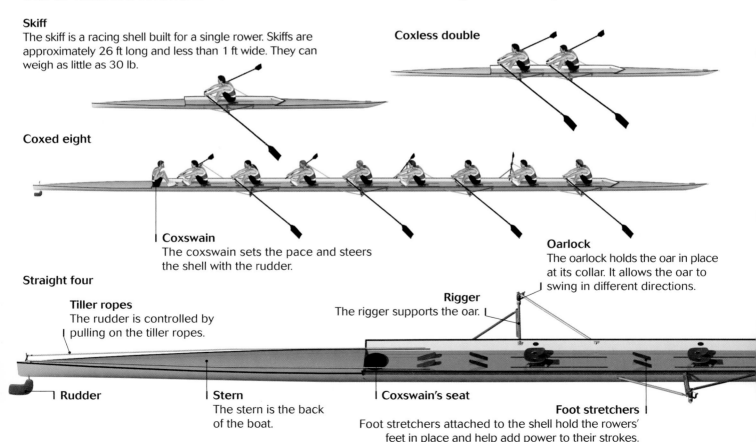

Coxswain
The coxswain sets the pace and steers the shell with the rudder.

Oarlock
The oarlock holds the oar in place at its collar. It allows the oar to swing in different directions.

Tiller ropes
The rudder is controlled by pulling on the tiller ropes.

Rigger
The rigger supports the oar.

Rudder

Stern
The stern is the back of the boat.

Coxswain's seat

Foot stretchers
Foot stretchers attached to the shell hold the rowers' feet in place and help add power to their strokes.

Rowing

The competition

The Olympic Games include the following rowing events for men and for women: pair oars without coxswain, eight oars with coxswain ("coxed eight"), single sculls, double sculls, quadruple sculls, and lightweight double sculls. Men also compete in the four oars without coxswain ("coxless double") and lightweight fours without coxswain events.

Shell

The long, narrow shape of a shell is what makes it cut through the water so fast. Shells can be made of wood, but most often are made of carbon fiber. This lightweight yet strong material enables the hull, which is the outer skin of the boat, to be very thin. Hulls as thin as 1/8 in. are no thicker than the shell of an ostrich egg!

Sculling technique

1. Catch
The rower leans forward with knees bent and arms extended. The oar blades are behind the rower. The blades are vertical, ready to enter the water.

2. Drive
The rower guides the blades into the water. Pushing against the foot stretchers, he leans backward and pulls his hands in toward his body. This pushes the blades back through the water and propels the shell forward.

3. Feathering
At the end of the stroke, the rower lifts the oars out of the water, turning the handles to reposition the blades.

4. Recovery
With the blades out of the water, the rower brings his hands forward and bends his knees. His seat slides back to the catch position.

Loudspeakers
Located next to each seat, loudspeakers amplify the coxswain's orders.

Splashguard
The splashguard keeps waves from entering the shell. Its tip is made of wood or carbon fiber.

Bowball
Made of white plastic or rubber, the bowball makes it easier to determine winners in photo finishes. It also protects the boat in case it is rammed.

Sliding seat
Rowers's seats slide back and forth on 2 rails making movements easier and strokes longer.

Bow
The bow is the front of the boat.

Canoeing and Kayaking

Canoes and kayaks are lightweight boats that are easily maneuvered. More than 6,000 years ago, Native Americans used canoes and kayaks to travel on large lakes and rivers. Today, men and women compete in two kinds of Olympic canoe and kayak events: flatwater racing and whitewater slalom. Flatwater racing takes place on calm water in a lake or lagoon with lanes marked. Whitewater slalom takes place on a course in a fast-moving river. Races are named after the first letter of the boat being used, *C* for canoe or *K* for kayak, followed by the number of athletes in each boat. A C2 race, for example, is a canoe race between teams of two in each canoe.

Flatwater competition

The goal in flatwater racing is to paddle a straight course and to cross the finish line first. Both canoes and kayaks are used in flatwater events. In the Olympic Games, there are C1, C2, K1, and K2 races of 500 m and 1,000 m, as well as K4 races over 1,000 m.

Equipment

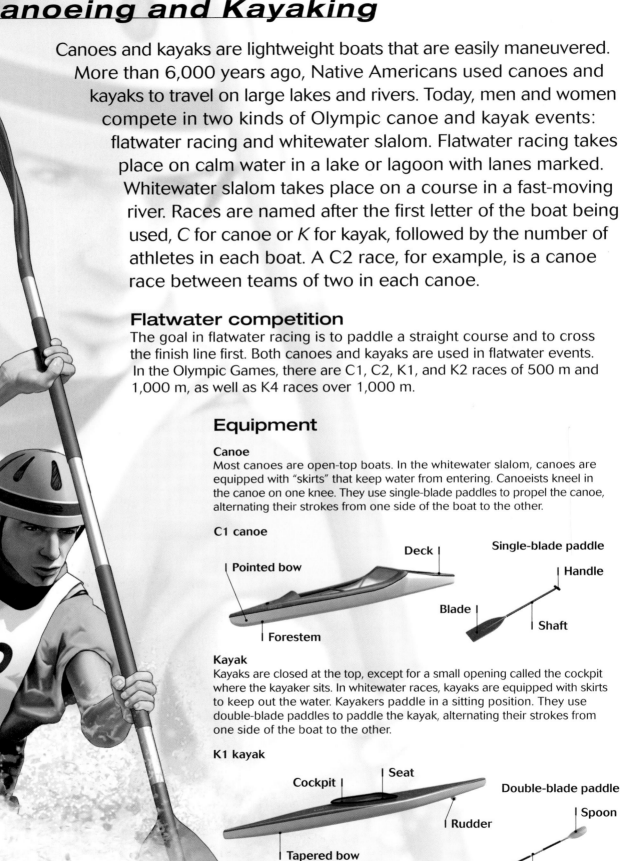

Canoe

Most canoes are open-top boats. In the whitewater slalom, canoes are equipped with "skirts" that keep water from entering. Canoeists kneel in the canoe on one knee. They use single-blade paddles to propel the canoe, alternating their strokes from one side of the boat to the other.

C1 canoe

Deck

Single-blade paddle

Pointed bow

Handle

Blade

Shaft

Forestem

Kayak

Kayaks are closed at the top, except for a small opening called the cockpit where the kayaker sits. In whitewater races, kayaks are equipped with skirts to keep out the water. Kayakers paddle in a sitting position. They use double-blade paddles to paddle the kayak, alternating their strokes from one side of the boat to the other.

K1 kayak

Cockpit

Seat

Double-blade paddle

Spoon

Rudder

Tapered bow

Handle

Back

Canoeing and Kayaking

Whitewater slalom competition

The whitewater slalom is a timed race. Athletes take turns paddling a winding course, called a slalom. The course features rapids, rocks, and a series of 25 gates to pass through. The gates are suspended over the river with wires. There are C1, C2, and K1 category events. Athletes must pass through the gates in a certain order, sometimes paddling with the current and sometimes against the current. The winner of the event is the fastest, strongest, and most agile paddler or pair of paddlers. Accidentally touching a gate means a 2-second penalty; missing a gate or passing through it in the wrong direction means a 50-second penalty!

Gate number panels

Gate number panels can be yellow or white. The numbers on the panels show the athlete the order in which to pass through the gates. A diagonal red line across a number shows the athlete that the gate must be entered from the opposite side.

Canoe paddling technique

1. Catch
With his arms extended, the canoeist prepares to put his paddle in the water.

2. Brace
The canoeist lowers the paddle into the water. Then he pulls the paddle back. This moves the canoe forward.

3. Recovery
At the end of the stroke, the canoeist straightens his back and lifts the paddle out of the water.

4. Return to catch
The canoeist returns to the first position to begin the next stroke.

Kayak paddling technique

1. Catch
The kayaker prepares to put her paddle in the water.

2. Brace and stroke
The kayaker lowers the paddle into the water. Then she pulls the paddle back. This moves the kayak forward.

3. Transition
The kayaker lifts the paddle out of the water after the stroke. She then brings the paddle into the catch position on the other side of the kayak. The transition must be made quickly in order to not lose momentum or speed.

Whitewater course

Gate judges
A judge stationed at each gate checks to see if the athlete has passed through without touching it.

Safety personnel
The 7 or 8 members of the safety team are equipped with cables, harnesses, and flotation devices. The team is on hand to rescue any athletes in danger.

Head referee
The head referee is responsible for all decisions made during an event.

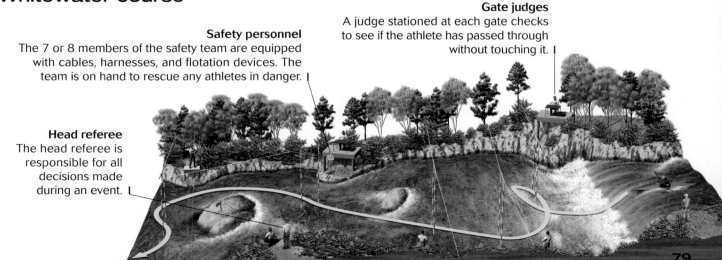

Sailboarding

Sailboarding is a sport that combines sailing and surfing. It was invented by surfers. Sailboards are light, fast, and easy to maneuver. Harnessing the power of the wind, men and women athletes can reach amazing speeds and perform spectacular acrobatic movements while riding on sailboards. There are three main categories in sailboarding competitions: long distance and slalom races, wave and freestyle competitions, and Olympic course races.

The competitions

Long-distance and slalom
In these types of races, the goal is to be the first across the finish line. Athletes in the slalom event follow a course marked by buoys and always sail with the wind at their backs. In a long distance race, the course may run from one point to another and then back. This means that for part of the race, the athletes have to sail facing the wind. Slalom races may last only five to ten minutes, while long-distance races may last two to four hours.

Wave and freestyle
Wave competitions are held on the ocean. The waves must be at least 6½ ft high and the wind must be blowing at least 16 mph. During the wave competition, sailboarders attempt to perform as many surfing moves, changes of direction, and jumps as they can in a 10- to 15-minute period.

Freestyle competitions may take place on lakes or in lagoons. In these events, athletes perform as many different acrobatic movements as they can without stopping. Three judges evaluate their performances for both artistic ability and technical difficulty, scoring both out of 10 possible points for each. The sailboarder with the highest score wins.

Olympic course
Olympic course races take place in an area marked out by two to four buoys. All athletes use the same type of sailboard— the Mistral One design. The sailboarders compete in a series of 3 to 12 heats that last from 20 to 60 minutes, depending on the speed of the wind. The athlete with the fastest average time in the heats is the winner.

Mast

Wishbone boom
The wishbone boom helps the sailboarder balance on the sailboard and steer.

Foot strap

Uphaul
The uphaul is a rope attached to the wishbone boom. It helps the sailboarder to lift up the sail when it has fallen in the water.

Sailboarding

Maneuvers

The jibe
This is a quick move designed to change the board's direction without losing speed when the wind is coming from behind the sailboard. Leaning in with her body, the sailboarder lets the sail turn around the mast. Switching the position of her feet on the board, she heads in a new direction.

Speed loop
The speed loop must be performed at high speed. The sailboarder pulls hard on the wishbone boom. Then he lifts the board with the help of the foot strap, and he transfers his weight forward. Crouching low, he quickly completes the rotation while looking back over his shoulder.

Types of sailboards

Slalom
The slalom board is built for speed and its ability to glide smoothly on the water.

Olympic
The Olympic board is long. It is designed for use in different wind conditions.

Wave
The wave board is strong, short, and light. Its sail is easy to control, even in high winds.

Sailing

Using only the power of the wind, sailboats can travel at amazing speeds—as long as the weather is in their favor. There are three main categories of sailing competitions: Olympic-type courses, regattas, and ocean races. Men and women sailors must be able to deal with changing weather conditions and plan strategies that will help them finish ahead of the competition. Depending on the direction the wind is coming from, sailors have different techniques for keeping their boats on course. Sailboats come in many models. The size of their sails, their shape, and their weight all help to determine how well they can perform in specific racing situations. Some boats are built for speed and their ability to change direction quickly in short races, while others are made for handling long, difficult ocean crossings.

The competitions

Olympic-course
Olympic course races are sailed in a team. The course is triangular and marked by three buoys. The boats must sail around the buoys in a certain order. The distance between the buoys varies according to the type of boats in the race.

Regattas
Regattas are generally held on the ocean close to shore, on a lake, or in a lagoon. Sailors try to outrace their competitors in a course marked by buoys. Course routes are planned in such a way as to allow sailors to use their most advanced sailing techniques.

Ocean races
Ocean races usually consist of crossing an ocean between two ports in the shortest time possible. The Europe 1-Star, for example, runs between Plymouth, Great Britain and Newport, Rhode Island. There is no shortage of adventure in this solo race. The sailor must choose the best route in order to avoid not only storms, but also areas where there may be no wind at all! Once the sailor is alone in the middle of the ocean, there is no one else to rely upon.

GPS (Global Positioning System)
The Global Positioning System enables sailors to know exactly where they are on the globe. Twenty-four GPS satellites orbit Earth, sending radio signals. The signals are picked up by the boat's GPS receiver and converted into information that gives the boat's precise position.

Sailing

Sailboats

Good sailors understand how their boats work, down to the smallest details. To rapidly change a boat's direction or to change sails requires a lot of skill, whether sailing in a crew or solo. In a regatta, this skill can help a crew stay ahead in the race. In a transatlantic crossing, the knowledge of one's boat can prevent a solo sailor from putting herself in danger.

Leech
The leech is the outside edge of the sail.

Mainsail
The mainsail is the largest sail of the boat. It is supported by the mast.

Port
Port is the left side of the boat looking toward the front.

Boom
The boom is a metal spar or pole that supports the foot of the sail.

Running rigging
The running rigging allows the sail to be adjusted.

Sheet car
The sheet car is a pulley that slides on a rail. It helps to guide the boom.

Stern
The stern is the back of the boat.

Tiller
The tiller is the handle attached to the rudder.

Halyard
The halyard is the cable used to raise the sails.

Mast
The mast is the metal spar or pole that supports the sails.

Luff
The luff is the part of the sail attached to the mast.

Shroud and stay
The shroud is the cable supporting the mast from the side. The stay is the cable supporting the mast from the front.

Spreaders
Attached to the mast, the spreaders keep the shrouds apart.

Jig
The jig is the triangular front sail.

Window
The window allows the crew to see through the sail to the other side of the boat.

Bow
The bow is the front of the boat.

Centerboard control
The centerboard control raises and lowers the centerboard.

Starboard
Starboard is the right side of the boat looking toward the front.

Rudder
The rudder is used to steer the boat.

Centerboard
The centerboard keeps the boat from moving sideways.

The 470
The 470 gets its name from its length, 4.70 m. The 470 is used in Olympic competition and is sailed by a crew of 2.

Hull types

Sailboats have different kinds of hulls, or bottoms. Catamarans and trimarans have more than one hull and are called multihull boats. Even though they are faster than single-hull ("monohull") boats, they are harder to handle, turn over more often, and are more difficult to put upright.

Monohull   **Catamaran**   **Trimaran**

Sailing

America's Cup

This world-famous regatta is named after a 100-foot-long racing boat called the *America*. Built by members of the New York Yacht Club in 1851, this new design of sailboat achieved international victory for the United States during the 1850s. The America's Cup race attracts sailboats from around the world. Each boat carries a crew of 16. The sailboats compete in a series of elimination races until one boat is left. This boat becomes the challenger and goes on to race against the previous year's winner. The two boats sail a minimum of seven races. The boat that finishes first in four races wins the cup.

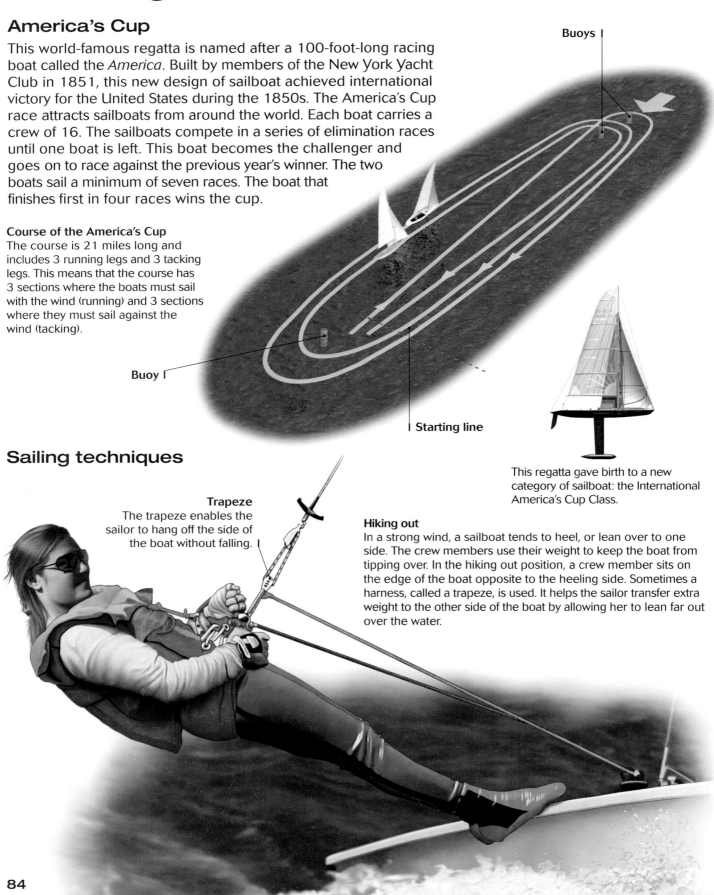

Buoys

Course of the America's Cup
The course is 21 miles long and includes 3 running legs and 3 tacking legs. This means that the course has 3 sections where the boats must sail with the wind (running) and 3 sections where they must sail against the wind (tacking).

Buoy

Starting line

This regatta gave birth to a new category of sailboat: the International America's Cup Class.

Sailing techniques

Trapeze
The trapeze enables the sailor to hang off the side of the boat without falling.

Hiking out
In a strong wind, a sailboat tends to heel, or lean over to one side. The crew members use their weight to keep the boat from tipping over. In the hiking out position, a crew member sits on the edge of the boat opposite to the heeling side. Sometimes a harness, called a trapeze, is used. It helps the sailor transfer extra weight to the other side of the boat by allowing her to lean far out over the water.

Equestrian Sports

The horse
Tack
Dressage
Jumping
Combined Eventing
Polo

The horse

In equestrian sports, human and horse form a team. Having an animal for a teammate is not easy. It takes many years of training until both horse and rider are ready to compete on an international level. The horse cannot be forced to perform—it must be convinced. The rider must gain the horse's trust and cooperation, which requires time and patience. Once the horse and rider understand each other, however, they can become a winning team. There are three equestrian events in the Olympics: dressage, jumping, and combined eventing. Both men and women riders compete in the same events.

Techniques

Although a horse can be guided using verbal commands, riders rely mostly on their legs and their hands for communication. The rider uses leg pressure on the horse's sides to instruct it to move forward. The horse can also be guided to turn or slow down by pulling on the reins.

Gaits

The way a horse places its feet when walking or running is called a gait. Horses have four gaits that they perform naturally: the walk, the trot, the canter, and the gallop—which is a faster variation of the canter. These are the natural gaits used most often in competition. Horses are trained to perform other gaits.

The walk
The walk is the slowest gait. The horse's feet touch the ground one at a time in a diagonal pattern.

The trot
In trotting, the horse's feet touch the ground 2 at a time in a diagonal pattern: the right forefoot with the left hind foot, and the left forefoot with the right hind foot.

The canter
The canter is an irregular gait. First 1 foot, then 3 feet, touch the ground, followed by a moment when all 4 feet are suspended in the air. The canter is faster than the trot, but slower than the gallop.

Equipment

Tack

Tack is the equipment used for riding the horse. The two most important pieces of tack are the saddle, on which the rider sits, and the bridle. The bridle, used to control the horse, is the harness that fits around the horse's head. It includes the bit, which is held in the horse's mouth, as well as the reins. Saddles and bridles are specially adapted for different kinds of equestrian events.

✳ A running mystery

When a horse canters or gallops, it is very difficult to detect the pattern of its leg movements. The horse's running style remained a mystery until the late 19th century, when photography became available. A photographer shot a series of pictures of a horse in motion. The camera captured the action in separate images, which revealed the horse's precise movements.

Racing saddle

Jumping saddle

Dressage saddle

Saddles

Saddles are designed to help riders sit in the position that is best suited for the event. The racing saddle is flat and very light. It gives the horse the most freedom of movement. The jumping saddle's seat is curved inward slightly to hold the rider in place. Its wide leg flaps give extra support to the rider's knees during a jump. The dressage saddle has a deep seat, which helps keep the rider stable. Its long, flexible leg flaps allow the horse to easily feel the rider's leg-pressure commands.

Horseshoes

Horseshoes are designed for specific activities and terrain. They are usually made from steel, but can also be made from aluminum or other metals. Horses need horseshoes to protect their feet and hooves from wear and injury. The farrier is the person who looks after shaping, fitting, and nailing the shoes to horses' hooves. Because horses' feet are fragile and need constant care, the farrier plays an important role in these four-footed athletes' ability to compete.

Jumping shoes

Jumping shoes are sometimes equipped with removable rubber pads. This helps lessen the shock of impact on the horse's legs when landing.

Racing shoes

Racing shoes are light and usually made of aluminum.

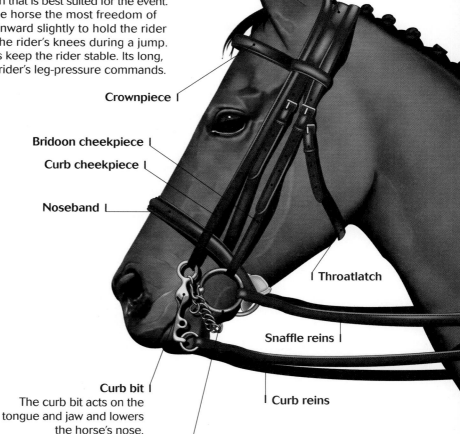

Browband

Crownpiece

Bridoon cheekpiece

Curb cheekpiece

Noseband

Throatlatch

Snaffle reins

Curb reins

Curb bit
The curb bit acts on the tongue and jaw and lowers the horse's nose.

Bridoon bit
The bridoon bit pulls on the corners of the horse's lips, which makes it raise its head.

Dressage

In dressage, the rider guides the horse through a series of complicated movements and steps, called figures. The horse uses its three natural gaits: walk, trot, and canter. The rider's commands must be invisible to the judges, and the horse must appear to be performing on its own, without orders. It takes many hours of practice to make the figures precise and the performance elegant.

The competition

The dressage competition takes place in a rectangular area called the show ring. Five judges evaluate the precision of the horse's movements and the regularity of its different gaits. They also watch for how easily the horse responds to the rider's commands. The judges score each movement out of 10. The winner is the rider with the best score calculated according to the results of three events: the grand prix; the grand prix special, which is more difficult; and the grand prix freestyle, which features music and choreography chosen by the rider.

Technique

Collection

Before competing in dressage, the rider must ensure that the horse finds the ideal carrying position. In the collection, the rider instructs the horse to rebalance her weight on its back. This improves the horse's own balance and ability to jump.

Equipment

The riders' clothing conforms to a strict dress code, which is a traditional set of rules about what riders can wear. Competitors in military service may wear their uniforms. Other riders must wear gloves, a white shirt and tie, a dark jacket, white or off-white riding pants, black boots, and a top hat. The horse's tack must also conform to the regulations.

Horse not collected
In this position, the horse's front legs and back legs are far apart. Its neck is stretched out and hanging down. Most of the rider's weight is being supported on the horse's front legs.

Horse collected
The horse brings its back legs closer to its front legs and raises its neck and head. The weight of the rider is now more evenly distributed between the front and back legs of the horse.

Advanced movements

Piaffe
The piaffe is a majestic, slow-paced trot. The horse appears to remain in one spot. It lifts its front legs high in the air and holds its head up.

Passage
The passage is a suspended trot in slow motion. It is called suspended because the horse's feet spend more time in the air and less time on the ground. The passage must be performed with the horse perfectly collected.

Show ring

The show ring surface is completely flat. It is covered in sand and sometimes shredded rubber to make it softer.

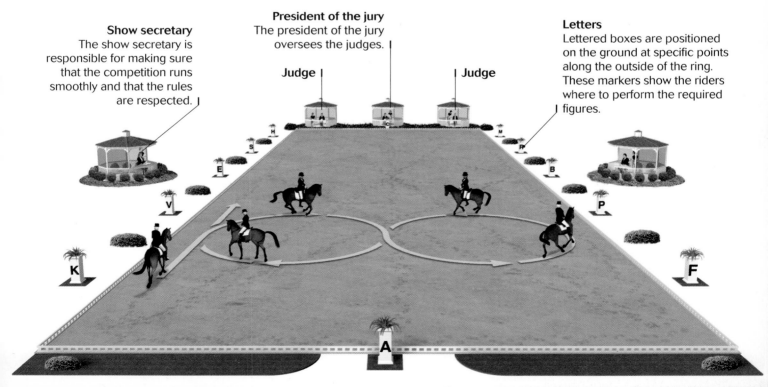

Show secretary
The show secretary is responsible for making sure that the competition runs smoothly and that the rules are respected.

President of the jury
The president of the jury oversees the judges.

Judge

Judge

Letters
Lettered boxes are positioned on the ground at specific points along the outside of the ring. These markers show the riders where to perform the required figures.

Jumping

In jumping competition, riders and their horses follow a course containing obstacles that must be jumped in a set order. The goal is to run the course without losing time and without knocking down any obstacles. The riders and horses must understand one another perfectly to perform the jumps with precision while avoiding dangerous falls. Although horses are naturally good jumpers, they need approximately four years of training not to be afraid of the obstacles and to confidently obey their riders' orders.

The competition

The course contains 12 to 15 numbered obstacles to be jumped in a predetermined order. The obstacles are marked with flags that show the rider the direction in which to jump. As the rider approaches the obstacle, the white flag is on her left side and the red flag is on the right. Before the competition, the rider may walk the course once to become more familiar with it. The horse does not have that privilege—it will only discover the obstacles the first time it faces them during the competition.

Belly pad
The belly pad helps keep the saddle in place. It also protects the horse from hitting itself in the stomach when it tucks up its front legs.

Breastplate
The breastplate keeps the saddle from slipping back when the horse jumps.

Padded jumping boots
The padded jumping boots support the horse's legs.

Bell boots
The boots are plastic and bell-shaped. They protect the hooves.

Jumping

Jumping technique

Riders try to not interfere with their horses' natural ability to jump. They adjust their positions in the saddle and shift their weight to help their horses maintain the necessary power and height for each jump.

1. Controlling the approach
Riders must let their horses know how fast to gallop and when to start a jump. The rider instructs the horse to lengthen or shorten its strides on approching the correct point for takeoff.

2. Controlling balance
Riders help their horses stay balanced while jumping by supporting themselves in the stirrups and leaning forward over the horses' necks.

3. Landing calmly
Horses become excited jumping. Their riders must calm them and keep them under control so that they do not rush nervously at the next obstacle.

The obstacles

An obstacle is a barrier a horse must jump over as part of a competition. There are different types of obstacles, such as gates, fences, walls, and oxers. Obstacles are usually made of wood and come in different heights and widths. Hedges as well as ditches filled with water are other obstacles.

Water jump
The water jump usually consists of a low hedge or fence, followed by a water-filled ditch. The ditch may be several yards wide. The horse must clear the entire obstacle without putting a foot in the water. A judge watches for errors.

Combination
A combination is a series of 2 or 3 obstacles placed close together. They are usually so close that the horse takes only 1 or 2 strides between them. The combination counts as a single obstacle.

Oxers
Oxers are composed of 2 barriers. For example, a horizontal rail followed by a hedge is an oxer. The horse must jump over the 2 sections at once. The 2 barriers can be spread apart to make a jump more difficult. However, the oxer cannot be wider from front to back than it is from top to bottom.

Combined Eventing

Combined eventing is a three-day challenge that demands courage and concentration. Horse-and-rider teams must demonstrate a variety of skills in three events: dressage, endurance, and stadium jumping. The riders are given penalty points for any faults they commit. The winner is the one with the least number of penalty points at the end of the three events. Combined eventing is so tough on horses that they are not allowed to compete more than three times a year.

✳ A team effort
Endurance events test how well the rider and horse communicate. It's often the horse that covers for the mistakes made by the rider!

Day 1
Dressage competition takes place on the first day. The purpose of this event is to demonstrate the horse's obedience and the good communication between horse and rider. The test consists of 18 movements and takes about 8 minutes to complete. It is not as difficult as a top-level dressage test.

Day 2
The endurance competition is held the second day. This is the most difficult event for both the horse and the rider. The competition has 4 timed stages. It includes 2 road and track races on a flat area, the steeplechase on a turf track with several low fences, and the cross-country race in the countryside with natural obstacles.

Day 3
The last competition is stadium jumping. This moderately difficult course features approximately 12 obstacles that are not more than 4 ft high. The course is designed to test the horses' powers of concentration. It also shows how well the horse has recovered from the difficult event of the previous day. The horses with the best results from the previous 2 days get to compete last.

Endurance competition: Cross-country race

Polo

In polo, two teams of four players on horseback use mallets to try to hit a ball through the opponents' goalposts. Polo is played on a grass field 300 yards long and 160 yards wide. Goalposts are spaced 24 feet apart, at both ends. The horses, known as polo ponies, are specially trained for the game. They know how to place their riders in good positions for hitting the ball. They stay calm in spite of their riders' acrobatic movements, without fear of contact with the other horses. The best polo players say that it is thanks to their horses that they are champions! Both men and women play polo in separate leagues, although women sometimes compete as the fourth member on a men's team.

Ball
The ball is made of willow root or plastic. It is about the same size as a baseball, but weighs only about 4 oz.

Equipment

Mallet
The mallet is made to be held in the right hand, wether the player is right- or left-handed. The bamboo handle's length depends upon the height of the player and the pony. Players hit the ball with the side of the mallet head, not with its end.

Saddle
The player's energetic movements and quick changes in direction can make the saddle slip off the horse. To help prevent this, the saddle has a second strap, called an overgirth, to hold it in place in case the main girth gives out.

Braided tail
The pony's tail is braided, folded in half, and then taped to prevent it from becoming entangled in the players' mallets.

Leg protection
Boots or bandages, called polo wraps, protect the horse's lower legs from mallet hits.

The game

The polo match is divided into 6 periods of 7 minutes each, called chukkers. Between each chukker, players must exchange their ponies for fresh ones, so as not to tire them out. This means that each player needs to have at least 7 ponies for each match. There are no time-outs, and the game continues even when players fall off their ponies. Two umpires on horseback and a referee on the sidelines ensure that the game is played according to the rules. A goal is scored when the ball is hit between the two goalposts of the opposing team.

Helmet
The helmet is usually equipped with a face protector.

Horse's mane
The horse's mane is shaved so that the rider's hands and mallet will not become caught in it.

Noseband

Martingale
The martingale is used to keep the horse's head from hitting the rider's head during sudden stops.

Knee pads
The knee pads protect the rider from ball and mallet hits.

Bell boots
Bell boots protect the top of the horse's hooves.

Polo

Wooden horse
Most of the top polo players use a wooden horse for practice. It allows them to concentrate on perfecting their mallet technique.

When is a horse a pony?
Originally, polo players rode ponies, which are a small, sturdy breed of horse. These short-legged animals could change direction easily as well as stop and start quickly. Even though most polo players ride full-size horses today, they still refer to their animals by the traditional name "ponies."

Forehand and backhand hits
The ball may be hit forward, backward, or diagonally. Because polo players play right-handed at all times, they must use backhand as well as forehand shorts. It is a forehand shot if the ball is hit on the right-hand side of the polo pony, and a backhand if the rider has to reach over and hit on the horse's left side. A good hitter can hit the ball the length of the field in two shots. Standing in the stirrups increases the power of the shot.

Forward forehand hit

Hooking mallets
Players may block an opponent's shots by hooking his mallet with their own. Hooking mallets is allowed when an opposing player is about to hit the ball—but hooking above shoulder level or in front of the horse's legs is a foul that is penalized by a free hit.

Perpendicular hits
Mallet hits taking place under the horse's neck or behind its tail are called perpendicular. The most difficult hit, called the millionaire's hit, is made right under the horse's belly.

Precision and Accuracy Sports

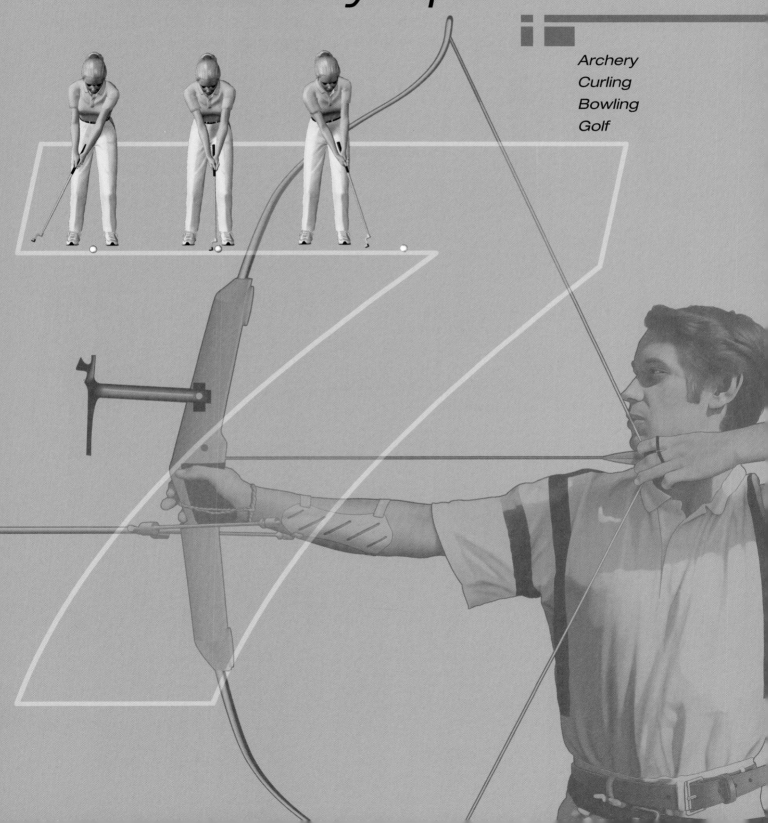

Archery
Curling
Bowling
Golf

Archery

In the sport of archery, athletes called archers stand on a shooting range and use bows to shoot arrows at distant targets. Both men and women compete in this mentally and physically challenging sport. When taking aim, archers must concentrate, stand perfectly still, and hold their breath until they release the arrow.

The competition

The targets are set up at distances of 30 to 90 m from the archers. Each arrow that hits the target is awarded points that correspond to specific areas on the target. In the Olympics and in world championships, archers shoot 144 arrows to determine the best 64 athletes. After another elimination round, eight athletes are left to compete in the finals. The two top archers compete one-on-one for the gold medal.

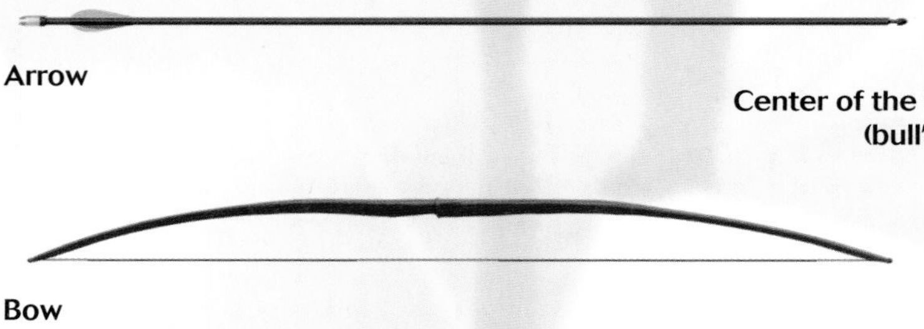

Arrow

Bow

Center of the target (bull's-eye)

22

Technique

The accuracy of a shot depends on the archer's ability to control his movements. Archers repeatedly practice the moves that make up the shooting sequence until they are automatic and perfectly smooth. The sequence, starting from taking the bow in hand to releasing the arrow, takes between 15 and 20 seconds.

The target

The target is composed of circles, one inside another, numbered from 1 on the outside to 10 in the center. The archers try to hit the center circle to win the most points.

1. Preparation before the shot **2.** Placing the arrow on the bow **3.** Taking aim **4.** Release **5.** Follow-through

Curling

In curling, two teams take turns sliding stones across an ice rink toward a target (the "house"). The goal is to place the stones closest to the target's center (the "button"). Curling teams can be made up of four women or four men. The two teams try to place ("throw") their stones into the same house. They try to position their stones in a way that will keep their opponents' stones out of the house. They also use their stones to try to knock those of their opponent out of the house. Concentration, control, and precision are the most important skills to have in curling.

The stone
Made of granite, the stone is carved into a circular shape, polished, and balanced so that it will follow a straight path when thrown. The player holds the stone by its plastic handle attached to the top.

The game

The game has 10 periods, called ends. The teams draw lots to see who plays first. The first player throws a stone. Then two team members help direct it by sweeping the ice in front of it. Every stone that is placed closer to the button than the opponent's stone wins a point for its team. The team that places a stone closest to the button wins that end. When all the players on both teams have each thrown 2 stones, the end is over and the players move to the opposite side of the rink. The team that accumulates the most points after 10 ends wins the game.

Sweeping
When heated up by the friction of the broom sweeping its surface, the ice melts, creating a thin layer of water that helps the stone slide more easily. Depending on how much and where the ice is swept, the stone can be directed to advance farther or even to change direction. Sweeping can add more than 1 ft to a stone's slide. The sweepers are directed by their team captain, called the skip, who watches the path of the stone as it approaches the target.

Rink
The playing surface of the rink is 146 ft long and 15.5 ft wide. The ice is scraped and watered regularly to keep it perfectly smooth and slippery.

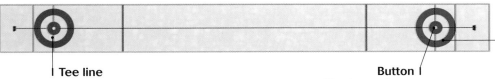

House
The house is a target area made up of three circles, one inside the other, with a "button" in the center. Only the stones that "enter" the house, either partially or completely, can give points to their team.

Tee line
As a stone approaches from the other end of the rink, players on the opposing team may sweep behind this line in an attempt to make the stone slide off course.

Button
The button has a 12 in. diameter.

Technique

Delivering the stone
The player slides the stone backward to gain momentum when she pushes it forward. The player slides along next to the stone, keeping her hand on it to send it straight. When she releases the stone, she gives it a slight rotation of the wrist. This makes the stone veer in a particular direction.

Bowling

In bowling, men and women players roll balls down wooden lanes trying to knock down 10 pins, which are set up in a triangle at the end. A game of bowling is made up of 10 frames. In a frame, every player gets two turns to knock down as many pins as possible. If the player knocks down all 10 with the first ball, it is called a strike. If it takes two balls to knock them all down, it is called a spare. Each pin knocked down is worth one point. Strikes and spares give players bonus points. The winner is the one with the most points at the end of 10 frames.

Equipment

Ball
The bowling ball is made of hard rubber, plastic, and Fiberglass™. It must be perfectly balanced to roll straight. Three holes in the ball permit holding it with the thumb, index, and middle fingers. The regulation weight of a ball used in competition is 16 lb.

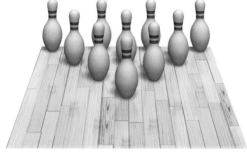

Pins
The pins are usually made of maple wood and are coated with plastic. Pins weight 3 lb.

Technique

Releasing the ball

The approach is the most important part of bowling. The player takes four or five steps, starting slowly and then accelerating until he lets the ball go. Each step is accompanied by an arm movement that readies the ball and helps the bowler keep his balance.

First step
Holding the ball with both hands in front of the body, the bowler moves his right foot forward slightly. The left-handed bowler starts on the left foot.

Second step
The bowler's left foot moves forward. He lets go of the ball with his left hand and then uses his left arm to stay balanced. The left-handed bowler does the same with his right foot and arm.

Third step
The player bends his knees to accelerate the ball's motion. His left arm is held out to help him keep his balance. The left-handed bowler balances with his right arm.

Fourth step
The player swings his right arm forward to release the ball. His fingers provide extra forward motion to the ball as his left foot ends its slide. The left-handed player swings his left arm and slides on his right foot.

Golf

In the game of golf, the winner is the one who ends with the fewest strokes. It is a sport played by men and women of all ages. Golfers use sticks, called clubs, to hit a small ball across a landscaped outdoor course. The goal is to get the ball into a hole, or cup, in the ground with as few strokes of the club as possible. To achieve a low score, golfers need to have a high level of confidence, calmness, and coordination. Becoming a top-level player means more than mastering the different strokes and rules of the game. Golfers must also learn to follow a very strict code of conduct, based on courtesy for fellow players and respect for the playing area.

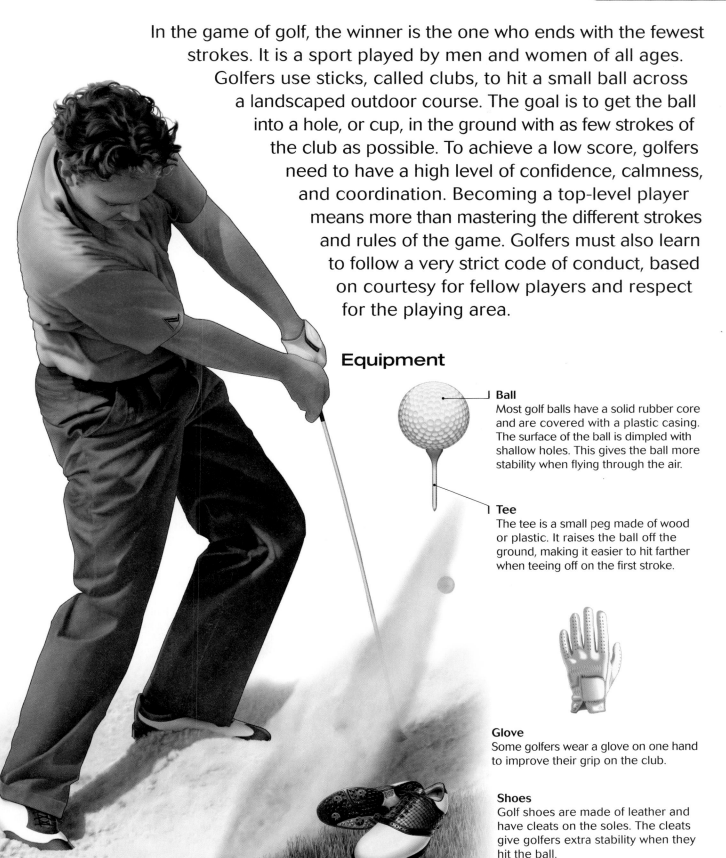

Equipment

Ball
Most golf balls have a solid rubber core and are covered with a plastic casing. The surface of the ball is dimpled with shallow holes. This gives the ball more stability when flying through the air.

Tee
The tee is a small peg made of wood or plastic. It raises the ball off the ground, making it easier to hit farther when teeing off on the first stroke.

Glove
Some golfers wear a glove on one hand to improve their grip on the club.

Shoes
Golf shoes are made of leather and have cleats on the soles. The cleats give golfers extra stability when they hit the ball.

Golf

The course

The golf course is a groomed landscape around natural obstacles like trees and bushes and human-made obstacles such as sand traps and water hazards. The course is divided into 18 areas called holes. Holes vary from 100 to 600 yards in length. Each hole is laid out with a starting area, called a tee. This is followed by a long grassy stretch, called a fairway, down which the golfer hits the ball. At the end of the fairway lies the green, where the hole, or cup, in the ground is located. Each hole is assigned par. Par refers to the number of strokes that the golfer is expected to take in order to hit the ball from the tee to the hole. A hole may be designated as a par 3, par 4, or par 5.

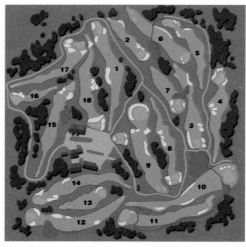

Diagram of a golf course, seen from above.

The competition

Golfers may compete as singles or in teams. They establish their rankings in world competition by accumulating points over a two-year period. During this time, they play at least 40 tournaments. Some of the major championships include the U.S. Open, which takes place on a different course every year; the British Open, played in Scotland or England; the Ryder Cup, in which an American team plays against a European team; and the Dunhill World Cup, made up of three-player teams from different countries. Golf is not an Olympic sport.

Birdie
If a ball lands in the hole in one stroke less than the par for that hole, or "one under par," it is called a birdie. For example, on a par 3 hole, the player gets a birdie if the ball lands in the hole in 2 strokes.

Bogey
If the ball lands in the hole in one stroke more than the par, or "one over par," it is called a bogey. For example, on a par 4 hole, the player gets a bogey if he takes 5 strokes to put the ball in the hole.

Eagle
If the ball lands in the hole in 2 strokes under par, it is called an eagle. On a par 5 hole, the player gets an eagle if it takes only 3 strokes to put the ball in the hole.

Hole in one
If a ball lands in the hole in one stroke (from the tee-off), it is called a hole in one.

Water hazards
Water hazards are streams or artificial ponds set up along the course. If the player hits the ball into the water, it is usually impossible to hit it out, unless the water is very shallow. The player usually drops a new ball next to where the first ball was lost, but takes a penalty stroke for doing so.

Hole (cup)
The hole, or cup, is 4 in. wide and at least 4 in. deep. A flagstick is set up in the center of the hole to help the player aim from a distance.

Bunkers
Bunkers are sand traps, usually located next to the green. If the player hits the ball into a bunker, he must then try to hit the ball out of the sand and back onto the green. Bunkers can be difficult to escape. The player is not allowed to push any sand away from the ball before hitting it.

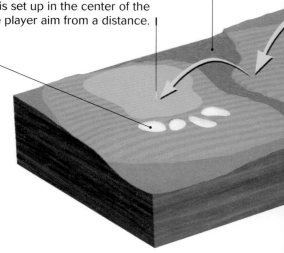

Par 3

On a par 3 hole, the player must try to hit the ball onto the green as close to the hole as possible with the first stroke. The player is allowed 2 additional strokes to make "par." Par 3 holes are usually the easiest.

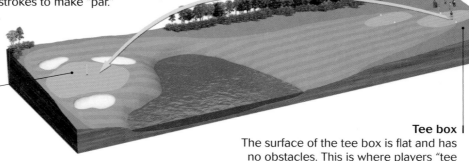

Green
The special grass on the green is cut short and carefully groomed so balls roll easily.

Tee box
The surface of the tee box is flat and has no obstacles. This is where players "tee off" to start playing the hole.

Par 4

On a par 4 hole, the player tries to place the ball on the green with the second stroke. The player then has 2 more strokes, or "putts," to par the hole.

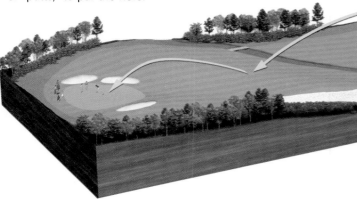

Fairway
The fairway is the longest part of the hole. It leads to the putting green. It may measure hundreds of yards in length, but is usually only 25 to 60 yd wide. The fairway is often bordered by tall grass, bushes, and trees. Hitting the ball down the fairway can be difficult because of its twists and turns.

Par 5

On a par 5 hole, the player tries to place the ball on the green with the third stroke. The player then has 2 additional strokes to hit the ball into the hole.

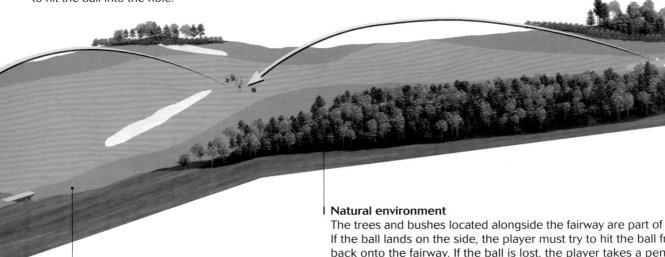

Rough
The rough is the longer grass located at the edge of the fairway. It is harder to hit the ball or make it roll when it is in the rough.

Natural environment
The trees and bushes located alongside the fairway are part of the course. If the ball lands on the side, the player must try to hit the ball from there back onto the fairway. If the ball is lost, the player takes a penalty stroke and must start over from the tee box with a new ball. If the ball is visible but impossible to hit, the player is allowed to drop a new ball close to it. The player is then allowed to play the new ball, but still gets a penalty stroke.

Golf

Golf bag

The golf bag is used for carrying the clubs. The player may use as many as 14 different clubs during the game, selecting them according to the type of terrain and the distance the ball must be hit. There are 3 main categories of clubs: woods, irons, and putters. Woods are usually used for the tee-off and for long shots. Irons are usually used for shots close to the green or on the green. Putters are used for rolling shots on the green, when the player needs maximum accuracy. Depending on the shape and slope of its head, a club can help the ball travel different distances and heights.

Fore!

When a flying ball might hit another player, golfers break the rule of silence on the course and yell "Fore!" This signal, which means "Watch out up ahead!" comes from an old military expression. When armies positioned their soldiers in rows on the battlefield, the soldiers in the rear would shout "Fore!" before shooting their guns. This warning was for the soldiers in front to be careful to duck their heads to avoid being hit.

Grips

Baseball grip

Overlapping grip

Interlocking grip

The way a golfer grips the club is very important. The golfer must find the most comfortable hand position. The grip should help the golfer remain flexible in his or her movements while maintaining accuracy.

Techniques

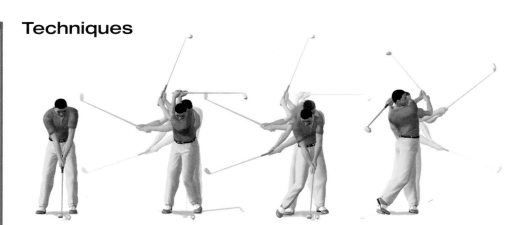

Long shot

When playing a hole, the first and second strokes are generally long shots. The golfer aligns his body with the ball and with the direction he will hit it. His body position as well as his arm and shoulder movements determine the distance and the accuracy of the shot.

Putting

Once the golfer gets the ball onto the green, she needs to hit the ball lightly so that it rolls into the cup. First, the golfer must see if the area has a hill or slope, which will affect how the ball rolls. She also estimates how the ball might roll depending on the condition of the grass. Using a swinging, pendulum type of stroke, the golfer then hits the ball to make it roll to the cup.

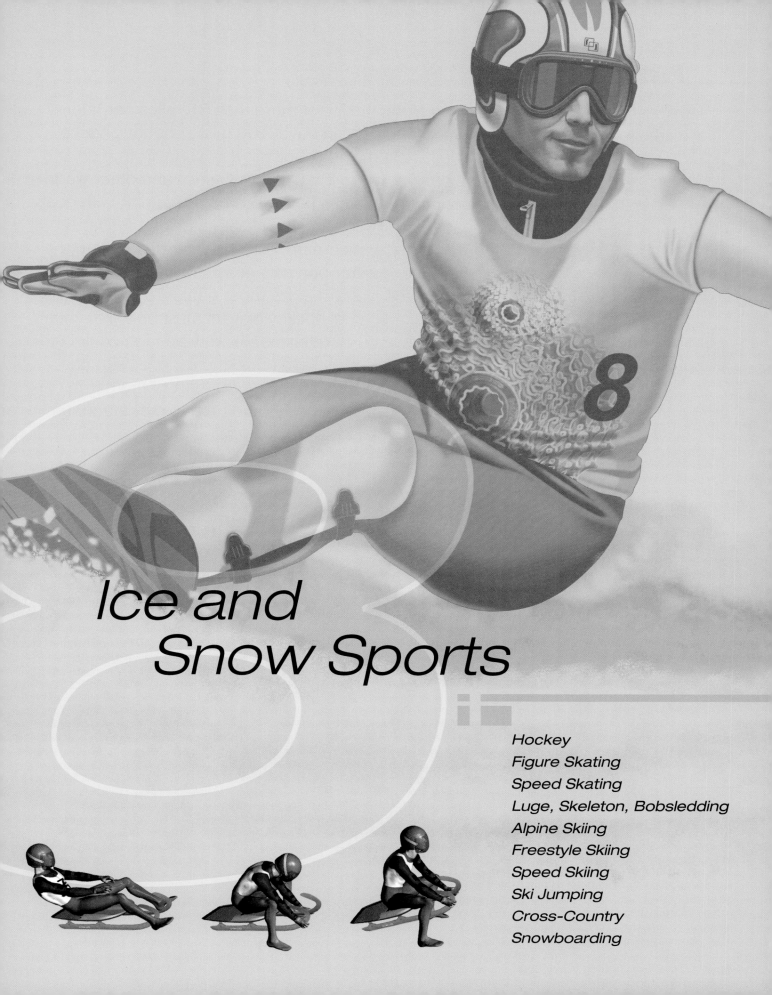

Ice and Snow Sports

Hockey
Figure Skating
Speed Skating
Luge, Skeleton, Bobsledding
Alpine Skiing
Freestyle Skiing
Speed Skiing
Ski Jumping
Cross-Country
Snowboarding

Hockey

With players skating along the ice at more than 35 miles per hour, chasing a rubber disk that can travel 100 miles per hour, hockey is one of the fastest-moving sports in the world. Both men and women play hockey in the Olympic Games and other world championships. Games take place on an ice rink, with goals at each end. Two teams on skates use long L-shaped sticks to try to hit a hard, black rubber disk, called a puck, into their opponent's goal. The winning team is the one that scores the most goals. To play this fastpaced game, hockey players must be agile skaters and have quick reflexes. Hockey is a high-contact sport. Body-checking—blocking a player with one's body—and stick-checking are part of the game. Players must be tough and able to stay standing when hit by opponents.

Equipment

Hockey players wear a wide assortment of equipment designed to protect their bodies. The equipment worn by goaltenders is especially important, since they must face fast-flying pucks that are shot at them.

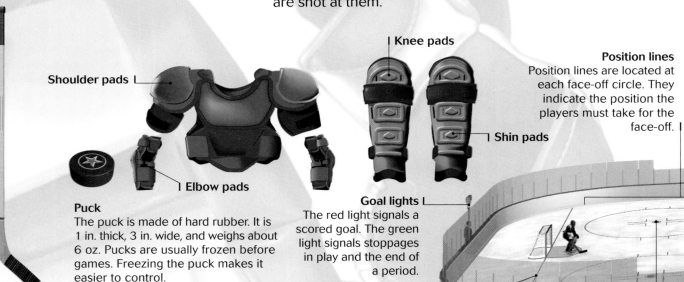

Shoulder pads

Elbow pads

Knee pads

Shin pads

Position lines
Position lines are located at each face-off circle. They indicate the position the players must take for the face-off.

Goal lights
The red light signals a scored goal. The green light signals stoppages in play and the end of a period.

Goal line
For a goal to be counted, the puck must cross the red goal line and go into the net.

Face-off circles and points
The 5 circles and 9 spots indicate where face-offs can take place.

Puck
The puck is made of hard rubber. It is 1 in. thick, 3 in. wide, and weighs about 6 oz. Pucks are usually frozen before games. Freezing the puck makes it easier to control.

Stick
The shaft of the hockey stick can be made of aluminum, wood, or man-made materials such as graphite or Kevlar. The blade, which is at the bottom of the stick, may be made of wood or man-made materials. The blade is curved to help the player maintain control of the puck.

The game

The game is played in three 20-minute periods with two 15-minute intermissions. The clock is stopped for goals, penalties, and injuries. A player who receives a penalty usually has to leave the ice and enter the penalty box for two to five minutes, depending on the rule that was broken. The team continues playing with one less player, giving the opposing team an advantage. The team with the most goals scored at the end of three periods wins the game. If the score is tied at the end of the three periods, the game may continue into overtime. This gives one of the teams a chance to score a goal and break the tie.

Off-side

Five lines across the hockey rink divide it into zones. These lines help to regulate the different areas of play. Players cannot advance across the blue line closest to their opponents' goal unless the puck has already crossed it. Players are not allowed to pass the puck to a team member who is more than 2 lines ahead. If either of these rules is broken, an off-side is called. The line judge stops play and orders a face-off.

Penalties

Referees signal penalties when players hold other players, trip them, or hook them with their sticks. To reduce injuries in a game, hockey players are penalized for raising their sticks higher than shoulder height. Interfering with an opponent who is not controlling the puck, or hitting an opponent will also earn a player a penalty. The most severe penalties may last 10 minutes or even for the duration of the game.

The face-off

In a face-off, 2 players face each other. The referee drops the puck on the ice between them and the players use their sticks to fight for control of the puck. Face-offs take place in the center face-off circle at the beginning of a game or period and when a goal has been scored. During the rest of the game, face-offs take place at one of the other 8 spots marked on the ice for this purpose.

Linesmen

The linesmen signal offsides and prevent fighting among players.

Referees

Referees supervise the game, drop the puck for a face-off, and make sure that the rules are followed.

Center line

The red center line divides the rink into two equal zones, one for each team.

Neutral zone

The neutral zone is the area between the two blue lines. Players must enter or exit the game from this area.

Goals

The goals are held in place with magnets that release easily if the goalposts are hit hard. This prevents players from being seriously injured if they are knocked into the goalposts.

Blue lines

The 2 blue lines divide the rink into 3 zones. The middle zone is neutral. The zone that a team protects is the team's defensive zone. The zone at the opposite end of the ice is the team's attacking zone.

Penalty box

Players who are penalized must sit on a bench in the penalty box and wait to go back on the ice.

The rink

The rink is rectangular and measures 200 ft in length. It is 85 ft wide in NHL (National Hockey League) hockey and 100 ft wide in Olympic hockey. Outside the perimeter of the rink are benches for officials, coaches, and players.

Hockey

The team

Hockey teams are made up of at least 20 players, but only 6 of them are allowed on the ice at the same time. These players have assigned positions. The center, left wing, and right wing make up the forward line. The job of the forward line is to score goals. The left and right defense players make up the defense line. The defense players try to keep the opposing team from scoring. Defense players also go on the attack sometimes, just as forwards may help with defense. The last line of defense is the goaltender. The goaltender remains in or near the goal, and tries to prevent the attacking team from putting the puck into the net.

Techniques and tactics

Hockey is made up of many quick passes of the puck among the players. To stay ahead in the game, hockey players continually use a combination of attack as well as defensive moves. Besides skating skills, hockey players must have a mastery of all types of shots, passes to other players, and ways of dodging opponents.

The passes

Passing the puck lets a team control it for attack or defense purposes. Passing requires accuracy and an ability to judge distances quickly.

Poke checking the puck
The goalie prevents an opponent from getting the puck by kneeling on the ice and "poking" his stick forward to push the puck away quickly.

Passing the puck off the boards
If a player is unable to pass the puck to his teammate directly, he may "bounce" the puck off the boards (the wall of the rink) and send the puck in his teammate's direction.

Deflecting the puck
An attacking player scores a goal by redirecting the puck that has been passed to him by a teammate.

The shots

Slapshot
The slapshot is the most powerful shot, but also the least accurate. The player raises his stick backward to gain the necessary momentum and power to hit the puck hard and fast.

Wrist shot
The wrist shot is fast and allows the player to shoot the puck in a precise direction. The player uses a snapping movement of her wrists to send the puck where she wants it to go. The wrist shot is very effective in front of the net as well as for long passes.

Backhand shot
The backhand shot is difficult because the player must strike the puck with the blade's outside curve. Goaltenders fear the backhand shot because they cannot accurately predict in which direction the puck will fly.

Flip shot
The player pushes the puck forward on the ice with the blade of the stick, and then uses the blade to "snap" the puck quickly off the ice.

Referees
The 3 referees wear skates and follow the game on the ice. This helps them to carefully watch the players and to step in quickly to enforce the rules.

Delayed penalty
The referee raises his arm to call a penalty but does not stop the game immediately. He may first wait to see the outcome of the play in progress. He may also need to delay the penalty if 2 of a team's players are already in the penalty box.

Hooking
A player has tried to make another player fall by hooking him or her with a stick.

Slashing
A player has hit another player with a stick.

Cross-checking
A player has body-checked an opposing player with the stick held in both hands.

Goal scored
The goal counts.

Goal disallowed
The goal cannot be counted.

Figure Skating

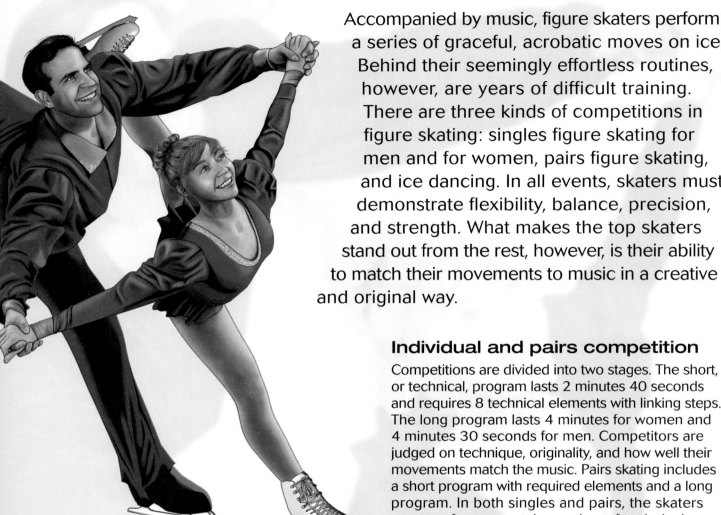

Accompanied by music, figure skaters perform a series of graceful, acrobatic moves on ice. Behind their seemingly effortless routines, however, are years of difficult training. There are three kinds of competitions in figure skating: singles figure skating for men and for women, pairs figure skating, and ice dancing. In all events, skaters must demonstrate flexibility, balance, precision, and strength. What makes the top skaters stand out from the rest, however, is their ability to match their movements to music in a creative and original way.

Individual and pairs competition

Competitions are divided into two stages. The short, or technical, program lasts 2 minutes 40 seconds and requires 8 technical elements with linking steps. The long program lasts 4 minutes for women and 4 minutes 30 seconds for men. Competitors are judged on technique, originality, and how well their movements match the music. Pairs skating includes a short program with required elements and a long program. In both singles and pairs, the skaters must perform a certain number of technical elements—spins, jumps, and spirals. Nine judges award each competitor a technical score and an artistic score, based on a scale of 0 to 6 points.

Blades
The blades are made of steel. There are 2 kinds of blades, one for figure skating and one for ice dancing. At the front of the blade there are several teeth, called toe picks. The longer toe picks on the figure skating blade make jumps, spirals, and spins easier to perform. The blade for ice dancing is shorter at the heel and has smaller toe picks, making dance movements less difficult.

Figure-skating blade

| **Toe pick**

Ice-dancing blade

Boots
The boots must be comfortable, hold the feet securely, and support the ankles firmly.

Figure Skating

Ice-dancing competition

In ice dancing, a couple performs dance moves to music. They must demonstrate perfect timing and harmony with each other and with the music. Unlike figure skating, which concentrates on acrobatic moves, ice dancing focuses on specific, recognized dance patterns. Artistic expression is a very important element to the judges in this event.

Figure skating techniques

The main movements in figure skating are spins, jumps, spirals, and steps. Under the direction of their coaches, figure skaters spend years mastering these movements.

Spins

To spin successfully, the skater must be able to turn around quickly and gracefully, perfectly centered on one spot on the ice. There are standing spins, sit spins, and combination spins. Spins can be performed on one foot, two feet, or while jumping.

Death-drop spin
The death-drop spin is a spectacular combination spin. It starts with what is called a flying camel spin and ends in a back-sit spin. The skater jumps off the outside front foot and lands in a sitting position on the other foot.

Figure Skating

Jumps

Each of the many different types of jumps, is defined by its takeoff and landing position. Jumps are also classified by the number of rotations the skater makes while in the air: single, double, triple, or quadruple.

The axel

The axel demands a lot of precision and is considered the most difficult jump. It is the only jump that starts with the skater facing forward. The axel can be performed as a single, double, or triple.

The lutz

The lutz is a unique and very physically demanding jump. It is similar to the flip, in that the right toe pick is used to make the skater take off from the left leg.

The toe loop

The toe loop is the simplest of the toe pick jumps. The skater takes off and lands backward.

Figure Skating

The flip
The flip is a toe pick jump performed in a straight line. The skater takes off facing backward.

Spirals
Spirals are high-speed spins. The best known are the front and back spirals, in which the single skater holds a skate with one hand, and the death spiral, in which the male skater makes his female partner spin while he holds her by one arm. The goal is to spin the woman as close to the ice as possible.

Outside back death spiral

Speed Skating

Skating on an ice track as smooth as a mirror, speed skaters can reach impressive speeds of 37 miles per hour. This is much faster than most people can ride their bicycles! In their quest to be the first across the finish line, skaters take off at a full sprint. Races take place on oval tracks. Skating quickly on a curved track is difficult. Athletes must lean sideways to maintain their speed, and risk falling if they lean too far. There are two kinds of speed-skating events for men and women: long track, in which two skaters compete, and short track, in which groups of four to six skaters compete.

Short-track competition

There are races for individuals as well as for relay teams. In the individuals race, all skaters start at the same time. They are allowed to pass, but are not allowed to slow down another skater in the process of passing. The winner is the one with the shortest time in the final. Men and women skate the same distances, which vary from 500 m up to 3,000 m. In the relays, women skate 3,000 m and men skate 5,000 m.

Finish judges and photo-finish officials
They make sure that the electronic timer works properly. They also time the races manually, in case the electronic equipment malfunctions.

Start judge
The start judge gives the signal with a starter's pistol.

Assistant referees
The assistant referees keep track of skaters' infractions, or faults. Two referees are on skates in the center of the rink. Two are at opposite ends, outside the rink.

Short-track rink
One complete turn around the track is approximately 110 m. It takes about 4½ turns to complete a 500-m course.

Coaches
The coaches give their skaters instructions during the race.

Chief referee
The chief referee supervises the assistant referees and makes sure that the rules are followed.

Speed Skating

Short-track techniques

Basic position

To be able to skate at high speed through the straightaways and curves, the athlete leans forward with knees bent. This position helps to maintain balance and adds power to the skater's strides.

Short-track skate

The long, thin, straight blade of the short-track skate is attached diagonally to the sole of the boot. The blade's position helps to give the skater more stability for leaning into the curves of the track.

Straightaway
The basic position.

Curve
Skaters are allowed to touch the ice with their hands to help maintain their balance in the curves. Hands cannot be kept on the ice for long, however, because this slows the skater down.

Start
The skaters take several running steps, digging their skate blades into the ice to help push off and to gain speed.

Safety padding
The boards are covered with padding to protect skaters who may crash into the sides. The padding is made of polystyrene covered with vinyl.

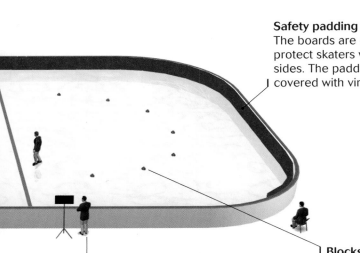

Lap counter
The lap counter indicates to the skaters how many laps, or turns around the rink, remain.

Blocks
The blocks are made of rubber or plastic. They are placed at the curves to help indicate the shape of the track. The blocks are not attached to the ice in case a skater hits one.

Speed Skating

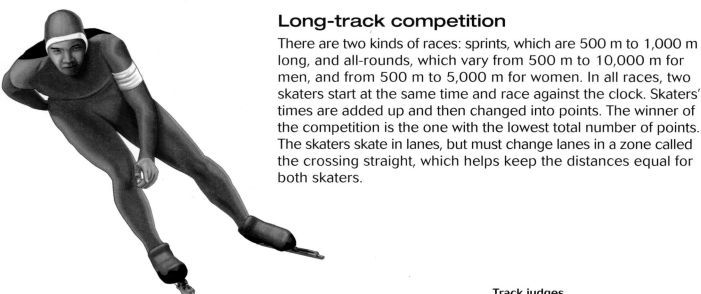

Long-track competition

There are two kinds of races: sprints, which are 500 m to 1,000 m long, and all-rounds, which vary from 500 m to 10,000 m for men, and from 500 m to 5,000 m for women. In all races, two skaters start at the same time and race against the clock. Skaters' times are added up and then changed into points. The winner of the competition is the one with the lowest total number of points. The skaters skate in lanes, but must change lanes in a zone called the crossing straight, which helps keep the distances equal for both skaters.

Long-track techniques

Basic position
Skaters lean forward. To reduce wind resistance, which will slow them down, they keep one arm behind their backs. Skaters use their other arm to help them balance in the curves. In sprint races, skaters swing both arms at the start and finish to add power and speed to their strides.

Straightaway   **Curve**

Long stride
To maintain a constant speed, skaters must use long strides. They use their arms and shoulders to help them balance, and lean forward throughout the race.

Track judges
Track judges make sure that the skaters are in the correct lanes, that they make their turns correctly, and that they do not get in each other's way.

Safety padding

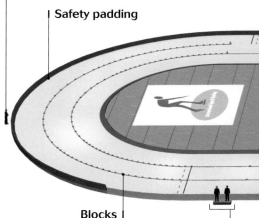

Blocks
The blocks indicate the lane that each skater must use.

Start judge and assistant
The start judge and assistant give the start signal and call back false starts. The start judge makes final decisions if there is a dispute regarding a start.

Speed Skating

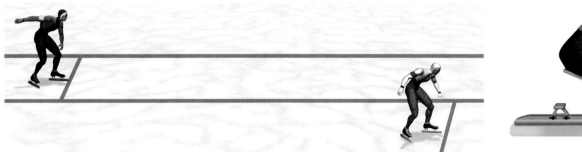

Start
The skaters need to have as powerful a push-off as possible. In the sprint race, the speed and power of the first strides can determine whether the skater wins or not.

Long-track rink

One complete turn around the rink is 400 m long. The track is divided into three lanes. The inside lane is reserved for the skaters' warm-ups.

Clap skate
The clap skate is used in long-track speed skating. Its long blade detaches from the boot at the heel which allows the blade to stay in contact with the ice while the skater takes longer, faster strides.

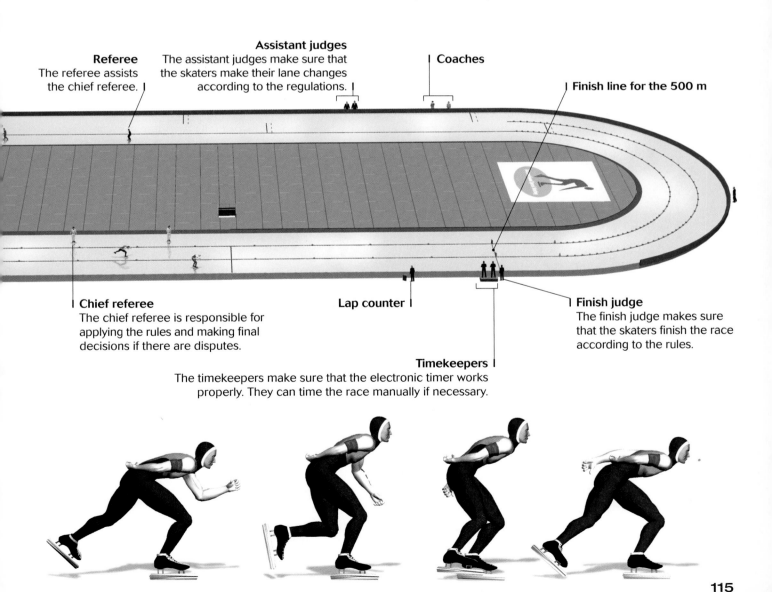

Referee
The referee assists the chief referee.

Assistant judges
The assistant judges make sure that the skaters make their lane changes according to the regulations.

Coaches

Finish line for the 500 m

Chief referee
The chief referee is responsible for applying the rules and making final decisions if there are disputes.

Lap counter

Finish judge
The finish judge makes sure that the skaters finish the race according to the rules.

Timekeepers
The timekeepers make sure that the electronic timer works properly. They can time the race manually if necessary.

Luge, Skeleton, Bobsledding

Tearing along an icy course at more than 80 miles per hour while lying on a small sled takes both courage and skill. With nerves of steel, the men and women who compete in luge, skeleton, or bobsledding guide their high-speed sleds through the many curves of the steeply banked course. The goal is to complete the course in the shortest time. Every fraction of a second counts! Bobsleds hold two or four athletes, luges hold one or two athletes, and skeletons are for one rider only.

Luge

Luge competitions are races against the clock. Each single competitor or team makes two to four runs, or descents, which are timed. The times are then added up, and the winner is the athlete or team with the shortest total time. The track is less than a mile long. It varies in length from 1,000 m to 1,300 m for the single luge, and from 800 m to 1,050 m for the double luge. In central Europe, where luge is especially popular, competitions sometimes take place on natural courses. These courses may consist of icy, winding roads, with no sidewalls to protect athletes from sliding off the edge.

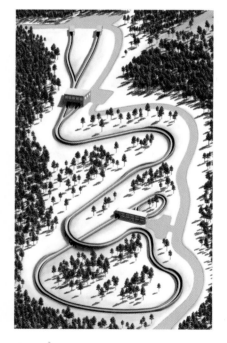

1. Start
Seated on the luge, the rider holds on to the starting handles on each side of the track.

2. Push off
The rider starts by pushing off the starting handles to move forward.

3. Acceleration
The rider gains speed by paddling (pushing against the ice with spiked gloves).

Track

The tracks are made of concrete and covered with ice. The ice is kept frozen artificially. Tracks may have different shapes, but they all have certain elements in common: a starting platform, straight sections, curves, banked turns, and, most important, a deceleration ramp, which is a straight section at the end of the course that allows the athletes to brake and slow down.

Luge, Skeleton, Bobsledding

Skeleton

In the skeleton event, athletes lie on their stomachs and travel down the course head first. The winner is the person with the shortest time.

1. Start
Riders grip the handles of the skeleton and run in this position for about 150 ft. Their shoes are equipped with cleats (spikes on the soles) to help them push off faster.

2. Loading
Riders lift their legs and fall onto the skeleton. This movement must be performed with precision or riders may be thrown off balance and lose control of their sleds.

3. Descent position
Riders steer by shifting their weight slightly to the left or right. At the finish, they may use their feet to help brake and stop their sleds.

Bobsledding

Unlike the luge and the skeleton, which are single-runner sleds, the bobsled is equipped with two sets of runners, or skis, one behind the other. The bobsled is steered by the rider in front, who uses handles connected to cables that are attached to the front runners. The athlete in back is in charge of using the brakes to slow and stop the sled. The winning team is the one with the shortest time.

1. Start
The riders push off, holding onto the starting handles on the outside of the shell.

2. Push
The riders run about 150 ft while continuing to push the bobsled.

3. Loading
Still running and pushing, the riders jump into the bobsled, starting with the driver. Team members push their starting handles inside the bobsled as they climb in.

4. Descent position
Except for the driver, who must steer the bobsled, the rest of the riders sit with their heads down to reduce wind resistance. They hold onto handles inside the sled and lean to the left or right on the curves to help the bobsled go faster. The rider sitting in back uses the brake to stop the bobsled once it has crossed the finish line.

4. Descent and steering
The rider lies back to reduce wind resistance. Riders can steer their luges by shifting their weight slightly to one side or the other, or by simply moving their heads or one of their shoulders.

5. Braking and stopping
After crossing the finish line, riders sit up and put their feet down on the ice while still in motion. Pushing down with the feet raises the front of the sled and forces the runners at the back of the sled to dig into the ice. This gradually brings the luge to a stop.

Alpine Skiing

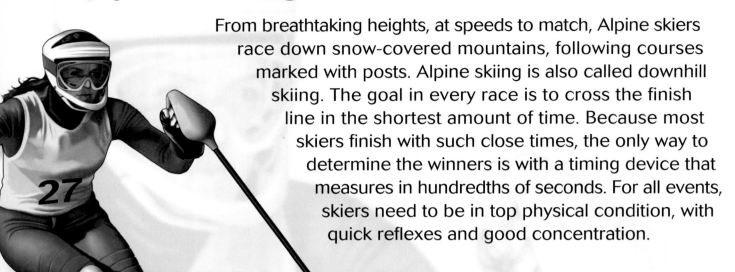

From breathtaking heights, at speeds to match, Alpine skiers race down snow-covered mountains, following courses marked with posts. Alpine skiing is also called downhill skiing. The goal in every race is to cross the finish line in the shortest amount of time. Because most skiers finish with such close times, the only way to determine the winners is with a timing device that measures in hundredths of seconds. For all events, skiers need to be in top physical condition, with quick reflexes and good concentration.

Equipment

Goggles
Whether the day is sunny or overcast, skiers can be easily blinded by the intense daylight reflecting off the snow. Goggles help to filter out the brightness, allowing athletes to see the course more easily.

Skis
A ski is made up of three sections, called the tail, the waist, and the tip. A ski's performance on the snow depends on its length, width, and shape. The longer skis used in Super-G and downhill are more stable. This is very important for high speeds. However, they are harder to control than slalom skis. Slalom skis have narrow mid-bodies, which allow the skier to change direction faster.

Boots
Ski boots are rigid, and made from a blend of plastics and other synthetic materials. They are attached to the skis at the heel and toe. The boots support the skier's ankles. This allows the skier to control the skis' direction by leg pressure and by leaning his body.

Edges
The metal edges along both sides allow the ski to "bite" into the snow to make turns. The edges are sharpened regularly to keep them working well.

Bindings
The bindings keep the boot attached to the ski. If the skier falls, the bindings are designed to release the skis. This helps to reduce injuries.

| Tail | Waist | Tip |

Downill and Super-G

Giant slalom

Slalom

Base
The base of the ski rides on the snow. The base is very smooth, and is made of synthetic materials. Ski bases are waxed before a race. There are different types of waxes designed to help skis slide faster in different snow conditions.

Alpine Skiing

Events

There are four kinds of events in Alpine skiing. The downhill and the super giant slalom (Super-G) are pure tests of speed. The giant slalom and the slalom or special slalom are races that focus on technique more than speed. Combined events allow skiers to demonstrate their skills in several different races—usually a downhill and a slalom event. The skiers' best combined results are measured.

Courses

Ski competitions take place in many parts of the world. Courses vary according to the type of mountain where the event is taking place. The clock tower, which shows the times, and the scoreboard, are always located at the bottom of the hill.

Officials
Officials are stationed at different areas along the entire length of the course to make sure that races proceed according to regulations.

Start
After getting a signal from the starting judge, the skier pushes off. The skier tries to pick up as much speed as possible in the first few yards by taking long skating strides while pushing with the poles.

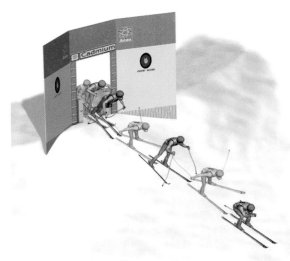

Finish line
The finish line is located at the bottom of the course. A clock reports each skier's time.

Suit
The suit is fitted tightly to the body to cut wind resistance, but is flexible enough to allow full movement.

Poles
The poles are light but rigid and made of aluminum or a combination of synthetic materials. The poles serve to push off, start the turns, and maintain balance.

Helmet
The helmet protects the skier's head from injury in case of a fall. Helmets must be worn in speed events, but skiers usually wear them in all other events as well.

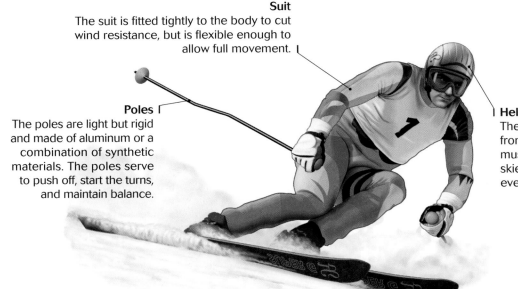

Alpine Skiing

Speed events

Speed events, which include the downhill and the super giant slalom, take place in one round.

Downhill

The downhill is the fastest of the Alpine skiing events. The race takes place on a very steep slope. It features long, straight sections and fast, sweeping turns through open gates. The skiers have three days of trials to study and to get used to the difficult course. On the day of the race, they descend the hill averaging speeds of 60 mph, and can reach top speeds of 85 mph!

Jumps

When skiing downhill, athletes are traveling so fast that the smallest bump on the course can cause them to jump into the air. To maintain both balance and speed, skiers try to stay low in a tuck position, similar to the schuss (below).

Super giant slalom or Super-G

The Super-G course is another fast race. It includes at least 35 open and closed gates through which the skier must pass. The Super-G combines the speed of a downhill race with the quick-turn techniques used in giant slalom. Competitors in this event learn the route of the course only the day of the race.

Gates

The gates' poles are made of plastic. They are jointed at the base so that they can bend when the skier hits them.

Schuss

The schuss is also called the "egg position." This position is used in downhill events and for skiing straight sections in the Super-G and giant slalom races. By bending over with a rounded back, knees bent, and elbows in, the skier creates less wind resistance and can ski faster.

Alpine Skiing

Technical events

Technical events take place on courses that are slower and have more gates. The skiers must make many turns without losing time or speed. Skiers have two runs each. The times from both runs are added together. The winner is the skier with the shortest overall time.

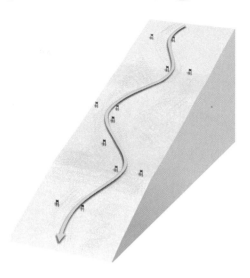

Slalom or special slalom

The positions of the gates in this race require skiers to make rapid turns. Skiers must make contact with the gates in order to stay on course. The course is made up of red open gates and blue closed gates that must be passed through alternately. Skiers are eliminated if they miss a single gate—and there may be as many as 75 of them on a course!

Slalom-type turns

The skier is in a standing position with her feet together. Her knees are slightly bent to help absorb the shock of the bumps. To turn quickly, the skier must pass as close to the gate as possible. Skiers often hit the gates while making their turns, and then push off with their hands or legs, if necessary. To avoid injury when hitting gates, skiers wear protective gear on their hands, shins, and face.

Giant slalom-type turns

Also used in downhill and Super-G, this turn is performed with knees bent, chest slightly forward, and feet and arms apart. The skier presses down with his outside ski to "cut" a turn with its edge, while using his arms and inside ski to maintain balance.

Closed gates

Closed gates are also called vertical gates. They are placed one in front of the other, going down the slope.

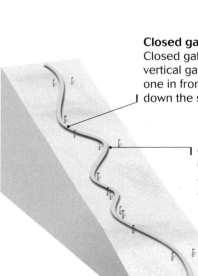

Open gates

Open gates are also called horizontal gates. They are placed side by side on the slope.

Giant or giant slalom

The giant slalom course features both open and closed gates. There are fewer gates, however, than in the special slalom, and the slope of the course is not as steep. With fewer gates, skiers can reach higher speeds.

Freestyle Skiing

Leaping through the air and performing quick and complex maneuvers, men and women freestyle skiers combine the speed of Alpine skiers with the agility of gymnasts. The three best-known events in freestyle are acro (for acrobatic), moguls, and aerials. Athletes usually specialize in one of the three, because each event demands a particular set of skills and requires much training. In the acro event, skiers perform a series of acrobatic figures and steps to music. In the moguls event, skiers descend a slope covered with bumps, called moguls, and must demonstrate both speed and style in the way they handle the course. In the aerials event, skiers perform figures in the air after launching themselves off a ramp. Both athletic and artistic, freestyle skiing demands great flexibility and a total mastery of one's movements.

Forward somersault
Somersaults can be performed with or without the help of the poles. When skiers use their poles, they often balance on them before returning their feet to the ground.

Acro

The acro event takes place on a smooth, gradual slope. Skiers use poles and short skis. In front of seven judges, the athletes perform their choreographed moves to music of their choosing. Moves are divided into three categories: spins, in which the skis stay on the ground; leverage (lifting) moves, which can be spins with the skis lifted off the ground; and somersaults. The different moves are linked together by steps choreographed to music. The variety of the figures and how well they go with the music are as important to the judges as the technical difficulty of the moves. At the end of the event, the competitors each receive a score of between 0 and 10.

Freestyle Skiing

Moguls

The moguls event takes place on a straight, steep slope featuring moguls as well as two jump ramps, called kickers. Athletes ski one at a time around the moguls and perform acrobatic jumps off the kickers in as short a time as possible. They are not allowed to perform the same acrobatic jump twice. In the dual moguls event, two skiers ski down the course at the same time and try to be the first to cross the finish line. Skiers are timed in all events. Their performances are judged according to how skillfully they perform the turns, how well they use the moguls, and the difficulty of their jumps. The skiers' finish times are converted into a final score of between 0 and 10.

Kickers
The kickers are located at least 165 ft from the top and bottom of the course.

Moguls
The moguls are spaced about 11 ft apart.

Finish line
The skiers' times are recorded with an electronic timer.

Turns
Despite the moguls, skiers try to keep their skis in constant contact with the slope. They hold their upper bodies straight and their knees and legs bent to keep going in the right direction and absorb the shock of the bumps.

Kicker

Helicopter
The rotation begins with the skier keeping his upper body straight and using his pelvis to turn his body. Spreading his arms out slows down the rotation. Keeping his arms close to his body speeds up the rotation.

Freestyle Skiing

Aerials event

In the aerials event, skiers launch themselves off ramps, called kickers and floaters, and perform difficult jumps and figures in the air. Events take place in two rounds. In each round, skiers perform two different jumps. Seven judges award the athletes points. The takeoff is worth two points, the aerial figure is worth five points, and the landing is worth three points. Skiers must maintain control at all times—losing their balance or falling upon landing loses points, even if their aerial figures are performed perfectly.

✳ Unique training methods

Training for the aerials competition takes a long time and must begin long before the competition season. Skiers often start training by jumping on trampolines—while wearing their skis!

Jump area

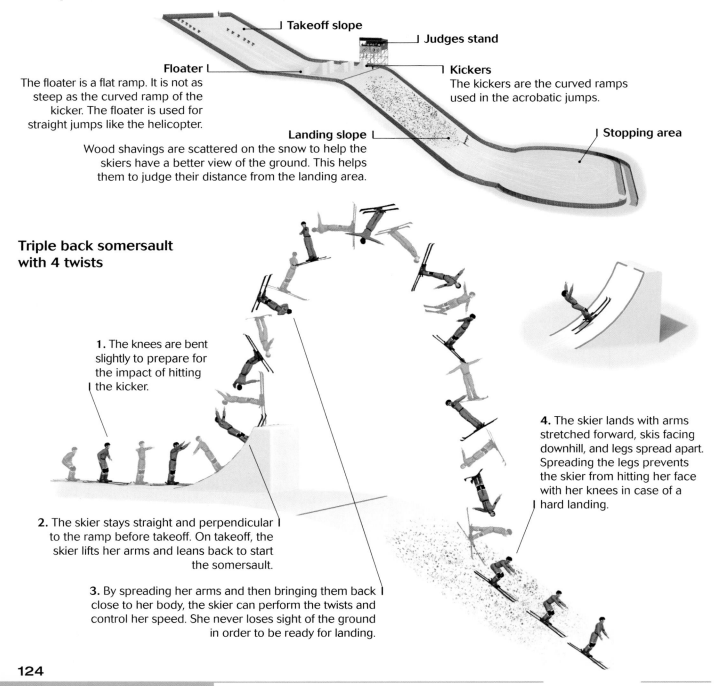

Takeoff slope

Judges stand

Floater
The floater is a flat ramp. It is not as steep as the curved ramp of the kicker. The floater is used for straight jumps like the helicopter.

Kickers
The kickers are the curved ramps used in the acrobatic jumps.

Landing slope
Wood shavings are scattered on the snow to help the skiers have a better view of the ground. This helps them to judge their distance from the landing area.

Stopping area

Triple back somersault with 4 twists

1. The knees are bent slightly to prepare for the impact of hitting the kicker.

2. The skier stays straight and perpendicular to the ramp before takeoff. On takeoff, the skier lifts her arms and leans back to start the somersault.

3. By spreading her arms and then bringing them back close to her body, the skier can perform the twists and control her speed. She never loses sight of the ground in order to be ready for landing.

4. The skier lands with arms stretched forward, skis facing downhill, and legs spread apart. Spreading the legs prevents the skier from hitting her face with her knees in case of a hard landing.

Speed Skiing

Speed skiing is the fastest nonmotorized sport in the world. Launching themselves from the top of a steep hill, men and women speed skiers can go from 0 to 125 miles per hour in less than six seconds. This is as fast an acceleration as a Formula 1 race car! Skiers descend the course one after the other. After accelerating for almost 500 meters, they are timed over a distance of 100 meters. The athletes' skis hardly touch the snow as they attempt to reach their top speeds. Many factors go into helping skiers achieve their best times. They hold their breath to help them maintain the correct body position. They use extra-long skis (almost eight feet long), and their suits and helmets are specially designed to reduce wind resistance. Above all, speed skiers rely on their courage and powers of concentration.

Tracks
The fastest tracks are in Europe, especially France. Tracks measure about 3,900 ft long and 1,470 ft high. The track's surface is prepared by a snow-grooming machine. The slope is so steep that the machine must be pulled up to the top by a cable.

Unique training methods
To practice positioning their bodies correctly, speed skiers must try to duplicate the wind conditions on the track. They achieve this by training inside a wind tunnel, facing an enormous fan that blows air at them at more than 125 mph!

Acceleration area
In the acceleration area, air pressure on the skiers increases. As they approach speeds of about 125 mph, their skis start to "float" on a cushion of air.

Braking area
Once they cross the red line at the end of the timing area, skiers lean forward and straighten out their legs. To slow down, they stretch out their arms. This creates more air resistance. They then ski 2 very wide turns to help them come to a complete stop.

Timing area
Reaching the timing area approximately 11 seconds into the descent, skiers may achieve speeds of 135 mph or more! Because their skis are, at this point, mostly riding on air rather than the snow, skiers steer themselves by varying their body positions slightly and adjusting themselves according to the air pressure on them.

Safety zone
The safety zone is a 65-ft area located on both sides of the track. It serves to protect the skiers in case they lose control and ski off course.

Ski Jumping

After a dizzying descent down a ramp, ski jumpers take off into the air, landing more than 300 feet away. That is almost the length of a football field! The goal is to jump as great a distance as possible. To achieve this, skiers must jump in the correct body position and hold that position while in the air. There is not much time to get it right—from starting gate to landing, the jump lasts only five to eight seconds—with only two to three seconds actually spent in the air. Both male and female ski jumpers rely on experience and a strong dose of courage to compete.

The competition

Ski jumpers compete in three events: the individual jump on a normal hill (90 m), an individual jump on a large hill (120 m), and a team jump on a large hill. A red line called a "K point" indicates the ideal landing position for the skiers. A jumper landing on the K point gets 60 points. In the 90 m jump, skiers gain two points for every meter they jump beyond the K point, and lose two points for every meter behind the K point. The five judges also award up to 20 additional points based on the jumper's position in the air and the landing. In individual events, the winner is the skier with the highest score after two jumps.

Technique

1. In-run
Going down the ramp, the skier crouches to reduce air resistance, holding that position until the takeoff point. Skiers reach speeds of more than 50 mph by the time they hit the ramp.

2. Takeoff
Taking off too early or too late will reduce the distance skiers can jump. At the takeoff point, skiers quickly straighten out their bodies and lean forward.

3. Flight
Skiers lean far forward toward the tips of their skis. The tips are spreadin a V shape that provides greater lift and adds distance to the jumps.

4. Landing
The force of the landing is equal to about three times the skiers' weight. Each skier lands with one leg in front of the other and knees bent to absorb the shock.

Cross-country

With lightweight, narrow skis and equipped with long poles to push them forward, men and women cross-country skiers race long distances, uphill as well as downhill, and over flat terrain. The goal in all cross-country ski races is to complete the course in the shortest amount of time possible. Races vary in length from sprints of about 90 miles to long-distance races of more than 900 miles! Especially popular in the Scandinavian countries are races of more than 50 miles, which can attract as many as 13,000 participants! Athletes need exceptional physical stamina for cross-country skiing. To keep from wasting their movements and energy, cross-country skiers must also master the most efficient ways of moving.

The competition

There are two styles of competition skiing. In the classical style, skiers push off with both poles and glide forward in two tracks in the snow. In the freestyle, skiers mainly use skating movements to propel themselves forward. All courses feature both hills and flat areas. For most races, competitors draw lots to determine in what order they will ski the course. Skiers leave the start at 30-second intervals. Races are against the clock. Classic races run from about 3 to 18 miles, while freestyle races are about 18 miles long for women and 31 miles long for men. In other races, like the relay (with teams of four skiers) and the sprint, the winners are the first to cross the finish line.

Equipment

Freestyle skis
Freestyle skis are wider and the tips are less curved than on classic skis. These skis make it easier for the skier to "skate" on them.

Classic skis
Classic skis are rigid and generally longer than freestyle skis. These longer skis distribute the weight of the skier more evenly across the snow.

Technique

Skating stride
The skier moves forward like a skater. Sliding one leg forward, the skier pushes off sideways with the other leg.

Snowboarding

Snowboarding combines the acrobatics of ocean surfing with Alpine skiing. Men and women snowboarders ride their boards on snow much the way surfers ride on water. Depending on the event, snowboarders may perform acrobatic moves similar to those done by ocean surfers, or they may "ski" their boards on a downhill course like Alpine skiers. Some events even feature moves that look like skateboarding. Although this free-spirited and fun sport looks easy, competitive snowboarding demands top physical condition, daring, and a perfect sense of balance.

Equipment

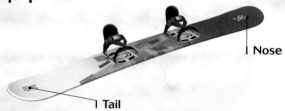

Nose

Tail

Freestyle board
Used in half-pipe events, the freestyle board is designed for smooth jumps and landings. The nose and tail are identical, to allow for takeoffs and landings in either direction. The freestyle board is used with flexible boots.

Alpine board
The Alpine board is designed for high speed. It is narrow, rigid, and slightly wider at the nose. The Alpine board is used with hard boots.

Flexible boot
The flexible boot allows snowboarders to move their legs freely in any direction without making the board unstable.

Hard boot
The hard boot is designed for the precise moves required in Alpine snowboarding. Snowboarders steer their boards by leg and body movements that are transferred to the boards by the rigid boots.

Snowboarding

The competitions

In freestyle, or acrobatic, snowboarding, athletes perform aerial figures inside special snow ramps called half pipes. In Alpine snowboarding events, which include slalom, giant slalom, and parallel (duel) slalom, athletes race downhill against the clock on a course with slalom gates.

Half-pipe competition

Snowboarders travel down the U-shaped, half-pipe course, accompanied by music. Switching from one side of the course to the other, they perform acrobatic jumps and twists in the air. Judges give each athlete a score from 0 to 10 based on the height of their jumps and the difficulty of their moves.

Half-pipe course
The course looks like a pipe that has been cut in half lengthwise. The course is sloped downward, and has sidewalls of about 10 to 13 ft in height to allow the boarders to perform their figures.

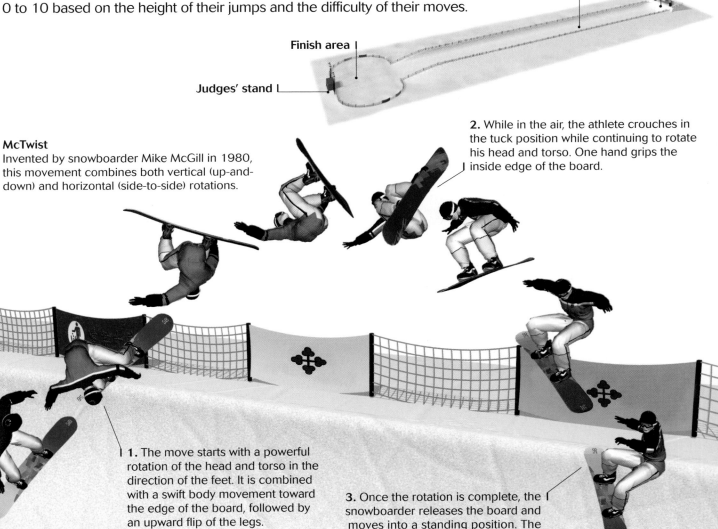

Start

Sidewalls

Finish area

Judges' stand

McTwist
Invented by snowboarder Mike McGill in 1980, this movement combines both vertical (up-and-down) and horizontal (side-to-side) rotations.

2. While in the air, the athlete crouches in the tuck position while continuing to rotate his head and torso. One hand grips the inside edge of the board.

1. The move starts with a powerful rotation of the head and torso in the direction of the feet. It is combined with a swift body movement toward the edge of the board, followed by an upward flip of the legs.

3. Once the rotation is complete, the snowboarder releases the board and moves into a standing position. The athlete is now in the correct position for sliding over to the other side of the half-pipe course.

Technique
Many aerial moves in snowboarding are inspired by skateboarding. For example, the backside air (jumping while holding the edge of the board), the corkscrew (twisting), and the McTwist.

Snowboarding

Giant slalom

The giant slalom is a timed race with two rounds. In each round, the boarder makes a descent and follows a set course marked with triangular gates. The athlete may fall without being disqualified, but is not allowed to miss any gates. The course has an equal number of left and right turns, making it fair for all boarders, those who ride with the right foot forward and those who surf with the left foot forward.

Technique

Turns can be performed two ways: the backside turn, in which the athlete turns by putting pressure on the heels, or the frontside turn, in which the athlete turns by putting pressure on the toes.

Backside turn
With the back held straight and the legs bent low, boarders lean into the turn with arms spread to maintain balance.

Frontside turn
At high speed, athletes bend their knees and lean their bodies toward the inside of the curve. They keep their eyes on the next gate to get ready to switch over for the upcoming curve.

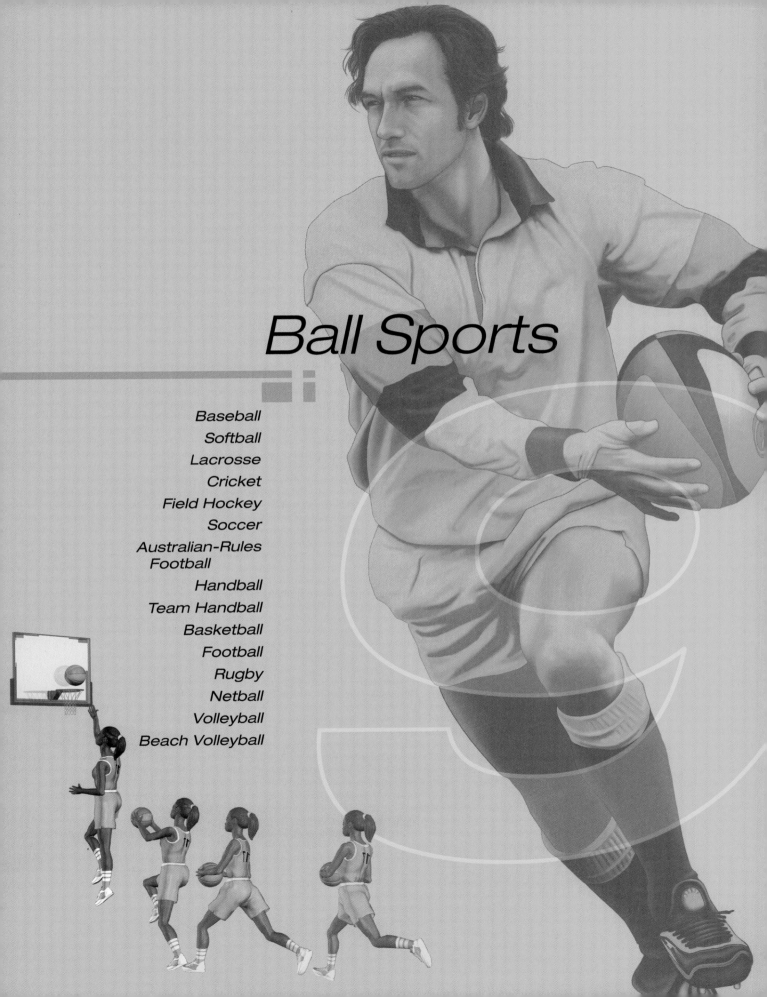

Ball Sports

Baseball
Softball
Lacrosse
Cricket
Field Hockey
Soccer
Australian-Rules
Football
Handball
Team Handball
Basketball
Football
Rugby
Netball
Volleyball
Beach Volleyball

Baseball

Baseball is a ball sport played between two competing teams of nine players each. Baseball is so popular in the United States that it is often called America's national pastime. Baseball demands quick reflexes and good coordination. The ball travels at high speeds. Thrown at up to 100 miles per hour, a ball often flies unpredictably when hit. In a baseball game, each player on a team takes a turn at trying to hit the ball with a bat. The opposing team's pitcher tries to make the batter swing and miss hitting the ball. The batter who hits the ball runs to the bases on the field while avoiding being tagged out by opposing players. A base runner who succeeds in touching all the bases scores a point, called a run, for his team. The team with the most runs at the end of the nine periods, called innings, wins the game.

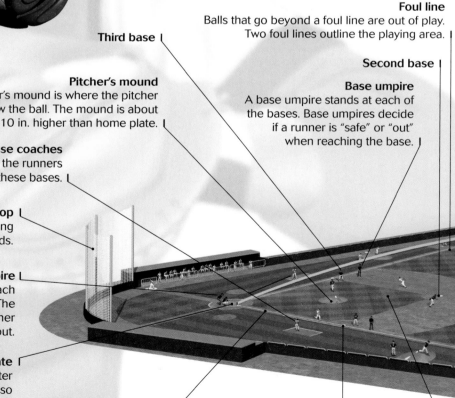

Foul line
Balls that go beyond a foul line are out of play. Two foul lines outline the playing area.

Third base

Second base

Pitcher's mound
The pitcher's mound is where the pitcher stands to throw the ball. The mound is about 10 in. higher than home plate.

Base umpire
A base umpire stands at each of the bases. Base umpires decide if a runner is "safe" or "out" when reaching the base.

First and third base coaches
The coaches signal instructions to the runners waiting on these bases.

Backstop
The backstop keeps the ball from being thrown or hit into the stands.

Home plate umpire
The home plate umpire judges each pitch and calls strikes and balls. The umpire also rules on whether a runner reaching home plate is safe or out.

Home plate
Home plate is where the batter stands to face the pitcher. It is also the last base in a run.

First baseline
A baseline marks the path the runner must follow to the base.

First base

Infield
The infield includes the diamond, which is the square area outlined by the 3 bases and home plate.

Baseball

Equipment

Ball

The hard ball measures about 9 in. around and weighs about 5 oz. It is made of cotton or wool yarn, tightly wound around a core of rubber or cork. Two pieces of leather sewn together form the cover.

Glove

The glove is made of leather and is padded inside. The size and shape of gloves vary according to players' positions.

Bat

The bat is a smooth, rounded wood or aluminum stick. It measures a maximum of 42 in. in length and 2¾ in. across at its widest point.

The game

Innings are divided into halves. Each team spends half an inning playing offense (batting and running), and half an inning playing defense (pitching, fielding, and catching). On offense, batters try to hit the ball for a base hit or a home run. They may also try to get to first base with a walk. Their base runner teammates try to run all the bases without getting tagged out. On defense, pitchers try to strike out the batters, and, along with their fielder teammates, try to tag out the base runners on the offensive team.

The field

The field is made of grass or artificial turf, with some sections covered in sand. The field is divided into two main sections, the infield and the outfield.

Ball

If a batter doesn't swing at a bad pitch, a "ball" is counted against the pitcher.

Walk

After 4 balls, the batter is allowed to proceed directly to first base for a "walk."

Strike

If a batter allows a good pitch to go by without swinging, or swings and misses, a strike is counted against the batter.

Out

After 3 strikes, the batter is declared "out" and must leave the field. A player can also be called out by being tagged by an opposing player with the ball before reaching a base, or by hitting a ball that is caught directly by a player on the defensive team.

Base hit

A batter who succeeds in hitting the ball and running to a base without being tagged out by the defensive team has a base hit.

Home run

A batter who succeeds in hitting the ball beyond the playing area, or who hits the ball without a player from the defensive team being able to retrieve it, gets a home run.

Grand slam

A grand slam is a home run that occurs when there are already 3 base runners on base. All runners then proceed to home plate, for a total of 4 runs.

Home run path
A home run is counted if the ball clears the fence.

Warning track
The warning track signals to the fielders trying to catch the ball that the fence is close by. This helps to keep them from accidentally running into the fence.

Outfield
The outfield is the playing area beyond the infield. It is bordered by the foul lines on 2 sides and the fence at the far end.

Fence

Foul pole (2)
The foul poles mark the ends of the foul lines.

Baseball

Batting

Every time the ball is pitched, the batter must decide whether to swing at the ball or not. To be counted as a good pitch, the ball must be thrown in the strike zone above home plate. If the ball is not in the strike zone and the batter does not swing, he is awarded a "ball." After four balls, the batter is allowed to proceed directly to first base. This is called a walk. A strike is called against the batter for not swinging at a good pitch. The batter also gets a strike for swinging and missing the ball or for hitting the ball outside the foul lines. A batter with three strikes is called out and must leave the field.

Strike zone
The area above the plate between the batter's knees and chest.

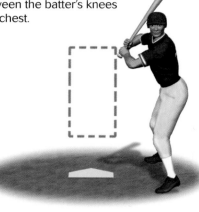

Batting technique
The player holds the bat at the narrow end with his 2 hands placed together. He grips the bat firmly but not too tightly.

1. Stance
The batter gets comfortable at the plate by placing his feet about shoulder width apart. The batter then holds the bat over his shoulder and waits for the pitch.

2. Swing
The batter shifts his weight forward and takes a short step toward the pitcher as he swings. The forward movement adds power to the batter's swing.

3. Follow through
If he hits the ball, the batter continues the arm, shoulder, and hip movement he started with the swing, and gets ready to run toward first base.

Pitching

Pitching technique
The pitcher takes his position on the mound and then throws the ball toward home plate.

1. Set position
The pitcher takes a step back, holding the ball close to his chest.

2. Wind-up position
Turning sideways, the pitcher raises his arm and balances on one leg.

3. Stride
The pitcher takes a step toward the batter as he starts to throw the ball. Transferring his weight forward adds power to his pitch.

4. Pitch
The pitcher throws the ball toward the batter, following through with his arm movement while taking one more step forward.

Baseball

Fielding

The defensive players try to prevent the offensive team from running safely from base to base. They do this by retrieving the hit ball and throwing it to a teammate guarding the base toward which the runner is heading.

Third baseman
The third basemen must have a powerful throwing arm to speed the ball to first base if necessary.

Catcher
The catcher indicates to the pitcher what type of throw he should use to try to trick the batter into missing the ball. The catcher uses secret hand signals that only his team understands.

Pitcher
The pitcher throws the ball, trying to get the batter to miss it. The pitcher also retrieves balls thrown by his teammates and tries to tag out runners.

First baseman
The first baseman is involved in most of the defensive plays. He tries to stop batters from reaching first base.

Left fielder
The left fielder, also called the outfielder, covers the area behind the third baseman.

Shortstop
The shortstop covers a large area of the infield. He retrieves the ball and usually throws it to the first or second basemen.

Center fielder
The center fielder covers the widest area of the outfield. He watches the catcher's signals and tries to figure out where the batter may hit the ball.

Second baseman
The second baseman covers the area between first and second base.

Right fielder
The right fielder plays behind the first baseman. He must be able to throw the ball as far as third base, if necessary.

Pitches

Types of pitches
Pitchers use a variety of pitches to try to trick batters and strike them out. A pitcher can make the ball fly through the air and change direction slightly, depending on the position of his fingers on the ball.

Curveball
By placing the fingers over the seams sewn on the ball, the pitcher can make the ball curve sideways and then drop.

Slider
The slider is similar to the curveball but travels faster. The 2 fingers on top are placed over the seams to make the ball spin. Just before the ball is released, the wrist is snapped sideways and the fingers on top are pushed straight downward. This makes the ball spin, then drop suddenly and curve to the right.

Knuckleball
The position of the fingers prevents the ball from rotating. This makes it difficult for the batter to predict how the ball will travel through the air.

Fastball
By placing 2 fingers on the top of the ball, the pitcher makes the ball travel straight and very fast. The fastball is a powerful pitch.

Change-up
The change-up is thrown with the same arm movement as the fastball. But because the hand covers more of the ball's surface, the ball travels more slowly through the air.

Softball

Softball is played with a bat and a ball on a diamond-shaped field with four bases. The object of the game is to score points, or runs, by hitting the ball and running around the bases. Although it resembles baseball in some ways, softball has only seven, not nine, periods called innings, and the ball is pitched underhand, not overhand. There are two common varieties of the game, fast-pitch and slow-pitch, each with its own set of rules. Women's fast-pitch is an Olympic event. Softball requires coordination, fast reflexes, and a mastery of throwing and catching.

The game

Two teams of nine players each take turns playing offense (batting and running) and defense (pitching, fielding, and catching). The positions are the same as in baseball. The pitcher tries to throw the ball and make the batter swing and miss hitting it for a strike call. If the batter does not swing at the ball because it was thrown incorrectly, it is called a ball. The batter who succeeds in hitting the ball can run to first base. To score runs, base runners must touch the three bases, in order, before returning to home plate. The team with the most runs at the end of seven innings wins the game.

The field

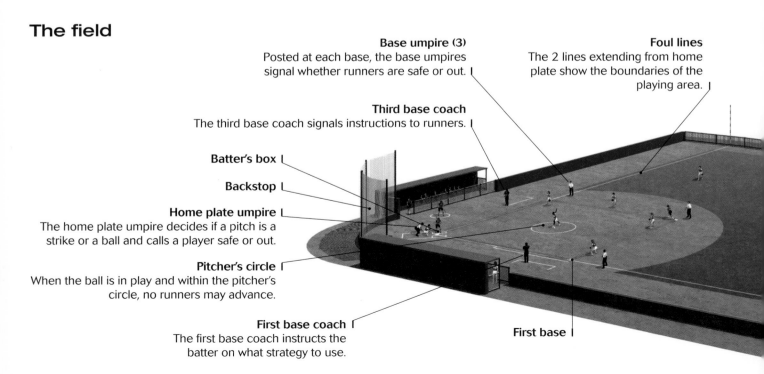

Base umpire (3)
Posted at each base, the base umpires signal whether runners are safe or out.

Foul lines
The 2 lines extending from home plate show the boundaries of the playing area.

Third base coach
The third base coach signals instructions to runners.

Batter's box

Backstop

Home plate umpire
The home plate umpire decides if a pitch is a strike or a ball and calls a player safe or out.

Pitcher's circle
When the ball is in play and within the pitcher's circle, no runners may advance.

First base coach
The first base coach instructs the batter on what strategy to use.

First base

Softball

Pitching technique

There are two styles of throwing the ball, depending on the type of game being played—fast-pitch or slow-pitch.

Fast-pitch
With both feet resting on the pitcher's plate, the pitcher waits for a sign from the catcher, who signals to her what kind of pitch to use. She does a "windmill" rotation with her arm, and then throws the ball underhand, releasing it at hip level. The ball must be thrown directly toward the batter's strike zone, crossing home plate between the height of the batter's front knee and her back shoulder.

Slow-pitch
The pitcher may have one or both feet on the pitcher's plate. She throws the ball underhand in one continuous movement. The ball arcs through the air at a medium speed. It must arc no higher than 12 ft and no lower than 6 ft, and it must drop in front of the batter.

Warning track
The warning track alerts the fielders trying to catch the ball that they are close to the fence.

Outfield

Equipment

Glove
The glove is used for catching the ball. It is made of leather and is padded to protect the hand.

Ball
Larger than a baseball, the softball measures 12 in. around. It is made of nylon thread wound around a core of rubber and cork covered with 2 pieces of leather sewn together.

Bat
The bat is often made of aluminum. It must be no more than 34 in. long.

Double base
A double base is used at first base. It is easier for the batter to touch the orange part with her foot when touching base. The wider base helps her avoid hitting the first baseman, who may be standing in her way.

Lacrosse

Lacrosse is a fast-paced field game played with a ball and a long-handled stick, called a crosse. Two opposing teams try to move the ball down the field and score points by throwing or kicking the ball through their opponents' goal. The object of the game is to score the most goals. Crosses are equipped with netted pockets on one end for catching, carrying, and passing the ball. There are several different versions of the game, played by both men and women. Men's teams have 10 players; women's teams have 12. Lacrosse is a sport that requires coordination and agility. While running, players must be able to catch and shoot the ball with accuracy. They also need endurance to stay in the game, which keeps them in constant motion over a large playing area.

Equipment

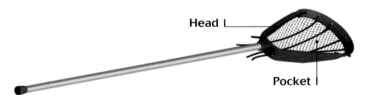

Head | ⌐

Pocket |

Crosse
The crosse can be made of wood, aluminum, or plastic. The netted pocket at the head is made of leather, linen, or nylon. The attacker's crosse is shorter than the defender's crosse. The goalkeeper's crosse has a much larger head.

Ball
The ball is made of hard rubber and may be yellow, white, black, or orange. It measures about 8 in. around and weighs approximately 5 oz.

Helmet
The helmet is equipped with a face mask and chin guard. Helmets are worn by all players in men's games and by the goalkeepers in women's games. Other women players do not wear helmets because there is less risk of injury in their no-contact game.

The field

International lacrosse is played outdoors on a field of grass or artificial turf. The playing area measures about 60 yd by 110 yd for men's games, and about 70 yd by 120 yd for women's games.

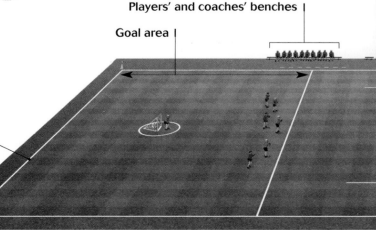

Players' and coaches' benches |

Goal area |

End line |

If the ball crosses the end line, it is called out-of-bounds. The team of the player who was closest to the ball when it went out-of-bounds gets to put the ball back in play.

Lacrosse

The game

An international lacrosse game is divided into 25-minute quarters with a 10-minute halftime. The umpire puts the ball in play in the center of the field at the start of each quarter and after a goal is scored. The rules of lacrosse vary according to the type of game. The players' hands must always be on their crosses. Breaking the rules results in penalties ranging from 30-second to 3-minute suspensions from the game. Physical contact, such as body checking, is carefully regulated to prevent injuries, and is allowed only in men's outdoor lacrosse. In women's lacrosse, the ball may not be kicked. In indoor lacrosse, which is played on covered ice hockey rinks during the off-season, there are no pauses during the game. This means that players may spend the entire game running from one end of the field to the other without a rest!

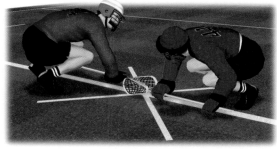

Face-off
Two players hold their crosses to the ground. The referee places the ball between the crosses. At the sound of the referee's whistle, the players each try to gain control of the ball.

Throw

Scoop

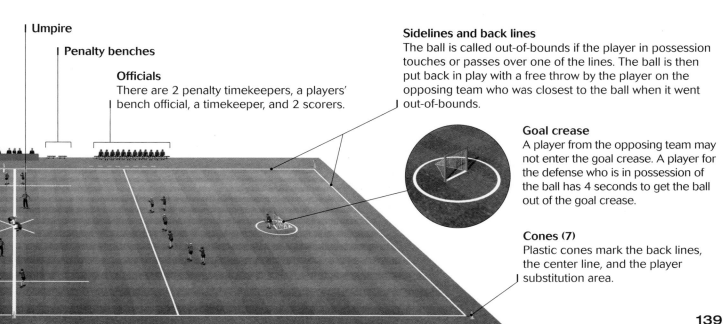

Umpire

Penalty benches

Officials
There are 2 penalty timekeepers, a players' bench official, a timekeeper, and 2 scorers.

Sidelines and back lines
The ball is called out-of-bounds if the player in possession touches or passes over one of the lines. The ball is then put back in play with a free throw by the player on the opposing team who was closest to the ball when it went out-of-bounds.

Goal crease
A player from the opposing team may not enter the goal crease. A player for the defense who is in possession of the ball has 4 seconds to get the ball out of the goal crease.

Cones (7)
Plastic cones mark the back lines, the center line, and the player substitution area.

Cricket

Cricket is an elegant and complicated game played with bats and a ball. Both men and women participate in the sport. In a cricket match, the 11 players on a team take turns going to bat and trying to score points by running in between two bases. The opposing team fields the ball and tries to end the batting team's turn at bat, called an innings, by getting the players out. There are two innings in a match. An inning ends when 10 players on a team are out. Because it can take a long time to get 10 players out, matches may last anywhere from one afternoon to five days!

The match

The match takes place on an oval field, with a rectangle in the center called the pitch. The pitch has two batting areas, called creases, and two sets of posts in the ground, called wickets. The pitcher for the defense, called the bowler, stands at one wicket along with a batsman for the offense. At the opposite wicket stands another batsman, as well as a wicketkeeper for the defense. The bowler throws the ball toward the opposite wicket and tries to "break" it (knock its bails down). The batsman standing in front of the wicket tries to protect the wicket by batting the ball away into the field. If the batsman hits the ball far enough, both batsmen then try to score runs, exchanging places as they run between the two wickets. Fieldsmen for the defense, positioned farther out in the field, try to get the batsman out. They may do this by catching the ball directly, throwing it at a wicket to break it, or throwing it to the bowler or the wicketkeeper, who then tries to break the wicket.

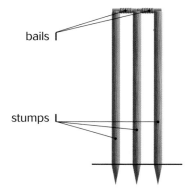

bails

stumps

Equipment

Ball
The cricket ball is slightly smaller than a baseball. It is made of string wound tightly around a core made of cork and covered in hard leather.

Bat
The bat is made of wood from a willow tree. The handle is covered with rubber. Batsmen use the flat side of the bat to hit the ball.

Wicket
The wicket consists of 3 posts, called stumps, on which 2 sticks, called bails, are balanced. If a stump is hit, the bails will fall down, getting the batsman out.

The players on the pitch

Bowler
The bowler runs an average of 20 ft before pitching the ball. He tries to make the batsman miss by throwing the ball very fast or with a curve.

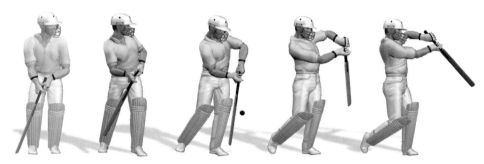

Batsman
The batsman is allowed to hit the ball in any direction on the playing field. The flat surface of the bat helps him to direct the ball wherever he wishes.

The pitch

Batsman (offense) (2)
The 2 batsmen stand in front of their wickets to protect them. One batsman faces the bowler and tries to hit the ball away. If he succeeds in getting a run, both batsmen exchange places, running to the opposite wicket to score points.

Wicketkeeper (defense)
The job of the wicketkeeper is to catch the ball thrown by the fielders, and to put the batsmen out by breaking the wicket.

Wicket (2)

Bowler (defense)
The bowler throws the ball toward the opposite wicket to try to break it, which puts the batsman out. The bowler may also catch the ball retrieved by one of the fielders on his team and then use the ball to break the wicket.

Popping crease
The pitch ends and the popping crease mark the area where the ball must be thrown and batted.

Umpire

Return crease

Pitch area

Batsman (offense)

Pitch ends

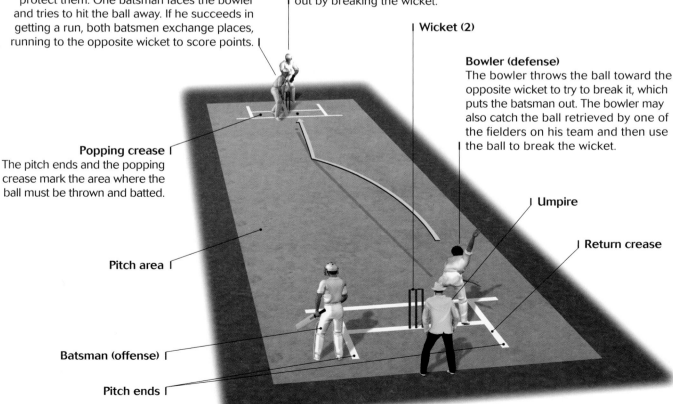

Field Hockey

In the game of field hockey, two opposing teams of women or men players use wooden sticks to hit a small ball across a field into the opponent's goal. The playing area resembles a soccer field with goals at either end. The object of the game is to score the most goals. Players may not use their bodies to block opponents, which makes it easier for opponents to take possession of the ball. This rule also adds to the game's action. There are many ball exchanges and lots of running in field hockey. To keep up with the game, players must be able to run fast, change direction quickly, and master their stick-handling techniques.

Equipment

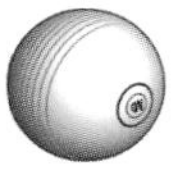

Ball
The ball is usually made of hard plastic. It measures close to 3 in. wide and weighs less then 6 oz.

Stick
The stick is usually made of wood. It has a long handle and a curved head. The length varies according to the height of the player. The stick is flat on one side and rounded on the other. Players may hit the ball using any part of the flat side.

The field

The field is rectangular. It is 60 yd wide by 100 yd long.

Sideline
When the ball crosses a sideline, it goes out of play. It is put back in play at the point where it went out by a player from the opposing team.

Officials' table
Three officials are responsible for checking players' equipment as well as their conduct on the bench. They also fill out the score sheet.

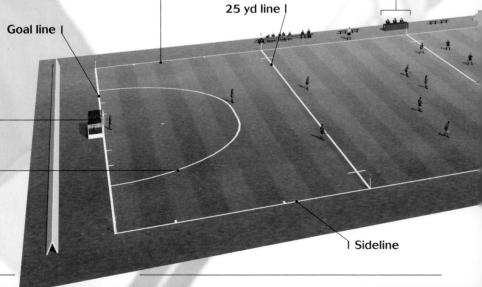

Goal line

25 yd line

Goal cage

Shooting circle
A goal counts only if an offensive player in the defending team's shooting circle shoots the ball into the goal.

Sideline

Field Hockey

The game

The game is played in two 35-minute periods with a 5- to 10-minute halftime. Following the game plan they have worked out, the teams spread out on the field as forwards, midfielders, backs, and goalkeepers. With the exception of the goalkeepers, players may have fouls called on them for raising their sticks too high or for stopping the ball with their bodies. Fouls result in penalty shots or free shots for the opposing team. With penalty or free shots, opposing team players can try to hit the ball directly into the goal or put the ball back in play in a position that gives them an advantage.

Techniques

Push
The push is a stroke used when the player wants to send the ball a short distance or get rid of it quickly. One hand is placed low on the stick to push the stick's head forward, while the other hand pulls the handle close to the player's body.

Hit
The hit is a powerful stroke used for long passes or shots on goal. The player raises the stick into a back swing to gain momentum. Then the player swings the stick forward, following through with the body to give the shot more power.

Penalty spot
The penalty spot is the position where the ball must be placed for a penalty shot. It is located 7 yd from the goal line.

Referee (2)
Each referee supervises half of the field and the closest sideline.

Flick
The flick is a stroke used for shots on goal or penalty shots. The movement is similar to that for a push except that the player straightens up to help send the ball upward and forward.

Corner flag (4)

5.5 yd line

25 yd line
If the ball goes out-of-bounds between the 25 yd lines, the teammates of the player putting the ball back in play can position themselves 1 yd away from that player until the ball is played. If the ball is put in play between the 25 yd line and the goal line, all players on both teams (except the person playing the ball) must position themselves at least 5 yd away from the ball.

Center line
The center line is where the ball is put in play at the beginning of each period and after each goal.

Soccer

Unlike other ball sports, soccer is a game in which players use their feet, and not their hands, to control the ball. Played by men and women in more than 200 countries, soccer is the most popular game in the world. Two good reasons for this are that hardly any equipment is needed and the rules are simple. The object of the game is to deliver the ball into the opposing team's goal. Players may use any part of their bodies to propel the ball—except their hands and arms. Soccer matches are played between two teams of 11 players each. Because the field is large and the ball is in constant motion, competitive soccer players need endurance to stay on the run and good coordination to control the ball with their feet while traveling fast.

The field
The field is rectangular. It must be between 50 and 100 yd wide and between 100 and 130 yd long.

Ball
The ball is made of leather with an inflatable air chamber inside. It measures about 28 in. around and weighs about 16 oz.

End line
If the defending team kicks the ball out-of-bounds across the end line on its own side of the field, the opposing team is awarded a corner kick. This is a chance for the opposing team to try to kick the ball from the corner of the field toward the goal or to a teammate. If the attacking team kicks the ball out-of-bounds, the defending team is awarded a goal kick. This is a kick taken from the defense's goal area to move the ball away from the goal.

Goal area
Players from the attacking team are not allowed to interfere with the goaltender inside the goal area.

Penalty spot
The penalty spot marks the place where the ball must be placed for a penalty kick.

Assistant referee

Corner flag (4)
A pole with a flag is placed at each corner of the field to mark the corner points.

Goal
A goal is scored when the ball completely crosses over the goal line between the 2 posts.

Soccer

The game

The game is divided into two periods of 45 minutes each, with a halftime of 15 minutes. A coin toss before the game determines which team will kick off. The kickoff takes place at the center of the field. Once the ball is in play, both teams try to gain control of it and send it into their opponents' goal. The players are in constant motion and the ball remains in play as long as it stays within the touch and end lines. There is a lot of contact between players, but their moves are carefully regulated by the referees to prevent injuries. A foul is called if a player pushes or trips the player with the ball or touches the ball with her hand. If the foul is committed within the penalty area, the opposing team is awarded a penalty kick at the goal from a spot 28 ft away. Only the goalkeeper is allowed to protect the goal. An offside is called if an attacking player receives a forward pass when fewer than two defenders are between him and the defenders' goal line. Offsides result in free kicks for the opposing team.

Cups and championships

Because soccer is played almost everywhere, there are championships that bring together the best teams from cities and countries around the world. In addition to the Olympic Games, soccer has a premier event, the World Cup, which is held every four years. More than 200 countries compete to become one of the 32 finalists. Women's World Cup competitions have been held since 1991. World Cup soccer attracts more than one billion television spectators!

Referee

Warning
The referee may hold up a yellow card, warning a player that he or she is breaking the rules.

Expulsion
The referee may hold up a red card, showing that a player is to be expelled, or thrown out of the game. Expulsions may be called for serious fouls, violence, rude language, or having more than 2 previous warnings.

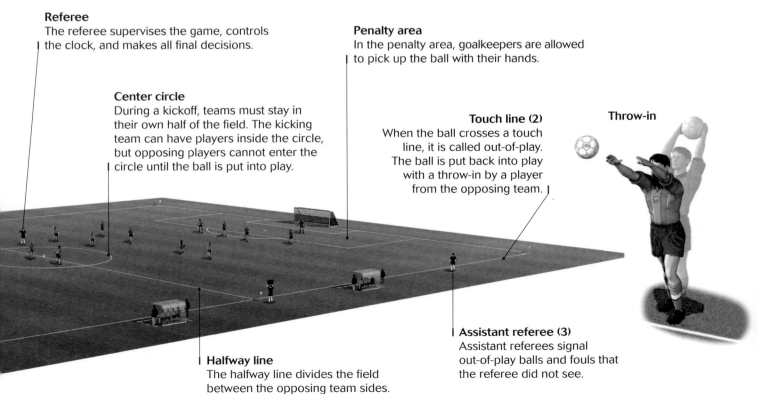

Referee
The referee supervises the game, controls the clock, and makes all final decisions.

Center circle
During a kickoff, teams must stay in their own half of the field. The kicking team can have players inside the circle, but opposing players cannot enter the circle until the ball is put into play.

Penalty area
In the penalty area, goalkeepers are allowed to pick up the ball with their hands.

Touch line (2)
When the ball crosses a touch line, it is called out-of-play. The ball is put back into play with a throw-in by a player from the opposing team.

Throw-in

Assistant referee (3)
Assistant referees signal out-of-play balls and fouls that the referee did not see.

Halfway line
The halfway line divides the field between the opposing team sides.

Soccer

Basic positions

The team takes the field according to the game plan organized before the match begins. The different formations are always variations on the basic positions.

Forwards

Forwards must take advantage of any ball that comes their way. They try to escape the defenders from the opposing team so that they can score goals.

Right and left fullbacks

Right and left fullbacks must slow or stop the progress of an opposing attacker in their zone while their own teammates get into defensive formation. In offense, fullbacks use their speed to start the play quickly on their side of the field.

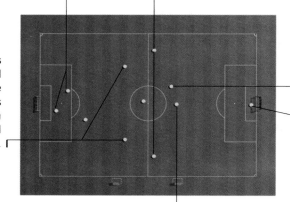

Midfielders

Midfielders play both offense and defense. In defense, they must take the ball away from opposing players trying to organize an attack. In offense, midfielders relay the ball and provide offensive support.

Stopper

Stoppers try to keep opposing forwards from getting into a scoring position.

Goalkeeper

Goalkeepers stop shots on the goal. They are their teams' last line of defense. Goalkeepers are the only players allowed to put their hands on the ball when it is in play.

Sweeper

Positioned behind the team, sweepers direct their teammates' defense and provide extra defense if necessary. They can also start their team's offensive play.

Skills

Dribbling

Dribbling is a way of moving with the ball using rapid foot movements and changes of direction to confuse the opponent.

Heading the ball

Players may hit the ball with their heads to direct it toward the net, hit it away from the net, or pass it to another player.

Technique

Sliding tackle
The sliding tackle is a defensive play, in which a player tries to kick the ball away from an attacker by sliding but without touching the attacking player.

Goalkeeping techniques

Throwing the ball
After stopping the ball, goalkeepers often put the ball back in play by passing it with their hands to a teammate. This move is more accurate than kicking the ball to a teammate, and helps the team to keep the ball in its possession.

Punting the ball
To send the ball deep into the offensive zone, goalkeepers kick or "punt" the ball. Their teammates rush to try to take possession of it where it lands.

1-2 relay
The 1-2 relay is a quick series of passes between 2 teammates that prevents the opponent from getting the ball.

1-on-1 defense
In 1-on-1 defense, each player on the defending team "covers" a player on the attacking team. A defending player follows his particular opponent's every move and tries to keep him from receiving, kicking, or passing the ball.

Lateral dive
The lateral dive allows a goalkeeper to stop or deflect a shot when he is not directly in the ball's path.

Australian-Rules Football

Australian-rules football, also known as "Aussie rules" or "footy," developed out of the English game of rugby and the Irish game of Gaelic football. Although mainly played in Australia, footy is rapidly becoming popular in other countries. The United States has a national league and about 50 clubs that operate in different cities. Both men and women play the game. Australian-rules football matches take place on the same oval field as cricket matches. Two teams of 18 players each try to score points by carrying or kicking the ball through either of the opposing team's two sets of goalposts, which are located at their end of the field. Players perform spectacular leaps to gain control of the ball, which is almost always in play. Although footy is a high-contact sport, with pushing, holding, and tackling, athletes wear very little protective gear.

Equipment

The ball is an inflated bag made of synthetic material, covered with 4 pieces of leather sewn together. It is slightly larger and rounder than an American football.

Techniques

Mark
A mark is a reward given to a team if one of its players catches a ball kicked from at least 32 ft away. The ball cannot touch the ground or another player before it is caught. The player who marked has a choice of playing the ball or taking a kick at the goal.

Handballing
Handballing is used in place of throwing. The ball is placed on the open palm of one hand, and then it is hit with the fist of the other hand.

The game

The game is divided into four 20-minute quarters. The field umpire puts the ball into play by bouncing it on the ground or throwing it in the air. Players on both teams try to get possession of the ball and take it to the opponent's goal across the field. Players can move in any direction, but cannot run with the ball for more than 49 ft without having it touch the ground. If the ball passes between a goalpost and a behind post, a one-point "behind" is scored. If the ball is kicked between the two goalposts without being touched by another player, a goal is scored, which is worth six points. The team with the most points at the end wins the game.

Scoring

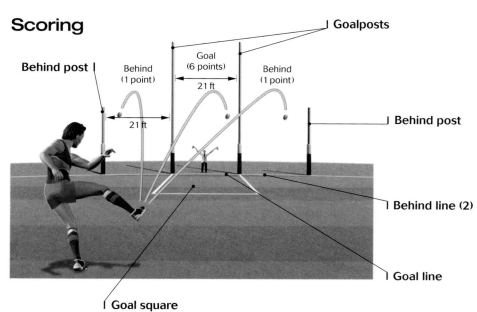

Goalposts

Behind post

Behind (1 point)

Goal (6 points)

21 ft

Behind (1 point)

21 ft

Behind post

Behind line (2)

Goal line

Goal square
When a behind is scored, the ball is put back into play by one of the defenders, who must kick off from within the goal square.

Handball

Handball is played on a court that has one, three, or four walls. Players use both arms and hands like tennis rackets to hit a rubber ball and make it bounce off the walls. The object of the game is to be the first player to score 21 points. Handball matches are played as singles (two players) or doubles (two teams of two players). Both men and women play the sport. There are approximately 10 countries participating in world championship games that are held every three years.

Equipment

Gloves
Players wear leather gloves to protect their hands from the impact of the ball. They may also wear bandages under the gloves for extra protection.

Ball
The ball is hollow and made of rubber. It is small, with a width of less than 2 in. It weighs about 2½ oz.

Protective eyewear
Players wear plastic goggles to protect their eyes from the ball.

Technique

Using the palm of the hand or a closed fist, the player hits the ball somewhere between knee and hip height. The wrist remains loose and the forearm swings sideways, parallel to the ground. Rotating the wrist makes the ball spin after it bounces off the ground.

Warm-up
To avoid being bruised by the ball, players try to increase blood circulation in their hands by clapping or warming them.

The court
The floor on a 4-wall court is about 40 ft long and 20 ft wide. The walls are often made of glass so spectators can watch the game.

The game

Players take turns serving the ball. The ball must touch the front wall before hitting the ground. It must be returned by the other player before it hits the ground a second time. This is called a volley. Players try to make their opponents miss the ball in one of three ways. They can force them to leave the center of the court, make them lose their balance, or return the ball too fast to be hit. Only the serving player may score a point. The receiver who wins a volley then becomes the server. The first player or team to reach 21 points wins the game. The winner of two games wins the match.

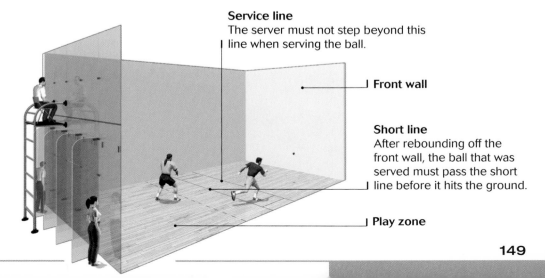

Service line
The server must not step beyond this line when serving the ball.

Front wall

Short line
After rebounding off the front wall, the ball that was served must pass the short line before it hits the ground.

Play zone

Team Handball

Team handball is a fast-paced game of skill and stamina. Matches take place on an indoor court with a goal net at each end. Two teams of seven players each try to score points by sending the ball into the opponent's net. Players can throw, push, hit, stop, and catch the ball using any part of their bodies—except the feet. Athletes need good coordination and great energy to throw, pass, and catch accurately while constantly on the run. Handball is an Olympic event played by men and women in many countries.

Equipment

Ball
Unlike a basketball, the handball is small enough for almost anyone to hold with one hand. Its small size also allows for hard, one-handed throws. It measures about 22 in. around and weighs about 15 oz. The outer casing is made of leather or a synthetic material.

Court

The handball court is larger than a basketball court, measuring 40 m x 20 m (approximately 131 ft x 66 ft).

Timekeeper

Scorekeeper
The scorekeeper keeps track of playing time, substitutes going on and off the court, and penalty time.

7 m throw (penalty throw)
This is a throw made directly on goal from the penalty mark. A player gets a 7 m throw (or penalty throw) when an opposing player has prevented him from throwing at the goal or trying to score; he also gets a penalty throw if a defender is in the 6 m area and blocking an attacker. The penalty thrower must not touch or cross the 7 m line until the ball has left his hands. All other players, except the goalkeeper, must stay outside the 9 m zone.

Secretary
The secretary assists the score keeper and referees.

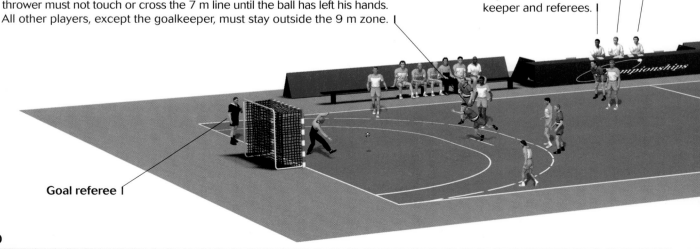

Goal referee

Team Handball

The game

The game is played in two 30-minute periods with a 10-minute halftime. A coin toss determines which team gets the throw-off, or first pass. The player throwing the ball stands at center court and throws the ball to a teammate. During the throw-off, each team must stay on its half of the court. Only the goalkeeper is allowed inside the goal area. Players may not hold the ball for more than three seconds, or takemore than three steps with the ball. A goal is scored when the ball goes entirely inside the net. The team with the most points at the end of the two periods wins.

Pass technique

The pass is a basic element of play in handball. There are many ways to pass the ball to a teammate. The speed and the accuracy of its passes show how good a team is.

Goalkeeper technique

The goalkeeper protects a goal measuring 2 m high by 3 m (6.6 ft x 9.8 ft) wide. The goalkeeper faces many powerful shots coming from a short distance away. Instead of trying to stop the ball, she hits or deflects it away from the goal. The goalkeeper moves toward the opponent with the ball and uses her entire body to block the shot. She must always be ready to react quickly by reaching out with her arms or legs to deflect the ball.

Sideline

When the ball crosses the sideline, it is thrown back onto the court by the team that did not have possession when it went out of bounds.

9 m line (free throw line)

When a free throw is awarded to a team, no attacking player may enter the 9 m area until the ball is in play.

Goal area

This area is defined by a semicircle 6 m away from the goal. Only the goalkeeper may enter this area. A player in possession of the ball may jump up over the line, however, when shooting at the goal.

Team coach

Only the coach is allowed to speak to the secretary, the timekeeper, and the referees.

6 m line

Goal

Goal line

Referee (2)

The referees control the match, taking turns being center referee and goal referee. When a team attacks, the referee on that team's side controls the court, while the other stands near the defending goal. When the defending team begins an attack, they switch roles.

Basketball

Basketball is the most widely played indoor sport in the world today. Because it is easy to organize and to play, it is a popular pastime for people of various ages and skill levels. As a spectator sport, basketball is exciting to watch. FIBA (Olympic), NBA (National Basketball Association), and WNBA (Women's NBA) games are demonstrations of great speed, unpredictable moves, and superior ball-handling techniques. Basketball is played on a rectangular court. The goals are baskets suspended 10 feet above the floor at each end. Two teams of five or six players try to score points by shooting the ball into the opposing team's basket. Players may use only their hands to control the ball. They can pass, throw, hit, or roll it, but cannot run with the ball unless they dribble it (bounce it repeatedly on the floor). The winning team is the one with the most points at the end of the game.

Court

The court used in NBA and WNBA games measures 94 ft by 50 ft.

Rule differences	NBA	FIBA	WNBA
Length of game	48 min (4 x 12 min)	40 min (4 x 10 min)	40 min (2 x 20 min)
Second clock	24 sec	24 sec	30 sec
3-point line	23.75 ft	20.5 ft	19.9 ft
Number of referees	3	2	3

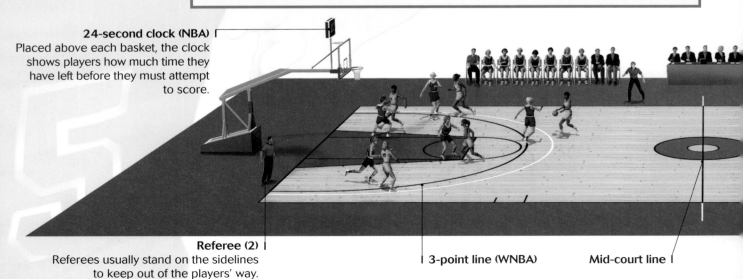

24-second clock (NBA)
Placed above each basket, the clock shows players how much time they have left before they must attempt to score.

Referee (2)
Referees usually stand on the sidelines to keep out of the players' way.

3-point line (WNBA)

Mid-court line

Basketball

The game

In the NBA, a game is divided into four 12-minute periods. The game begins with the referee tossing the ball up into the air between two opposing players. The two players jump for the ball and try to tap it to a teammate. The player who gets the ball has only eight seconds to move it forward across the mid-court line, and 24 seconds to take a shot at the basket. A player who is blocked by an opponent must move the ball by dribbling, throwing, or passing it within five seconds. The referees call fouls if time limits are exceeded. The opposing team is then given the ball. Fouls are also called against players who handle the ball incorrectly or who interfere with opponents. Fouls can result in free throws or throw-ins for the opposing team. These shots allow a team to take possession of the ball and throw it to a teammate (throw-in) or at the basket (free throw) without interference from the other team.

Scoring

A field goal is worth two points. This is a basket taken from inside the 3-point line during the normal course of the game. If the shot is taken from behind the 3-point line on the court, the field goal is worth three points. A successful free throw, taken from behind the free-throw line and inside the free-throw circle, is worth one point. Free throws are an important part of scoring in the game. Because a high number of fouls are called during a game, with free throws awarded as a result, these shots can help a team score many points.

NBA Ball
The ball is inflated and covered with leather or a synthetic material. The ball is almost 30 in. around and weighs approximately 20 oz. The ball used in the WNBA is slightly smaller.

Backboard
The backboard is made of a hard, transparent plastic. This allows spectators sitting behind the goal to have a better view of the game.

Hoop
Players often hit the hoop when performing dunk shots. This causes vibrations that can shatter the backboard. To reduce vibration, the hoop is mounted on springs.

Coach
The coach directs the players continuously during the game. The coach keeps an eye on the refereeing, works out game plans, and decides who plays and who sits on the bench.

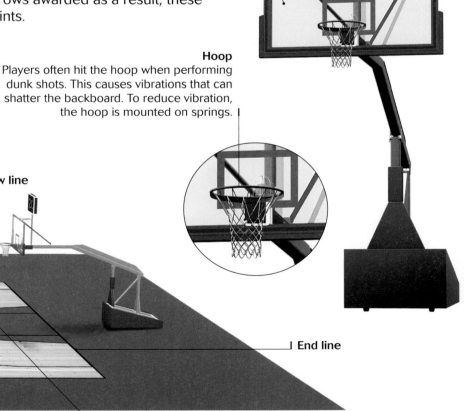

Assistant coach

Free-throw line

End line

Sideline

3-point line (NBA)

The key
A player in possession of the ball can remain in this area for no more than 3 seconds at a time.

Basketball

Player positions

Forward

Rear guard

The rear guard covers the strongest opponent, helps the point guard, and shoots for the basket whenever possible.

Center (inside player)
Often the tallest player, the center protects the basket from the opponent's shots. The center also tries to retrieve the ball when it bounces off the basket after a missed shot by the opponent.

Forward
Forwards are the team's most dependable shooters. They act as a link between the rear guard and the center. They play either defensively or offensively, depending on which team has the ball.

Point guard
The point guard is the team's best ball handler, sets the pace of the game, and leads the offense.

Referees

Basketball is difficult to referee. The rules are complicated, and the game is fast-paced. Referees must make split-second decisions to call fouls or let the game continue. They use hand signals to communicate with the scorer and other officials.

Charging
Pushing or moving into an opponent's torso.

Traveling
Taking one or more steps while holding the ball.

Double dribble
Resuming a dribble after touching the ball with both hands or allowing the ball to come to rest.

Foul   Time-out

Passes

Players try to keep their passes short and direct. They usually pass without looking at the player receiving the ball. This keeps opponents off guard and reduces their chances of getting the ball.

Chest pass
The chest pass is used when there are no opponents between the thrower and the receiver. The ball is gripped in front of the chest with both hands and then thrust forward with the arms and wrists.

Bounce pass
The bounce pass is used to get past an opponent standing between the thrower and the receiver. The ball is passed downward into the area least protected by the opponent and caught by the receiver after one bounce.

Baseball pass
The baseball pass gives the thrower a better angle for passing when being pressed by an opponent. Using his free hand (the hand not holding the ball), the player protects the ball as he winds up for the throw.

Basketball

Shots

The accuracy of a shot at the basket depends on a player's speed, balance, and ability to jump and throw.

Jump shot
The jump shot is the most common shot. The player holds the ball in place with one hand and uses the other hand to shoot the ball toward the basket. The player releases the ball at the highest point of the jump.

Layup
After charging past opponents, the player jumps close to the basket and "lays the ball in." The player's wrist remains straight while her other hand pushes the ball up from underneath.

Dunk
The dunk is the most spectacular shot in basketball. Using one or both hands, the player dunks—or shoves—the ball into the basket from above. This move prevents opponents from blocking the ball.

Dribbling

Players are not allowed to run with the ball by carrying it, but they are allowed to move freely with it by dribbling. In dribbling, the hand taps the ball with flicks of the wrist and keeps the ball bouncing. Dribbling players keep their eyes on their opponents and signal to their teammates. They do not watch the ball. Stopping and restarting a dribble is against the rules.

★ Harlem Globetrotters
The legendary Harlem Globetrotters are ambassadors for the sport of basketball. Playing and promoting the game around the world, the Globetrotters have been entertaining audiences with their acrobatic antics since 1927. In 1998, they played their 20,000th basketball game. No other professional sports team in history has achieved this record.

Low dribble
The low dribble is used to get away from opponents, or to try to get through the opponent's defense. The ball is bounced knee-high and is shielded by the player's free hand and body. The low dribble is effective in keeping the ball away from the opponent because it allows the player to switch hands or change direction quickly.

High dribble
In a high dribble, the ball is bounced at waist or shoulder height. A player who is in the clear can use the high dribble to travel quickly across the court, taking long strides.

Football

In football, planning the game is as important as playing it. Behind the show of raw power is a series of complex moves, or plays, memorized by every team member. Two teams of 11 players each try to score points by advancing the ball down the field to the opposing team's end zone. The opposing team does everything it can to prevent the advance. Players push, shove, and tackle to stop the advancing team and get possession of the ball. If the advancing team succeeds in bringing the ball into the end zone, it scores a touchdown, worth six points. The other way to score points is by kicking the ball through the opponent's goalposts. The team with the most points at the end of the game wins.

Helmet
All players wear helmets for protection. The quarterback has a radio receiver in his helmet so that he can hear his coach's instructions.

Shoulder pads and tooth guards
Players must wear these for protection because the game can get very rough.

The Field
The field measures 53⅓ yd by 120 yd.

Goalposts
The 2 posts stand slightly more than 18 ft apart, with a crossbar 10 ft off the ground. The flags attached to the top of the posts show which way the wind is blowing. This helps the player trying to kick the ball between the goalposts.

Crossbar

End line
Players must not go beyond the end line.

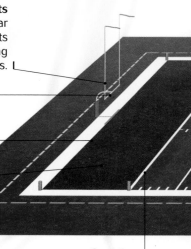

End zone
Each team defends its end zone, found at opposite ends of the playing field. The end zone is 10 yd deep.

Goal line

Football

The Game

The game is played in four 15-minute periods, called quarters. With all the suspensions of play, games often last three hours or more. Each team has a maximum of 45 players, divided into three formations: offense (the attackers), defense (the defenders), and "special teams." Special-team players include kickers, for kickoffs, and punters, for drop-kicking. In a drop kick, the punter lets the ball fall and kicks it the moment it hits the ground. A coin toss determines which team will kick off to start the game and which team will receive.

Officials

There are 7 officials on the playing field. Each one watches a specific part of the game. The referee, who wears a white cap, makes the final decisions.

Holding
A player has illegally held an opposing player.

First down
The offensive team has covered at least 10 yd in 4 downs (tries) or less. It can now continue its advance.

Points scored
A touchdown, field goal, or other goal has been scored.

Offside
A defending player has illegally started moving forward before the ball is played.

Kickoff

At the beginning of the game, after halftime, and after each touchdown or field goal, one team place-kicks the ball as far as it can toward the other team's zone. In a place-kick, the ball is made to stand on one of its two pointed ends, and, then kicked. The team receiving the kicked ball (the attackers) tries to bring the ball back to their opponent's side of the field. Play stops when the player receiving the kicked ball is tackled.

Lines
The lines divide the field into 5-yd zones and are used to measure the advance of the attacking team. Hashmarks between the lines mark each yard.

50-yd line
The 50-yd line marks the center of the playing field. Each side of the field is defended by one of the teams. At the end of the first and third quarters, the teams change sides.

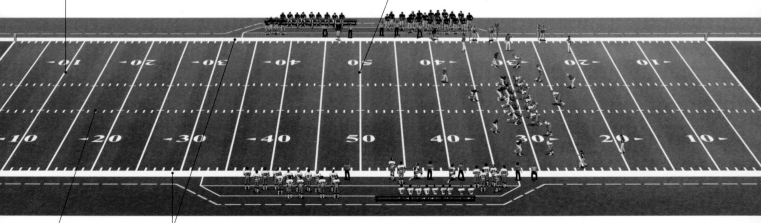

Hashmarks   Sidelines

Football

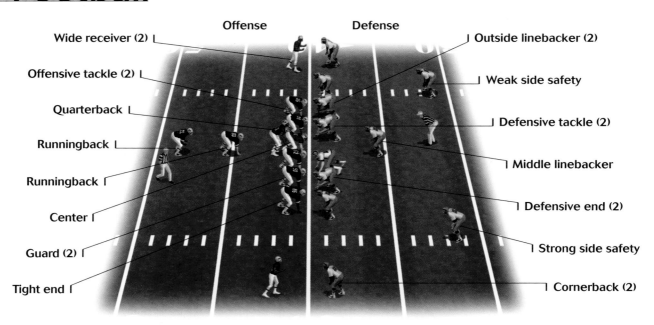

Wide receiver (2) — Offense — Defense — Outside linebacker (2)

Offensive tackle (2) — Weak side safety

Quarterback — Defensive tackle (2)

Runningback — Middle linebacker

Runningback — Defensive end (2)

Center — Strong side safety

Guard (2) — Cornerback (2)

Tight end

Offense

Quarterback
The quarterback leads the attack and tells the team which play (strategy) they will use. To keep the other team from understanding what the plays will be, the quarterback uses coded signals to communicate with his team members.

Center
The center snaps the ball to begin a play.

Runningback (2)
The runningbacks include the halfback, who usually carries the ball on running plays, and the fullback, as a blocker.

Tight end
The tight end helps the offense control the line of scrimmage.

Wide receiver (2)
Wide receivers catch passes and use their speed to force the opposing defense to cover them over long distances.

Guard (2)
The guards are the key blockers during running plays.

Offensive tackle (2)
The offensive tackles are placed at the ends of the line of scrimmage and protect the quarterback when he passes.

Offense

The attacking team has four tries, called downs, to advance the ball 10 yd into the defending team's zone. If the team does not succeed, the ball is turned over to the defenders, who then become the attackers. A down will end when the ballcarrier fumbles, loses control of the ball, or goes out of bounds. A down also ends when a pass is intercepted by a defender or when a defender tackles the ballcarrier. The center puts the ball in play by passing it through his legs to the quarterback, while the rest of the attackers face the defenders on the line of scrimmage. The line of scrimmage is where the two teams line up before putting the ball in play. Several players protect the quarterback, who must pass or hand the ball to a teammate using a play decided on in advance. The attackers may run with the ball or the quarterback may throw a long forward pass to the wide receiver. Other offensive plays include field goals (kicking the ball through the goalposts) and extra point conversions.

Exchange
The center "snaps" the ball to the quarterback, who is directly or a few yards behind.

Quarterback pass
While the quarterback is being protected, he spots the receiver and passes the ball to him. The pass may be short or very long, sometimes more than half the length of the playing field.

Football

Pass reception

The receiver tries to get away from the defense so that the quarterback can throw the ball to him. Once the receiver catches the ball, he protects it by cradling it in his arm and continues running toward the defense's end zone.

Defense

The defending team tries to keep the attacking team from reaching its end zone or kicking the ball between the goalposts. The defenders must figure out which play the attackers are likely to use. They try to tackle the quarterback or the ballcarrier as quickly as possible during a running play. The defenders also try to intercept passes thrown to the receiver.

Tackle

The tackler's main target is the player with the ball. He makes the tackle by grabbing the ballcarrier and forcing him to the ground.

Pass coverage

Cornerbacks and safeties defend against passes. They watch the quarterback to figure out where the pass will go.

Field goal and extra point

A 3-point field goal can be attempted from anywhere on the field. The center snaps the ball back to a teammate. The teammate holding the ball sets it upright for the place kicker, who tries to kick it through the goalposts. After a touchdown, a team may attempt a 1-point conversion kick. It takes place 2 yd from the goal line and is performed the same way as the field-goal kick. The team may, instead, try for a passing or running conversion, scoring 2 points for taking the ball across the goal line.

Defense

Defensive tackle (2)
Defensive tackles try to keep the offense from advancing forward by tackling the quarterback or the runningback with the ball. They also force the offensive line to use 2 of their own players to block them.

Middle linebacker
The core of the defense, the middle linebacker moves sideways quickly to attack the ballcarrier.

Defensive end (2)
The defensive ends try to contain and control the offense. Defensive ends force any running offensive players toward the inside, or center, of the field and try to prevent the quarterback from escaping toward the sidelines.

Outside linebacker (2)
Outside linebackers put pressure on the quarterback and cover the ballcarrier and tight end.

Weak side safety
The weak side safety is used mainly for his skill in breaking up any attempted passes to the receiver, either by catching or intercepting the ball or by tackling the receiver.

Strong side safety
The strong side safety is placed on the side where the offense is more likely to attack.

Cornerback (2)
The cornerbacks must be as fast as the wide receivers. They are often the last line of defense against a touchdown.

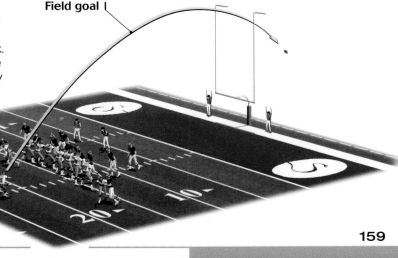

Field goal

Rugby

Rugby is a sport that resembles both soccer and football. Popular with men and women, rugby is played in more than 100 countries around the world. Different rugby leagues have their own sets of rules. The IRB (International Rugby Board) is the oldest and most widely known rugby association for the game of Rugby Union. It includes some 92 national unions with both amateur and professional teams. Rugby matches take place on a field, called a pitch, with goalposts at both ends. In Rugby Union games, two teams of 15 players try to score points by sending the ball into the opposition's goal. Players move the ball by running with it, throwing it, and kicking it. Although players may kick the ball forward, they may only pass the ball sideways or behind them. Only the player carrying the ball can be tackled—other kinds of hitting and blocking are not allowed. As in soccer, the game moves freely around the field and there are few time-outs.

Pitch

The pitch is usually covered in grass. The playing area is larger than a football field, measuring about 75 yd by 110 yd.

Scoring

A player can score points for the team in several ways.

Try (5 points)
A player must carry the ball over the goal line and ground it in the opposition's in-goal area.

Penalty kick (3 points)
The penalty kick allows a player from the opposition to kick the ball directly through the goalposts of the team that committed a foul.

Conversion (2 points)
A player may, following a try, attempt to send the ball directly through the opposition's goalposts with a place-kick or dropkick.

Drop goal (3 points)
A player may drop-kick the ball through the opposition's goalposts at any time during play.

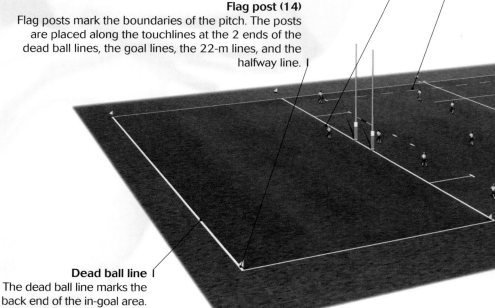

Touchline
Balls crossing the touchline are out of bounds and must be put back in play with a line-out.

Goal line
The goal line marks the front end of the in-goal area.

Flag post (14)
Flag posts mark the boundaries of the pitch. The posts are placed along the touchlines at the 2 ends of the dead ball lines, the goal lines, the 22-m lines, and the halfway line.

Dead ball line
The dead ball line marks the back end of the in-goal area.

The Game

A Rugby Union match consists of two 40-minute periods with a five-minute halftime. The team that wins the coin toss kicks off from the center of the halfway line. The ball must cross the opponent's 10 m line to be in play. Both teams then attempt to get control of the ball to score points. The ball may be carried into the opponent's in-goal area and then grounded (touched to the ground) or kicked through the goalposts. If a player sends the ball out of bounds, a player from the opposing team puts it back in play with a throw-in. At least two players from both teams form two lines, called a line-out. The ball is thrown between the lines, and all the players then try to get control of it. Fouls result in penalty kicks or free kicks for the opposing team. A penalty kick is an attempt to kick the ball directly through the goalposts. With a free kick, a player has the choice of kicking the ball or playing it by hand, but cannot try for a goal. The team with the most points at the end of the game wins.

Cups and championships

Rugby World Cup (RWC)
Alternating between the Northern and Southern Hemisphere, the RWC is held every 4 years. Twenty countries take part in the finals.

Six Nations Tournament
England, Scotland, Wales, Ireland, France, and Italy compete in this tournament. Every country gets to play one game against each of the other 5 countries.

Equipment

Did you know?
Although rugby is not currently an Olympic event, it once was. The United States won gold medals in rugby in both the 1920 and 1924 Olympic Games.

18 ft

10 ft

Ball
The ball is inflated, covered in plastic or leather, and treated to shed water and mud. Shaped like an American football, it is slightly larger with rounded ends. It measures about 11 in. long, with a 30 in. around. It weighs about 15 oz.

Lock line
The lock line is 15 m from the touchline. It indicates the farthest position that may be occupied by the lock, the last player in line, during a line-out.

Goalposts

In-goal area
A try is scored within the in-goal area.

Halfway line
The halfway line divides the 2 teams' zones.

10-m line
During a kickoff, the team not in possession of the ball must not cross this line. The team putting the ball in play must send the ball beyond this line.

22-m line
A drop-out kick may be used to restart play after a defending player stops a ball in the in-goal area.

Throw-in line
The throw-in line is 5 m from the touchline. It indicates the position to be taken by the first player in line during a line-out.

Rugby

Techniques and tactics

Passing
Passing helps a team keep control of the ball. A pass must always be made to the side or behind. A series of quick passes among teammates helps to create openings in the other team's defense. This allows the attacking team to advance toward the opponent's in-goal area.

Mark (fair catch)
A mark occurs when a player, who is in between his own in-goal and 22-m line, catches a forward kick or pass made by the opposing team. The player shouts "Mark!" when he catches the ball. He is then allowed a free kick at the opponent's goal.

Scrum
A scrum is formed after a foul has been called. Eight players from each team form a group and wait for the ball to be thrown on the ground between them. The team that did not foul puts the ball back into play. The hooker (front row center) heels the ball toward the back of the scrum. Players must not leave the scrum before the ball comes out.

Maul
A maul is formed when the ballcarrier has been stopped by a defender without being tackled to the ground. Players from both teams surround the ballcarrier and try to get possession of the ball. The maul breaks up when the ball is released, if the ballcarrier breaks free, or if a scrum is called.

Ruck
Players form a ruck to take possession of the ball after a tackle. Joining arms, they huddle around the ball and try to push it back with their heels.

Rugby

Player positions

Each player wears a numbered shirt. The number identifies the athlete's playing position on the field.

Three-quarters (4) (centers and wingers)

When playing defense, the three-quarters must be good tacklers to prevent the opposing team from moving across the field. When playing offense, they pass the ball around quickly to keep it away from the opposition's defense.

Winger

Fly half

The fly half is the link between the scrum half and the three-quarters. The fly half starts the team's attacks.

Second row (locks) (2)

The second row players support the front row during a scrum. The second row tries to win or recover the ball during throw-ins or scrums.

Tight head prop

Hooker

The front row is in contact with the opposition during a scrum. The hooker is responsible for winning (getting) the ball and heeling it (pushing it with the foot) to the teammates behind.

Fullback

The fullback is the last line of defense when an opponent is attempting to score a try. The fullback must be able to intercept a ball kicked by an opposing player. The fullback must also restart his or her team's attack, either by handling the ball or by kicking it away.

Centers (2)

Winger

Scrum half

The scrum half is the link between the offense and defense. During scrums, the scrum half must recover the ball and put the three-quarters into an attacking position.

Third row (3)

The third row makes up the last line of players in a scrum. Third row players must keep the ball between their feet until the scrum half can recover it. During play, they must relay the ball from the front row to the halves.

Loose head prop

Front row (3)

The 2 prop forwards (tight head and loose head) push their opponents to try to move the scrum forward. They also try to stop the opposing team from advancing and winning the ball during scrums.

Dropkick

The kicker drops the ball and then kicks it as it bounces up from the ground.

Tackle

The tackle is a defensive move to block an opponent who is carrying the ball and to prevent him from advancing. The tackler is allowed to grab the opponent between the knees and the torso. The tackled player must release the ball when he hits the ground.

Netball

Netball is a variation on the game of basketball. It is played mainly by women. Like basketball, netball is played on a court with basket goals, called rings, suspended on posts at both ends. The object of the game is to score points by shooting the ball through the opponent's ring. What makes netball very different from basketball, however, is the movement of the players. The seven members of the team must stay in their designated zones on the court. They are not allowed to run with the ball or dribble it, and only two of the players are allowed to shoot the ball to score points. Netball players have to make up for these restrictions with strong teamwork based on fast and accurate passing and catching.

The court

The court is divided into three equal parts, with five zones. The playing area is approximately 98 ft long by 50 ft wide, about the size of a basketball court.

Goal defense (GD)
The GD's direct opponent is the opposing goal attack (GA) in zones 1, 2, and 3. The GD and her goalkeeper (GK) defend the goal zone and provide support for attacks. The GD tries to figure out where the ball will be thrown. She tries to intercept the ball as it is passed or bounced by opposing players.

Wing attack (WA)
The WA covers zones 3 and 4 and tries to pass the ball to the goal shooter (GS) and the goal attack (GA). The WA also receives center passes. The WA must be good at avoiding opponents and passing the ball.

Umpire (2)
The umpires control the game. Each is responsible for half of the court.

Goal attack (GA)
She moves in zones 3, 4, and 5 and can shoot at the ring.

Teams
Usually composed of 12 players, only 7 of them are on the court at one time. Players can be substituted only during stoppages in play.

Goal shooter (GS)
The GS must stay in zones 4 and 5. To shoot at the ring, she must get clear of the goalkeeper (GK) from the opposing team. The GS does not have much time or room to throw the ball at the ring.

Center (C)
The center plays in zones 2, 3, and 4. As the link between her team's attack and defense zones, she passes the ball and sets the pace of the game. Her central position keeps her active during most of the game.

Netball

The Game

The game is divided into four 15-minute periods. The team that wins the coin toss gets to make the first pass from the center circle. Each player has a precise role corresponding to her position on the court and wears initials on her shirt to identify her position. Only the goal attack (GA) and the goal shooter (GS) may shoot at the ring, and only from inside the goal circle. Players may catch the ball, then tip, bat, or bounce it to another player. Once a player has the ball, she cannot keep it more than three seconds. Players may not run with the ball, but may spin around on one foot or take one step with it. Fouls are called for stepping incorrectly and for blocking other players. The winning team has the most points at the end of the four periods.

Ball
The ball is made of leather, rubber, or a similar material. Resembling a soccer ball, it measures 27 to 28 in. around and weighs 14 to 15 oz.

Passes
The ball can be thrown, bounced, tipped (hit lightly with the fingers), or hit with one or both hands. It cannot be rolled or kicked.

Defense
Defending players must remain at a minimum distance of 3 ft from attackers. Any contact that blocks the player who is carrying the ball is a foul.

Goalkeeper (GK)
The GK defends zones 1 and 2 and protects her team's ring from attackers, especially the goal shooter (GS). The GK has to anticipate where the ball will come from and be able to intercept it. She provides one-on-one defense.

2

1

Boundary
When the ball crosses the boundary, it is thrown back into the game at the same spot by a player from the team that was not in possession of the ball when it was sent out of bounds.

Wing defense (WD)
The WD plays in zones 2 and 3. To defend against the wing attack (WA), she must be an expert in one-on-one defense. The WD also takes part in attacks that start in zone 3.

Shooting at the ring
The player aims for the ring on the opposing team's side. To throw the ball, the player holds the ball over her head with both hands and jumps. This gives the ball the necessary height to make it arc high and drop directly into the ring.

Volleyball

Volleyball is played on a court divided in half by a net. Two men's or women's teams of six players each are positioned on respective sides of the net. Players take turns at serving, using their hands to hit the ball over the net to the opposite side. They try to score points by making the ball hit the ground on the opponent's side. The opponent tries to hit the ball and return it. Points are scored by the serving team if the other team fails to return the ball over the net, hits the ball out-of-bounds, or commits a foul. Players may hit the ball but never hold it. They must return the ball over the net by the third hit. Teams play 15-point sets, or games. The winner of the match is the team that wins three out of five sets. Volleyball is an Olympic World Cup event.

Equipment

Ball
The ball is inflated and covered with soft leather. It is smaller than a basketball, measuring approximately 26 in. around. It is also much lighter, weighing approximately 9.5 oz.

Knee pads
Players must often drop to their knees to return the ball. They wear knee pads to protect themselves from the shock of hitting the hard floor.

The court

The playing area measures 18 m by 9 m. It is surrounded by a free zone measuring 3 m or 5 m wide. Players are permitted to step into the free zone to hit the ball if necessary.

Scorekeeper
The scorekeeper records points scored, interruptions in play, time-outs, and player rotations.

Coach

Line judge (4)
The line judges use red flags to signal service faults, contact with the antennas, balls outside the antennas, and balls out of bounds.

End line

Volleyball

The game

The team that wins the coin toss has the choice of serving or receiving the ball. The players stand in two rows of three, covering the front and back of their part of the court. The ball is served by a player standing behind the end line. This player hits the ball with one hand or arm and tries to send the ball over the net. If the receiving side fails to return the ball, the serving team scores a point. If the receiving team returns the ball and makes the serving team miss the return, the receiving team becomes the serving team. Teams lose their serve if they hit the ball out of bounds or if the ball touches the net. Except for the Libero (a special defense player), team members play in rotation. They take turns playing in different positions on the court so that all have a chance to serve.

Tennis serve

The serves

In the tennis serve, the player uses his arm like a tennis racket to serve the ball overhand. In the jump serve, the player throws the ball into the air, and then takes a running jump toward it and hits it overhand. Although an underhand serve is allowed, international level players use an overhand (tennis) serve.

Second referee

The second referee rules on faults at the center line and attack line, as well as net faults (illegally touching the net). The second referee also checks the position of the players on the team receiving the serve, and assists the first referee.

Scoreboard

Sets
Number of sets won by the team.

Libero

Each team can select one player to be the Libero, a specialized player in defense. The Libero may be called in to replace any back row player as needed.

Points
Number of points scored per team in the current set.

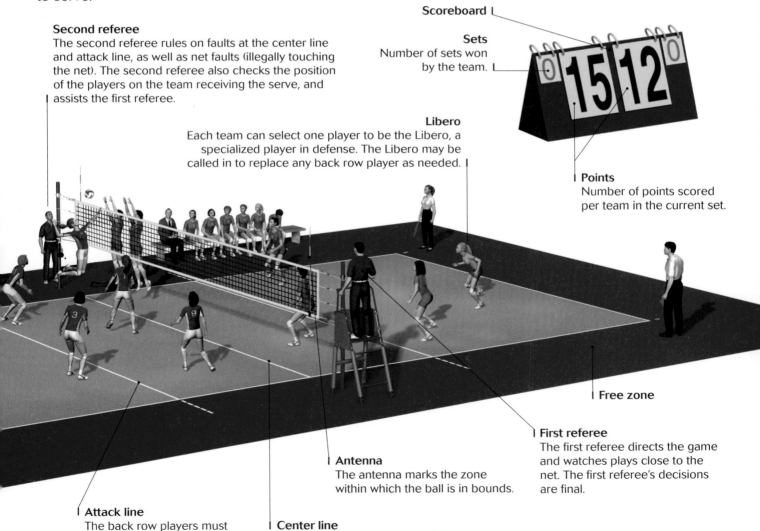

Free zone

First referee

The first referee directs the game and watches plays close to the net. The first referee's decisions are final.

Antenna
The antenna marks the zone within which the ball is in bounds.

Attack line
The back row players must attack the ball from behind this line, without touching or crossing it.

Center line
The center line separates the 2 sides of the court. A team loses a point if one of its players crosses the center line.

Beach Volleyball

Beach volleyball is an outdoor variation of volleyball. The playing area is slightly smaller and covered with sand. Participants often play barefoot. Teams are made up of two or four players. The ball is inflated to a higher air pressure than in indoor volleyball. This makes the ball heavier and more stable in the wind.

The bump
The bump is used to retrieve a serve and to redirect the ball to another player.

The dig
The dig is used to retrieve a ball that otherwise would be impossible to play. The player dives for the ball close to the sand and performs a 1- or 2-hand bump.

The block
The block is an effort to prevent the ball from being spiked over the net. It is performed by 1, 2, or 3 players. To block, a player must be able to jump high as well as anticipate where the ball will come from.

The spike
The spike is used to smash the ball down over the net. The player jumps high and forward to give the spike more power, making the ball difficult to retrieve.

Playing surface
The sand must be at least 15 in. deep.

First referee
The first referee supervises the game.

Second referee
The second referee assists the first referee and signals all net faults (players illegally touching the net).

Line judge (4)
Line judges signal balls hit out of bounds.

Scorer

Rest area

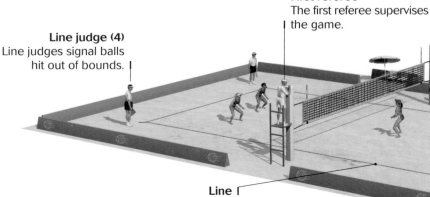
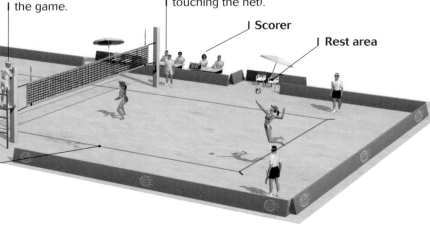

Line
The limits of the playing area are marked with a brightly colored cord anchored in the sand. There is no center line.

Racket Sports

Tennis
Badminton
Table Tennis
Squash
Raquetball

Tennis

Tennis is a racket sport played by two opposing players (singles) or two teams of two players each (doubles). Matches take place on an outdoor or indoor court divided by a net. Players take turns hitting the ball back and forth over the net, which is called rallying. The object of the game is to score the most points by making the opponent fail to return the ball over the net and in bounds. Tennis is a popular game because it can easily be played by people of all ages and skill levels. In Olympic and professional tennis, the game is lightning-fast and demands quick reflexes. Players must be able to hit a ball traveling over 100 miles per hour.

Equipment

Racket
The frame is made of a combination of synthetic materials. The strings are usually nylon. The handle is often covered with leather or rubber.

Ball
The ball measures about 2.5 in. around and weighs about 2 oz. It is hollow and made of rubber covered with yellow or white felt (a wool or synthetic fiber).

Chair umpire
The chair umpire makes sure the rules of the game are upheld and gives out penalties to players who disobey them. He or she can reverse a judge's decision in case of error. The chair umpire also announces the score after every point.

The court

The tennis court measures 78 ft long by 27 ft wide (36 ft wide for doubles matches). The surface may be clay, grass, asphalt, concrete, wood, or synthetic materials.

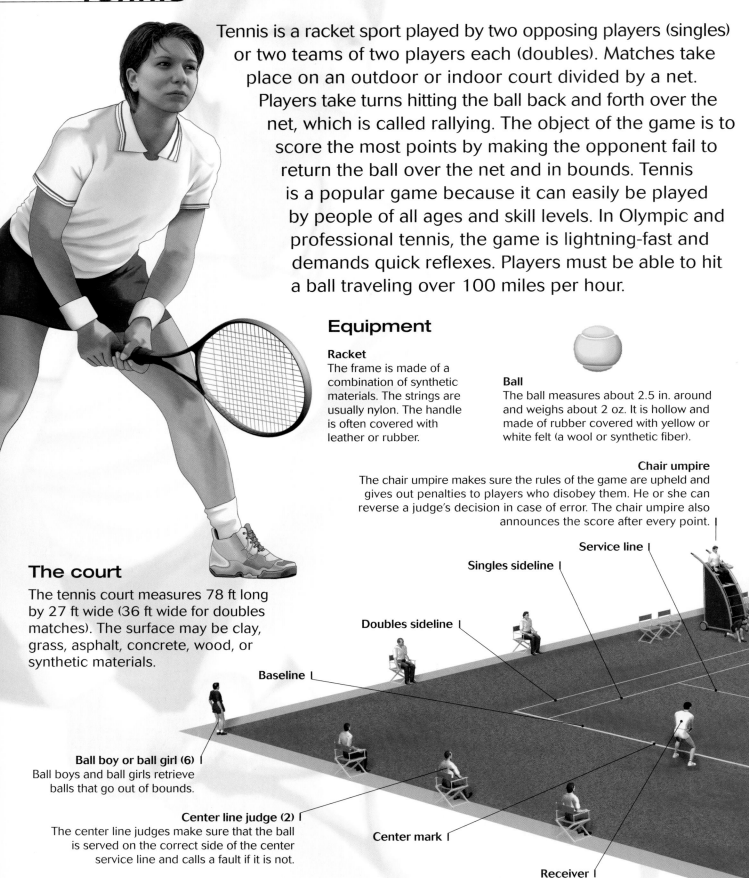

Service line

Singles sideline

Doubles sideline

Baseline

Ball boy or ball girl (6)
Ball boys and ball girls retrieve balls that go out of bounds.

Center line judge (2)
The center line judges make sure that the ball is served on the correct side of the center service line and calls a fault if it is not.

Center mark

Receiver

The match

The players spin a racket to choose which side of the court they will occupy and who will serve first. The racket is made to spin on its head (the top of the frame). The side of the court on which the racket falls decides the players' positions and serving order. The server has two chances to serve successfully. A served ball must always be returned over the net after one bounce. During the rest of the play, players may return the ball before or after it bounces once.

Tournaments

A number of important tournaments draw top tennis players from around the world: the US Open, held in New York; the Australian Open; the French Open; and Wimbledon, held in London, England.

Scoring

The match is divided into sets, games, and points. A game consists of a series of points. Players start at "0" (also called "love"). The first player to score four points and have a two-point advantage over the other player wins the game. The four points are named "15," "30," "40," and "game." The first player to win six games wins the set, as long as the player has won by at least two games. Otherwise, an additional tie-breaking game must be played. Matches usually consist of three sets. The winner of the match is the first player to win two out of three sets.

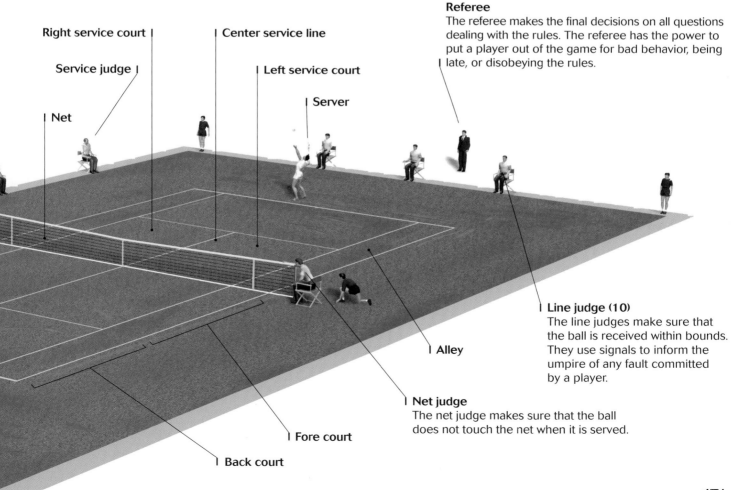

Referee
The referee makes the final decisions on all questions dealing with the rules. The referee has the power to put a player out of the game for bad behavior, being late, or disobeying the rules.

Right service court | Center service line | Left service court | Server | Service judge | Net

Line judge (10)
The line judges make sure that the ball is received within bounds. They use signals to inform the umpire of any fault committed by a player.

Alley

Net judge
The net judge makes sure that the ball does not touch the net when it is served.

Fore court | Back court

171

Tennis

Serve

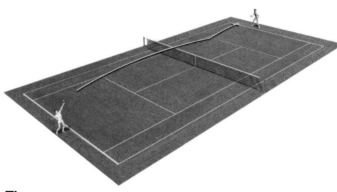

The serve
The server puts the ball in play by tossing the ball in the air and hitting it before it bounces. The server stands behind the baseline and has 2 tries to send the ball into the service court on the opposite side of the court. The first serve is made from the right side of the court. After a point is scored, the players change their positions from one side of their court to the other.

Strokes

Approach stroke
In an approach stroke, the player hits the ball from about the middle of the court to the opponent's back court and then advances toward the net. An approach stroke can be used when the opposing player's ball has landed in the fore court.

Ground stroke
In a ground stroke, the ball is hit so that it travels low and hard. It is a powerful and accurate attack during a rally. Ground strokes are usually played from near the baseline.

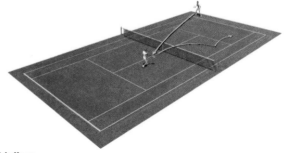

Volley
In a volley, the player returns the ball before it has bounced on the ground. Volleys are usually made close to the net. When they are made from midcourt, they are called approach volleys, because they allow the player to move closer to the net.

Special strokes

Lob
The ball is sent high and far so that it bounces as close as possible to the baseline. The lob may be used to trick an opponent who has come close to the net.

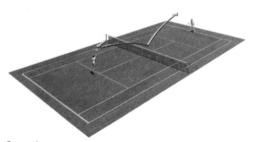

Smash
The smash is a powerful overhead stroke. It is usually made in response to a lob. The smash makes it difficult for an opponent to return the ball.

Doubles match

Doubles partners must work as a team. Each player has a particular role to play as the game progresses: server, server's partner, receiver, and receiver's partner. One player may hit the ball several times in a row, without the other player stepping in. Once the ball is in play, both partners position themselves to cover different areas of the court, depending on where the ball is being sent. Doubles partners take turns serving.

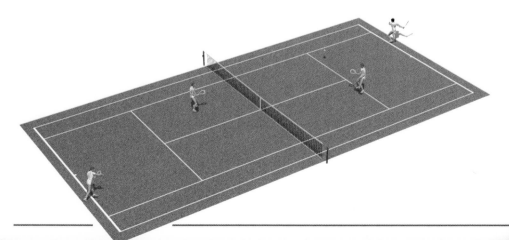

Racket grips
Tennis players change their grips on their rackets to make the ball travel in different ways.

Two-handed grip
There are many variations of this type of grip, which is mainly used for backhand strokes. In a backhand stroke, the back of the hand that grips the racket is facing the ball.

Eastern forehand grip
The Eastern forehand grip is used for high volleys and ground strokes. This grip usually makes the ball travel straight with a slight forward spin.

Continental grip
The continental grip is mainly used for volleys and serves. It makes the ball spin backward as it flies forward through the air.

Western and semi-western grips
The western and semi-western grips are used for ground strokes. These grips can make the ball spin forward as it flies through the air.

Badminton

In badminton, opposing players use lightweight rackets to hit a cone-shaped object, called a shuttle, back and forth over a net. Matches are played by two opposing players (singles) or two teams of two players each (doubles). Men and women play separately or in a mixed doubles team consisting of one man and one woman. The object of the game is to score points by hitting the shuttle over the net in such a way that the opponent will be unable to return it. In badminton, the shuttle must be kept from hitting the playing surface. The first player or team to score 15 points wins the game. Badminton is an Olympic event.

Equipment

Shuttle
A competition shuttle is made of 14 to 16 goose feathers attached to a cork base. A piece of lead or a screw is sometimes added to the base to make it more stable and easier to hit. For informal play, shuttles can also be made of nylon with a cork base.

Feathered shuttle

Synthetic shuttle

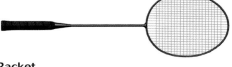

Racket
The racket is made of lightweight, strong materials such as aluminum, graphite, or titanium. The strings are usually made of nylon.

The court

The playing area measures about 39 ft by 17 ft for singles matches and about 44 ft by 20 ft for doubles matches.

Service judge
The service judge checks that the players serve and hit the shuttle correctly and are playing in the correct areas of the court.

Line judge (10)
Line judges make sure that the shuttle is within bounds and inform the umpire of any faults committed by the players.

Short service line

Umpire
With the assistance of the line judges and service judge, the umpire makes sure that the match is played according to the rules. The umpire's decisions are final.

Long service line

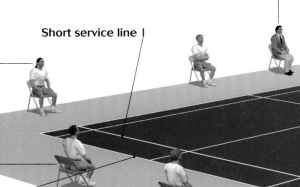

Badminton

Techniques and tactics

In singles matches, players try to surprise their opponent by jumping, moving quickly, and hitting the shuttle hard. In doubles matches, the two players on a team try to get the opposing players to move into awkward positions. They do this gradually, by hiding what type of shots they are about to use until the last moment, so that the opponent cannot guess where the shuttle is going to go.

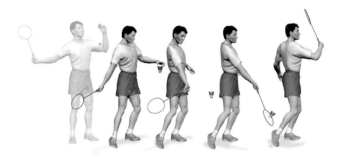

The serve
The serve must be an underhand stroke. The popular long serve falls near the long service line; it forces the opponent to the back of the court, leaving the server more time to prepare for the return.

Smash
In a smash, the shuttle can travel at more than 120 mph when it is first hit by the racket, but its speed is quickly reduced. The smash is the most powerful attack shot. It is performed when the shuttle is high in the air, and it is aimed to land far forward of the opponent.

Net
The holes in the net are small so that the shuttle cannot pass through it.

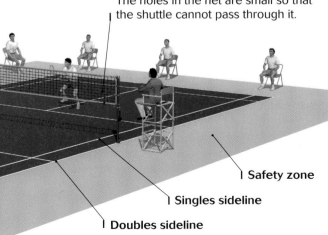

Safety zone

Singles sideline

Doubles sideline

Clear
The clear is a forehand stroke. A forehand stroke is made with the palm of the hand turned in the direction in which the hand is moving. The shuttle is supposed to land far back in the opponent's court. As a defensive shot, it slows down the play and gives the player a chance to get back into a good position. When hit hard, it becomes an offensive shot, forcing the opponent to reach up high to return it.

Table Tennis

Table tennis is a fast-moving game played on a table divided by a low net. Players use small wooden paddles to hit the ball back and forth over the net. The object of the game is to score points by hitting the ball over the net so that the opponent is unable to return it. Table tennis is played in singles matches (two opposing players), doubles matches (two teams of two players each), and mixed doubles matches (two teams of a man and a woman on each). Table tennis is an Olympic event.

Equipment

Ball
The hollow ball is made of celluloid, a type of plastic. It measures about 1½ in. wide and weighs less than 1 oz.

Paddle
The paddle is made of wood. The wide, flat part, called the blade, is covered on both sides with layers of foam and rubber.

Table

The table measures about 9 ft long by 5 ft wide and stands almost 30 in. high. The net is almost 6 in. high. Tables are usually painted dark green.

Assistant umpire
The assistant umpire posts the points announced by the umpire and watches for incorrect serves and out-of-bounds balls. If a ball being served touches the net before touching the table on the opponent's side, the ball must be served again.

Floor
The floor is made of wood or a synthetic material that does not reflect light. A shiny floor could make it more difficult for the players to spot the ball.

Umpire
The umpire controls the match, announces points, and calls out-of-bounds balls.

Center line
The center line is used only in doubles matches. In a doubles match, the ball must be served from one side of the center line diagonally across the net.

Panels
The panels are about 30 in. high. They mark the boundaries of the floor play area, which measures about 46 ft by 23 ft. They also help prevent balls from rolling away.

Table Tennis

The match

After the ball bounces once on their side, players must hit it back onto the opponent's side of the table. A point is won if the opponent cannot return the ball or if it is played before the first bounce or after a second bounce. Each player serves five times in a row. In doubles, players take turns serving. During rallies in a doubles game, team members must each take a turn hitting the ball, no matter where it lands on the table. The first player or team to score 21 points wins the set. Generally, the first team or player to win two out of three sets with an advantage of at least two points wins the match.

The shots

Topspin (forehand)
The forehand topspin is the perfect attack shot. It is used during rallies (when both players hit the ball offensively) or as a way of returning a serve that has landed close to the body. In a forehand topspin, the palm of the hand faces the ball.

Paddle grips

Penholder grip
The penholder grip is very effective for playing offensively. However, it is more difficult when performing a backhand shot. In a backhand shot, a player has to reach across his or her body to the side opposite from where the paddle is normally held.

Orthodox grip
The orthodox grip is the most common way to hold the paddle. It allows the player to hit the ball offensively or defensively.

Sidespin
Putting a sidespin on the ball makes it change direction, making it difficult for the receiver to return it.

Topspin (backhand)
With topspin, the ball drops quickly then speeds up after the bounce. It usually rises as it hits the receiver's paddle. In a backhand topspin, the back of the hand faces the ball.

Squash

Squash is a racket game played with a small rubber ball on a boxed-in court that has four walls and a ceiling. Two players (singles) or two teams of two opposing players each (doubles) take turns hitting the ball and making it bounce off the walls, and the floor. The court is marked off in zones that indicate where the ball must be served as well as where it must bounce after a serve. Players do not have their own sides on the court—they share the same playing area. The object of the game is to score points by making the opponent miss returning the ball or allowing it to bounce twice. Squash is played by both men and women.

The court

The playing area measures about 32 ft long by 21 ft wide for a singles game and 32 ft long by 25 ft wide for a doubles game.

Scorer
The scorer calls the play, signals faults, and announces the score.

Referee
The referee decides on fair scores and rule violations.

The serve

The ball is thrown up in the air and then hit with the racket. The ball must bounce off the front wall, cross the service line in the middle of the court, and then bounce off the back court opposite the server's side. Serves do not usually win points; they are for putting the ball in play and forcing the opponent to make a defensive return.

Squash

The game

A return is considered correct if the ball touches the front wall before bouncing on the floor. The ball is allowed to bounce any number of times on the side and back walls. A match is played in five 9-point games. Only the server can score a point. When the server misses a return or allows the ball to bounce twice, the receiver becomes the new server. Professional tournaments are played in 15-point games. In professional tournaments, players win points for making the opponent miss a shot, whether or not the player is the server or receiver.

Equipment

Goggles
Players may wear plastic goggles to protect their eyes from the ball.

Balls
The balls are hollow and made of hard black rubber. They measure between 1½ in. and 1¾ in. across and weigh about 8.5 oz.

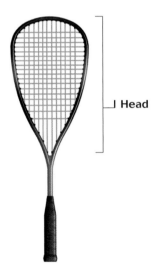

Head

Racket
The racket must be less than 27 in. long. It is about 8.5 in. wide at the head. It weighs about 5 oz. The frame and handle are made of mixed synthetic materials such as graphite. The strong, elastic strings are also synthetic.

Cut line
The cut line marks the bottom of the service zone. This area is where the ball must first hit when it is served.

Out lines
Out lines mark the areas that are out of bounds for the ball.

Front wall

Service line

Service box (2)
Players alternate serving from the service boxes. Until the ball is hit, one foot must stay in contact with the floor inside the box and not touch any of the lines.

Racquetball

Similar to squash, racquetball is played in a completely enclosed court with a ceiling and four walls. Players use short-handled, wide-headed rackets to hit a small rubber ball off the walls, floor, and ceiling of the court. The object of the game is to serve or return the ball so that the opponent is unable to return it properly. Players take turns hitting the ball. It must be hit before the second bounce on the floor. The ball must touch the front wall before touching the floor. Matches can be singles (two opponents) or doubles (two opposing teams of two players each). Both men and women play racquetball, which is recognized by the International Olympic Committee as a developing sport.

The game

Matches consist of two sets of 15 points each. If there is a tie, a third set of 11 points determines the winner. A point is earned if a server makes a receiver miss a shot. Only a server can score a point. A server who misses a return loses the serve and becomes the receiver.

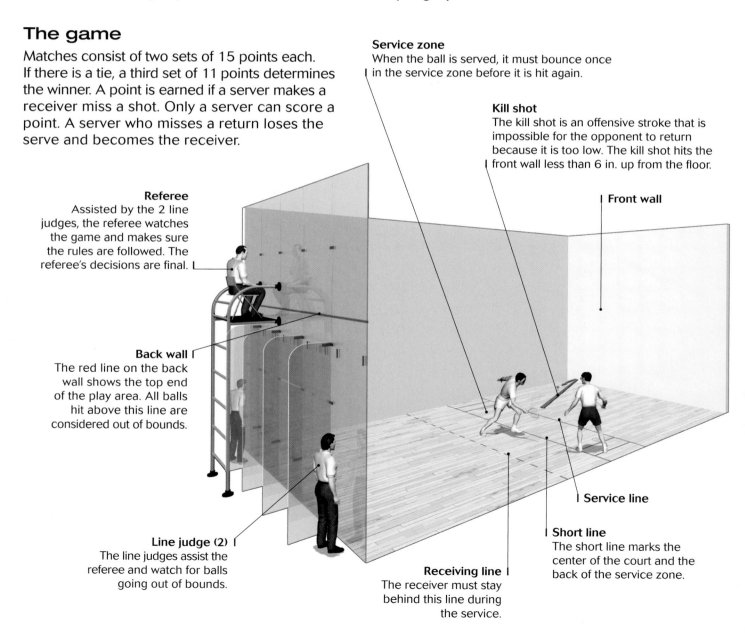

Service zone
When the ball is served, it must bounce once in the service zone before it is hit again.

Kill shot
The kill shot is an offensive stroke that is impossible for the opponent to return because it is too low. The kill shot hits the front wall less than 6 in. up from the floor.

Front wall

Referee
Assisted by the 2 line judges, the referee watches the game and makes sure the rules are followed. The referee's decisions are final.

Back wall
The red line on the back wall shows the top end of the play area. All balls hit above this line are considered out of bounds.

Service line

Short line
The short line marks the center of the court and the back of the service zone.

Line judge (2)
The line judges assist the referee and watch for balls going out of bounds.

Receiving line
The receiver must stay behind this line during the service.

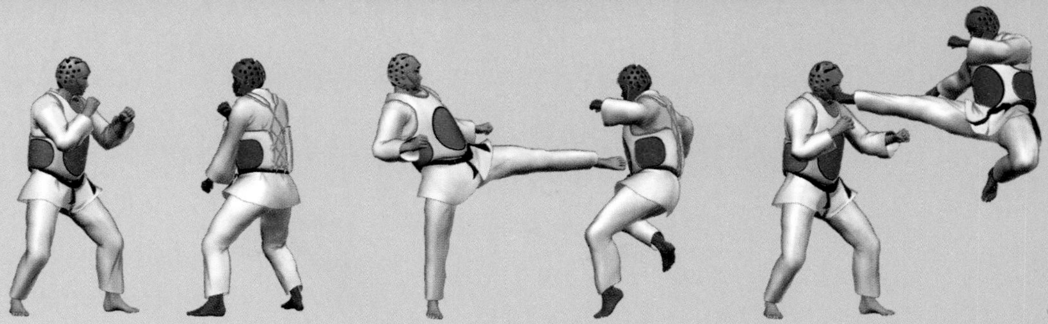

Combat Sports

Karate
Judo
Tae Kwon Do
Fencing
Wrestling
Boxing

Karate

Karate is a Japanese style of fighting that combines combat and self-defense techniques. Both physical fitness and mental training are equally important to a karate fighter. In karate, the hands, elbows, arms, feet, knees, and head serve as weapons. Competitive karate takes several forms. In tameshi wari demonstrations, athletes break objects such as wood planks, cement slabs, or blocks of ice using their hands or feet. In kata demonstrations, athletes perform a series of combat moves against imaginary attackers. In shiai competition, two athletes fight against each other. Karate is practiced in a classroom called a dojo, which means seat of wisdom. Training often begins in childhood, and mastering the various techniques takes years of practice. Athletes must develop speed, power, and especially flexibility. There are more than 70 styles of karate being practiced today. Both men and women compete on an international level.

Table of honor
Several karate experts sit at the table of honor and view the match. They have the power to overrule any decision made by the officials.

Head referee
The head referee supervises the match and awards points, warnings, and penalties. The head referee announces all decisions as well as the start and end of the match.

Competition area
Matches are held on the ground or on a mat. The competition area measures approximately 26 ft by 26 ft.

Officials
There are between 3 and 7 officials who watch the match and make sure the rules are followed.

The competition

In a kata demonstration, the competitor is graded by the judges on technical precision, breathing, strength, coordination, rhythm, balance, and concentration. Competitions may be individual or team events. In the team events, participants try to coordinate their moves and perform them at the same time.

A karate blow can seriously injure or kill an opponent. In combat events, participants generally demonstrate their fighting techniques without actually hitting their opponents, although some contact may be allowed in certain events. Athletes earn points, called ippons, for technique, position, precision, and rhythm in their movement. The first participant to score two ippons wins the match.

Technique

No matter what style of karate is being performed, kata demonstrations always begin with a defensive move followed by a counterattack. This is followed by several sequences that alternate between defensive moves and attacking moves in various directions.

Shotokan-style grading system	
Grades	**Belt color**
9th to 6th kyu (beginner)	white
5th kyu	yellow
4th kyu	orange
3rd kyu	green
2nd kyu	blue
1st kyu	brown
1st to 8th dan (advanced)	black
9th and 10th dan	red

Grades

Athletes move from one grade to the next as their knowledge and technique improve. It can take several years to advance to the higher grades. The modern Shotokan style of karate features a system of grading karate fighters, who wear belts of various colors to show their level of expertise. White belts are for beginners and red belts are for the most advanced athletes. The lower levels are called kyu, and the higher levels are called dan.

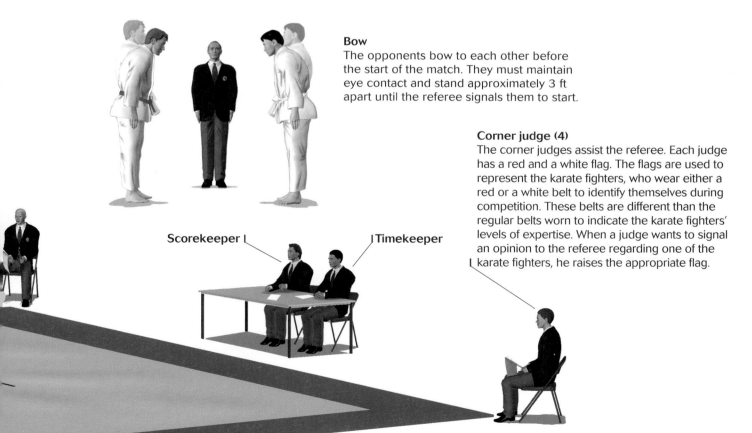

Bow
The opponents bow to each other before the start of the match. They must maintain eye contact and stand approximately 3 ft apart until the referee signals them to start.

Corner judge (4)
The corner judges assist the referee. Each judge has a red and a white flag. The flags are used to represent the karate fighters, who wear either a red or a white belt to identify themselves during competition. These belts are different than the regular belts worn to indicate the karate fighters' levels of expertise. When a judge wants to signal an opinion to the referee regarding one of the karate fighters, he raises the appropriate flag.

Scorekeeper

Timekeeper

Karate

Combat training moves
These sequences demonstrate attack and defense techniques used both in training and in combat.

1. Direct punch
The attacker (left) throws a fist forward. The punch lands at the same time as the forward foot is put down. The rear leg is extended backward. The shoulders remain low during the entire movement.

2. Forward kick
The attacker (right) holds his chest straight and his shoulders relaxed. His rear fist protects his chest. His hips shift along with his leg, which extends forward only at the moment of impact. This gives maximum power to his kick.

3. Dodging
The defender (right) tries to avoid being hit by the attacker. He combines his ability to move quickly with subtle hip movements in order to dodge the opponent. By avoiding contact, the defender can save his energy for a counterattack.

4. Counterattack with the outside of the hand
This move is used when an opponent is off balance. The defender (right) rotates his hips and swings his arm toward the opponent. His upper arm and elbow remain relaxed, while from the elbow to the hand his arm forms a solid block. His hand then strikes the opponent's temple or neck with a whipping motion.

Heian Godan
The Heian Godan is a basic Shotokan-style kata. It consists of a sequence of 23 movements. It takes approximately 50 seconds to complete the sequence, which must be performed without any hesitation. Three of the 23 movements are illustrated here:

Start of the kata
The participant concentrates intensely, never taking her eyes off her imaginary opponent. She bends her legs to help her remain steady on her feet. Performing a block with her left wrist, she rotates her hips, which helps to increase her speed.

Intermediate phases
Every block is followed by a counterattack. The participant inhales while preparing for each movement, then exhales while performing the movement. The shoulders remain relaxed. The abdominal muscles are contracted to help the athlete stay balanced.

End of the kata
After meeting the imaginary attacks coming from four different directions, the athlete goes back to the starting position.

Judo

In judo, unarmed athletes attack by throwing their opponents to the ground. The defender does not resist the attacker's force. Instead, the defender takes the attacker's power and turns it back on the attacker. Judo means "gentle way" in Japanese. In competitive judo, the goal is to throw an opponent on his back and pin him to the ground for a certain length of time. If the throw is performed correctly and the opponent is pinned down long enough, the attacking player is awarded enough points to win the match. Athletes are ranked according to their weight and level of experience. They must master certain techniques before they can progress to the next level. Judo is an Olympic sport practiced by both men and women.

The competition

Two contestants from the same ranking are selected by a random drawing of names. The contestant who loses the fight is eliminated from competition, unless it is the semi-final round, in which case the two contestants compete for the bronze medal. The two finalists fight for the gold and silver medals. Athletes may fight five to six matches in the same day before reaching the final. The two athletes bow to each other before moving to their positions on the mat. The referee signals the start of the fight by calling *Hajime!* The fight ends when one of the contestants scores a 10-point ippon or when the time limit is reached (5 minutes for men and 4 minutes for women in international competition). If an ippon is not scored, the contestant with the highest point total wins the match.

Competition area

The competition area measures approximately 30 ft by 30 ft. It is surrounded by a safety area approximately 10 ft wide. The safety area protects athletes who may be thrown outside the competition area during combat. The surface consists of small mats placed side by side, called tatami. The tatami help to cushion the athletes' falls.

Mat judge
The mat judge watches the fight, insures that the referee and corner judges observe the rules, and helps make judgments fair.

Scorers and timers

Referee
The referee stands in the fight area. If a dispute arises, the final outcome must be agreed upon by the referee and the two corner judges.

Tatami

Safety area

Corner judges

Judo

Scoring

If no ippon is scored before the match time runs out, points can be earned by a koka, a yuko, and a waza-ari. These points are added to determine the winner. During a match, kokas and yukos canot be combined for the required 10 points. The accumulation of two waza-aris is equivalent to one ippon (10 points), and ends the contest.

Koka

There are two ways to score a koka: 1) throwing the opponent onto a shoulder, leg, or buttock with control, force, and speed; 2) pinning the opponent to the ground (osaekomi) for 10 to 14 seconds. A koka is worth 3 points.

Yuko

A yuko is a controlled throw of the opponent that is missing two of the elements necessary to score an ippon, or achieving an osaekomi of only 15 to 19 seconds. A yuko is worth 5 points.

Waza-ari

A waza-ari is scored if an opponent is pinned to the ground (osaekomi) for 20 to 24 seconds or if a throw is missing one of the four elements necessary to achieve an ippon. The four elements are: landing the opponent on her back, and performing the throw with control, force, and speed. A waza-ari is worth 7 points.

Equipment

Judogi

In international competitions, the judogi consists of a white or blue cotton jacket and pants. The first participant called to fight wears a blue judogi, while the second wears a white judogi. The clothing is designed to allow participants to get a proper grip on their opponents in order to throw them to the ground. Women wear a white T-shirt or leotard under their jacket. All competitors are barefoot.

Ippon

There are three ways to score an ippon: 1) throwing the opponent onto her back with control, force, and speed; 2) forcing the opponent to submit using an arm-lock or choking technique; 3) pinning the opponent to the ground (osaekomi) for 25 seconds. An ippon is worth 10 points.

Violations

When a contestant is penalized, her opponent receives a corresponding number of penalty points. If a contestant commits more than one violation of the same level of seriousness, she receives a higher penalty. Some of the violations that are penalized by the officials include: intentionally leaving the tatami, fighting too defensively, faking attacks, striking the opponent, intentionally falling to the ground, or disobeying a judge. Any actions intended to injure the opponent are not allowed.

Techniques and tactics

Athletes try to take the lead at the start of the contest and maintain their position in order to control the fight's pace and progress. A good judo fighter tries to take advantage of the smallest error committed by the opponent so that she can throw her off balance and counterattack. The athletes study their opponents' styles, and, with the help of their trainers, prepare two to five special moves they can use during the fight, which will give them the best advantage against their opponents. The moves are designed to best suit the size, body shape, and skills of the contestants.

Rank	Belt color
6th kyu (beginner)	white
5th kyu	yellow
4th kyu	orange
3rd kyu	green
2nd kyu	blue
1st kyu	brown
1st to 5th dan (advanced)	black
6th to 8th dan	white and red
9th and 10th dan	red

Throwing and grappling: standing on the mat

1. Ready position
The contestant tries to grab the opponent quickly and throw her off balance by moving or pretending to perform a certain move before attacking. At the same time, she tries to avoid giving her opponent a good angle for getting hold of her.

2. Gripping
The contestant who successfully grips her opponent gains the advantage. Achieving a good grip requires short but powerful arm movements and solidly locked wrists.

3. Positioning
The opponent who is grabbed tries to escape, while her attacker prepares for the throw. The attacker checks her grip, repositions her feet, and corrects her position. She needs to be sure she has the necessary stability and control for throwing the opponent.

4. Throwing
In throwing her opponent off balance, the attacker prevents her from being able to defend herself. The attacker throws the opponent onto her back with force and control. The thrown athlete tries to turn onto her stomach, roll herself into a ball, or get up on her hands and knees.

5. Pinning
The attacker increases the pressure on her opponent's body, especially on the shoulders. When pinning an opponent, the attacker is not allowed to use her legs.

Tae Kwon Do

Tae kwon do is a Korean art of self-defense and unarmed combat. *Tae kwon do* means "the art of punching and kicking." Rapid action and spectacular moves are features of the sport, in which the feet do most of the hitting. Tae kwon do is a sport that requires power, endurance, and speed. Athletes test their strength during training by striking and breaking objects. There are two types of tae kwon do competition. The first is a demonstration of forms called poom-se, a series of techniques performed while facing one or several imaginary opponents. The second type of competition, kyoruki, is combat between two single competitors. The goal in tae kwon do combat is to score the most points within the time limit of the match. Points are scored by striking the opponent in specific areas of the body. Only kyoruki is part of international competition. There are world championship events for both men and women. Tae kwon do is also an Olympic sport.

Equipment

Head protector

Trunk protector

Timekeeper
The timekeeper times the periods.

Recorder
The recorder takes note of the judges' decisions.

Competition area

The competition area measures approximately 40 ft by 40 ft.

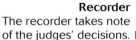

Referee
The referee supervises the contest. He also calls out the start and the end of each round.

Tae Kwon Do

The contest

In kyoruki, or competive tae kwon do, a random drawing determines the pairing of competitors, who take part individually or in a team. A kyoruki consists of three 3-minute periods. Participants earn one point by hitting the opponent's face with a foot or by hitting a specific area of the opponent's chest with a foot or fist. Participants are penalized with warnings and point deductions for committing faults. These include: attacking below the waist with the hand or the foot, striking the back or back of the head, hitting with the knee or the head, punching the face, and holding the opponent. The winner is the one who has scored the most points by the end of the three periods. In team competition, the winning team is the one with the most victories by its individual members. If there is a tie, the referee decides in favor of the fighter whose quality of performance is judged to be superior.

Fighting technique

The fighter must be able to attack and defend himself in all possible positions, both on the ground and in the air.

Roundhouse kick
Jumping into the air, the defender attempts a kick to the head that is known as a roundhouse kick. The power from this kick comes from the hips. Maximum power is reached when the leg is completely extended.

Foot technique
The attacker prepares to deliver a foot blow. A relaxed movement of the leg combined with rotation of the hips gives the blow more power. As the attacker delivers the blow, the defender begins to jump out of the way.

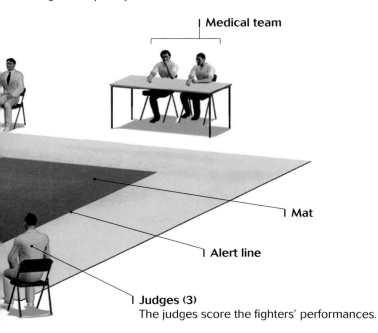

Medical team

Mat

Alert line

Judges (3)
The judges score the fighters' performances.

Fighter level	Belt color
10th keup (beginner)	white
9th keup	white with yellow stripes
8th keup	yellow
7th keup	yellow with green stripes
6th keup	green
5th keup	green with blue stripes
4th keup	blue
3rd keup	blue with red stripes
2nd keup	red
1st keup	red with black stripes
1st to 10th dan (advanced)	black with gold stripes

The ranks
Demonstration of increased skill in techniques allows athletes to rise through the ranks, symbolized by different colored belts. There is also a black band on the collar of black belt athletes' jackets.

Fencing

Fencing is an elegant combat sport in which two men or two women fight each other using swordlike weapons called foils, épées, or sabers. Matches take place on a rectangular track, called a piste. The goal in fencing is to touch the opponent's body with the tip of the weapon, while the opponent tries to dodge the weapon and counterattack. Fencers score a point for each touch or hit. The first fencer to score 15 hits wins the match. Fencing is a sport in which concentration is as important as strength. In addition to technique and quick reflexes, fencers must be able to spot their opponents' weaknesses and plan their attacks accordingly. As in boxing, skillful footwork allows the fencer to move quickly into a good attack position and to dodge or block the opponent's attacks. Fencing is an Olympic event.

Piste

The piste measures approximately 46 ft long and is about 5 to 6 ft wide.

Fencing outfit
The main part of the fencing outfit is made of Kevlar™, a strong, flexible material that protects the fencer from being pierced by the opponent's weapon. Fencers wear metallic scoring jackets over their outfits so that valid touches, which count for points, leave a mark and be can recorded.

Electrical scoring apparatus
The scoring apparatus records the number and location of touches. Each fencer is linked to the scoring apparatus with an electrical body wire. When a weapon registers contact with an opposing fencer's suit, a light is activated. A red or green light (depending on which fencer is hit) indicates a valid touch, which counts for points. A white light registers an invalid touch, which does not count for points.

Timers
The timers keep track of the time and record the touches.

Floor judge (2)
The floor judges assist the referee. They check to see if the fencer is making touches out of bounds.

Raised piste
In major competitions, the raised piste gives spectators and television crews a better view of the match. Pistes' heights may vary.

Referee
The referee supervises the match.

The movements

The step forward and step back are the basic fencing movements for the lower body. In both cases, the upper body remains upright and the legs are bent.

The salute
The salute is a traditional sign of courtesy. It is made with the face uncovered before and after each match. The fencer salutes his opponent, the referee, the jury, and the public.

The foil

The foil measures approximately 3½ ft long and weighs less than 1½ lbs. Touches are made with the tip of the foil only.

Blade

Electrical tip

Guard
The guard is rounded and smooth on the outside and is about 4 in. wide. The guard protects the fencer's hand from the opponent's weapon.

Handle

Additional equipment

Mask
The mask is traditionally made of a metallic mesh of thin wires that protect a fencer's head during a match. Masks are also equipped with a bib to protect the neck.

Gloves
The gloves are lightly padded. The cuffs extend up the arms.

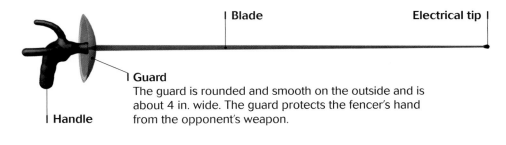

Body wire
The body wire connects the fencer to the electric touch-signaling system. The wire runs through the back of the fencer's jacket, down the sleeve, and across the glove. It is connected to a plug inside the weapon's guard.

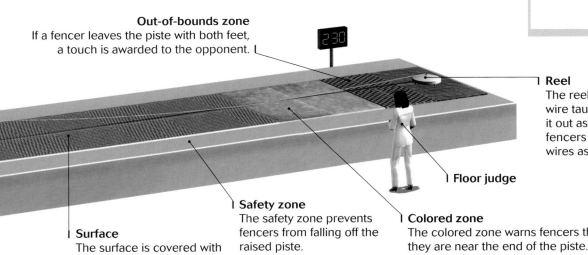

Out-of-bounds zone
If a fencer leaves the piste with both feet, a touch is awarded to the opponent.

Reel
The reel keeps the electrical body wire taut, pulling it in and letting it out as necessary. It prevents the fencers from tripping on their wires as they advance or retreat.

Floor judge

Surface
The surface is covered with an anti-slip metallic mesh.

Safety zone
The safety zone prevents fencers from falling off the raised piste.

Colored zone
The colored zone warns fencers that they are near the end of the piste.

Fencing

Techniques

The attack and the parry are the two basic techniques used in fencing. Attacks and parries always start in the on-guard position: the knees are bent, the free arm is bent upward and held behind the body, and the armed hand is held out toward the opponent.

The attack
The attack is a continuous offensive move toward the opponent. With the arm extended, the movement is often accompanied by a leap forward, called a flèche.

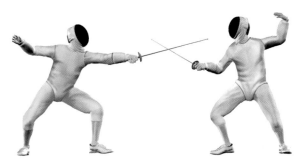

The parry
The parry (performed by the fencer on the right) is a defensive move. It can be performed in a variety of ways. The parry is a way of deflecting, or pushing off, an opponent's weapon using one's own weapon.

The riposte
The riposte (performed by the fencer on the right) is the counterattack after a parry. The riposte can be performed in a variety of ways, from a standing or moving position.

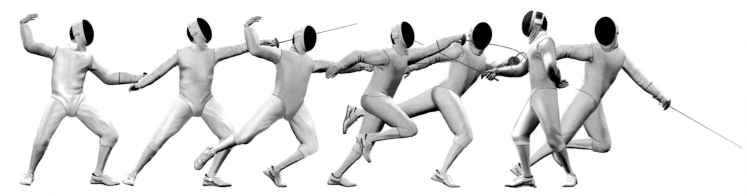

The flèche
The flèche is a rapid and spectacular attack technique in which the attacker attempts to score a hit while rushing forward and attacking his opponent. The armed hand is extended as the attacker rushes forward on his front leg. The tip of the attacker's weapon must touch the opponent before the attacker's other foot touches the ground.

Wrestling

Wrestling is a barehanded combat sport in which two opponents try to throw each other to the ground and pin, or hold, each other down using a series of special moves. Greco-Roman and freestyle wrestling matches are held in a competition area made up of a square mat with a circle inside it. The goal in wrestling is to put the opponent on the ground within the circle and pin his shoulders down long enough for the referee to count it as a fall. A fall means that the attacking wrestler has complete control over the opponent. Wrestling is a sport that requires flexibility, balance, and overall strength. Athletes must use all their muscles to grasp their opponents, secure holds, and score falls. Freestyle and Greco-Roman wrestling are Olympic events for men only. Both women and men participate in freestyle wrestling on a professional and world championship level.

Competition area

Mat chairman
The mat chairman settles any disagreements between the referee and the judge. He may also interrupt the match.

Referee
The referee works closely with the judge. The referee wears a blue band on one arm and a red band on the other. The colors correspond to the colors of the two wrestlers' uniforms. The referee raises one arm to show which wrestler has earned points. The number of fingers raised by the referee shows the number of points earned. The judge then confirms those points.

Judge
The judge follows the match, awards points for each move, and records the points on the score sheet. Both the judge and the mat chairman are responsible for confirming the number of points awarded.

Passivity zone
The passivity zone is a neutral area. It serves mainly to remind wrestlers that they are close to the edge of the combat zone.

Protection area
A match is stopped when a wrestler accidentally touches the protection area in the following ways: by placing one foot in the area while standing, by placing both hands in the area while kneeling, or by touching the area with his head while lying flat on his stomach.

Wrestling area
At the beginning of the match, the wrestlers stand on each side of the white circle in the center.

Wrestling

The competition

An Olympic freestyle or Greco-Roman match is composed of two 3-minute periods with a 30-second pause in between. The two wrestlers stand in their designated corners, which are colored red or blue to match the athletes' uniforms. Athletes are checked to make sure they are not hiding anything in their hands that could injure their opponents. They must carry handkerchiefs to wipe away sweat. Sweat and greasy substances on the skin are not allowed, because these make it difficult for wrestlers to hold their opponents. The wrestlers salute each other and shake hands before the referee signals the start of the match. In Greco-Roman wrestling, unlike freestyle, only holds above the hips are allowed. The wrestlers may not use their legs to pin each other down. The match ends when one of the wrestlers is pinned to the ground at the shoulders, and held there long enough for the judge to declare the move a fall.

Starting positions

Standing position
In Greco-Roman wrestling, the match starts with the athletes in the standing position.

Crouching position
In freestyle wrestling, the match starts with the athletes in the crouching position. The wrestlers move from the starting position into a scrimmage, in which each wrestler tries to gain control over his opponent. The goal is to upset the opponent's balance and throw him to the mat.

Techniques

In Greco-Roman wrestling, there are two types of holds for throwing and pinning an opponent: 1) standing holds, in which the athletes are both on their feet at the start; 2) mat holds, in which one or both athletes are down on the ground. Freestyle wrestling features standing holds, mat holds, and also leg holds, in which athletes use their legs to pin their opponents.

Double leg tackle (leg hold)

1. The attacker crouches slightly to grab the opponent's legs.

2. With one knee on the mat, he locks his arms around the opponent's thighs and begins to lift him up.

3. With both knees on the mat, he throws his opponent off balance and lifts him over his shoulders.

Gut wrench (mat hold)

1. The attacker places himself behind the opponent.

2. He puts his arms around his opponent from behind and places a knee down to one side.

3. He pulls his opponent toward him and puts his knee under his opponent's body.

4. The attacker arches his back and pushes his hips forward and up.

5. He then makes a bridge with his body. While holding the opponent, he pivots, or turns sideways, and pins the opponent's shoulders to the mat.

Hip toss (standing hold)

1. In this move, the attacker puts the opponent's right arm under his left armpit and grabs the opponent's head firmly with his right arm.

2. Pivoting, the attacker unbalances his opponent by holding him and pushing him off his feet using his hip. This move throws the opponent forward.

3. The attacker then drops to the ground with the opponent. This move puts the opponent into the fall position.

Reverse hip toss (mat hold)

1. The wrestler on top firmly seizes the opponent's hips by taking hold of the opponent's thigh on the far side of him.

2. He then raises the opponent's body toward him, placing his bent right leg under the opponent to support his weight.

3. From this position, the attacker throws himself backward, flipping the opponent.

4. The attacker pivots, puts one foot on the mat, and turns his opponent toward the mat, falling on top of him.

5. The attacker then locks his opponent in place by pinning his shoulders to the mat.

Boxing

Boxing is a combat sport of skill and stamina in which two opponents hit each other using only their fists. The boxers wear padded gloves to protect their hands and reduce injuries to their opponents. Fights take place on a raised square platform surrounded by ropes, called a ring. The goal of a boxing match is to score the most points within the time limit of the fight. Boxers earn points for their fighting technique and for the number of punches they land on their opponents. Punches "below the belt" (below the hips) are not allowed. Punches delivered to the back, the back of the head, or the back of the neck are forbidden and can result in penalties. Boxers need strength for punching, endurance to withstand blows, and quick reflexes. Boxers' footwork is as important as their fists. It enables them to move quickly into good attack positions and to dodge their attacking opponents' blows. Boxing is an Olympic event as well as a professional sport.

The ring

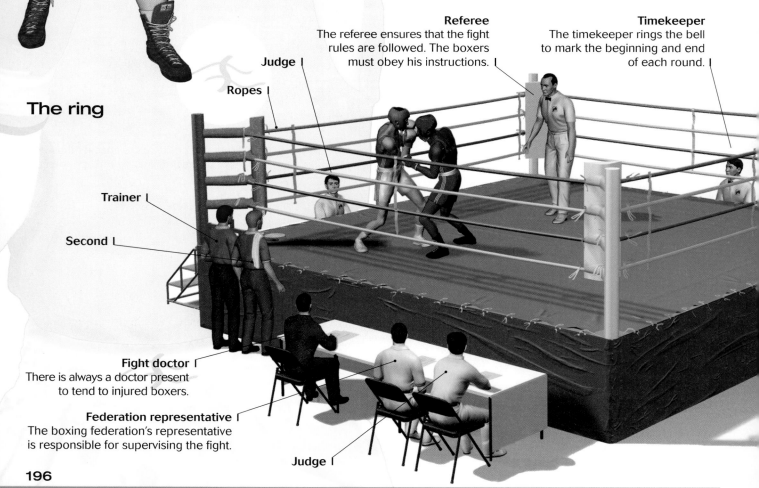

Referee
The referee ensures that the fight rules are followed. The boxers must obey his instructions.

Timekeeper
The timekeeper rings the bell to mark the beginning and end of each round.

Judge

Ropes

Trainer

Second

Fight doctor
There is always a doctor present to tend to injured boxers.

Federation representative
The boxing federation's representative is responsible for supervising the fight.

Judge

The fight

A boxing match is divided into rounds, separated by 1-minute rest periods. Professional matches may consist of four to twelve 3-minute rounds. In Olympic boxing matches there are only three or four 2-minute rounds. There are a number of ways to win a fight. It can be won by judges' decision, based on the number of points a boxer has achieved within the time limit of the match. It can be won by a knockout, which occurs when a fighter is knocked down and cannot get up within 10 seconds. If the referee stops the fight because one of the boxers is judged to be too injured to continue, the other boxer wins the match. A boxer may also win if his opponent gives up the fight or gets disqualified. A boxer can be disqualified for showing unsportsman-like conduct or for committing too many technical faults (mistakes that go against boxing rules).

Men's professional and amateur boxing weight divisions

Division	Maximum weights	
	Amateur (Olympic)	Professional
Strawweight	not recognized	105 lbs
Junior Flyweight	108 lbs	108 lbs
Flyweight	112 lbs	112 lbs
Junior Bantamweight	not recognized	115 lbs
Bantamweight	121 lbs	118 lbs
Junior Featherweight	not recognized	120 lbs
Featherweight	130 lbs	126 lbs
Junior Lightweight	not recognized	130 lbs
Lightweight	139 lbs	135 lbs
Junior Welterweight	147 lbs	140 lbs
Welterweight	156 lbs	147 lbs
Junior Middleweight	167 lbs	154 lbs
Middleweight	180 lbs	160 lbs
Super Middleweight	not recognized	168 lbs
Light Heavyweight	194 lbs	175 lbs
Cruiserweight	not recognized	190 lbs
Heavyweight	209 lbs	over 190 lbs

Trainer
Each boxer has a trainer who gives him advice during the match.

Second
Each boxer has a helper, called a second, who attends to his needs between rounds.

Judge
Three or 5 judges watch the boxing match. At the end of each round, the judges award a score to each boxer based on the number of points earned for successful punches.

Equipment

Gloves

Olympic boxing gloves
Olympic boxing gloves are leather and lined with foam to soften the force of blows. They are fastened to the hands with laces. Gloves weigh 12 oz for all weight classes of boxers. Punches must be delivered with the white part of the glove.

Professional boxing gloves
Professional boxing gloves are also made of leather and lined with foam. They are fastened to the hands with Velcro straps. Professional gloves range in weight from 8 to 12 oz, depending on the boxer's weight classification.

Mouthpiece
The mouthpiece protects the boxer's teeth.

Amateur and professional boxing
There are several differences between the rules of amateur or Olympic boxing and the those of professional boxing. Professional boxers do not wear a shirt or a protective helmet. Professional boxing matches have more rounds than Olympic-category matches. All boxing matches have the following rules in common: boxers must wear gloves and be weighed. Boxers are classified by their weight and fight only in their weight category. The size of the ring is standard. Ten seconds must be counted if a boxer is knocked down. If he does not get to his feet within 10 seconds, the opponent is declared the winner.

Boxing

Offensive moves

The three basic punches are straights (which include jabs), hooks, and uppercuts.

1. Straight
A straight (left or right) is a swift, direct punch delivered with the arm extended straight out from the body. A right straight is said to be the most powerful punch. A jab is a straight punch in which the arm is not fully extended. Jabs are used to keep the opponent at a distance.

2. Hook
A hook is a short, powerful punch delivered from the shoulder with the elbow bent.

3. Uppercut
An uppercut is a punch in which the arm swings upward and hits the opponent under the mouthguard.

Defensive moves

The three basic defensive moves are weaving, parrying, and blocking.

1. Weaving
The boxer slips away from his opponent's punch by twisting his hips and turning his body. This move prepares the boxer for a counterattack.

2. Parrying
The boxer stops his opponent's punch with his hand. He uses the hand that is on the same side of his body as the oncoming punch. This move throws the opponent off balance, allowing the boxer to counterattack.

3. Blocking
The boxer uses both gloves or forearms (the lower part of the arms from the elbows to wrists) to prevent the opponent's punch from hitting him.

Sports on Wheels

Skateboarding
In-line Skating
Roller Hockey

Skateboarding

Skateboarding is an acrobatic sport in which athletes ride small four-wheeled wooden platforms called skateboards. Creativity is as important as technical skill in skateboarding. Men and women athletes seem to defy gravity while they jump, spin, and rotate their boards in the air. Skateboarding requires flexibility, strength, balance, and fearlessness.

Half pipe

The half pipe event is named after the competition area, a huge U-shaped structure that looks like a pipe cut in half lengthwise. After a series of qualifying matches, the finalists compete in best-out-of-three events. Athletes have 45 seconds to perform a series of moves either on the verts, the vertical sides of the half pipe, or in the air above the half pipe. The skateboarders are awarded points for technical performance, originality, and difficulty. The skater with the most points wins.

Street

Street competition requires a course with an area of about 1,200 sq yds. Courses have some of the features of a typical city street, with sidewalks, stairs, and other obstacles of different shapes and sizes. Three to five judges rate the skateboarders' performances and give them each an overall score between 0 and 100 points. Athletes are judged according to their technique and style.

Equipment

Skateboard
The skateboard is a platform made of wood that curves upward at the edges.

Grip tape
The grip tape on the surface of the board helps keep the skateboarders' feet sticking to the board.

Wheels
The polyurethane wheels come in several sizes and vary in hardness. They are designed to suit the different types of events and courses.

1½–2 in.

Tail
Back part

Nose
Front part

Truck

30 in.

Skateboarding

Street moves

Ollie

The ollie is a basic move for jumping over obstacles. In the approach, the athlete bends his legs, puts his weight on his toes, and moves his feet back on the board. As he begins the jump, he puts pressure on the tail of the board. To maintain contact with the board, he scrapes his feet along the grip tape surface. He bends his knees and flexes his ankles to make a stable landing.

Halfpipe moves

There are three types of acrobatic moves: lip tricks, aerials, and plants. Lip tricks are performed on the coping of the half pipe. Aerials are performed in the air above the half pipe. Plants are performed with a hand or foot on the coping. All moves can be performed front side (with the skateboarder's back toward the inside of the half pipe) or back side (with the skateboarder facing the inside of the half pipe).

5/0 grind

The 5/0 grind starts with an ollie; the athlete then slides along a metal bar on the trucks of the skateboard. The trucks are the frames that hold the wheels. His body and the skateboard must be perfectly in line with the bar. The athlete balances by bending his legs and moving his arms. He must stay focused on heading in the right direction and anticipate his landing.

Coping

The coping is the rounded edge at the top of the vert.

Grab 540 backside

The skateboarder rolls up the vert at high speed. He presses on the board with his back foot to help stay in contact with it as he takes off over the edge of the half pipe. He crouches in the tuck position, holds the skateboard with his right hand, and swings his left arm around to help him turn in the air. He completes the turn as he descends, keeping his eyes on the half pipe. He must anticipate when he will come into contact with the half pipe and know when to let go of the skateboard. Being able to perform this move smoothly depends on the flexibility of the legs, which are bent at takeoff and during flight, and extended during the landing.

Vert |

In-line Skating

In-line skating is both a popular recreational activity and the basis of several competitive sports: acrobatic skating, speed skating, and roller hockey. In-line skating is also called Rollerblading. In in-line skating, men and women athletes perform a series of moves on courses that feature ramps, stairs, and other obstacles. In speed skating, athletes race against the clock as individuals or teams on an oval track. Roller hockey is played on a surface similar in size to the traditional ice hockey rink. Any sport in which in-line skates are used requires excellent balance, coordination, and reflexes. World championships in speed skating and acrobatic skating are held each year.

Acrobatic skate
The boot of the acrobatic skate is made of hard plastic and is fastened with a combination of laces and buckles. The boot has a shell inside to help absorb the shock of landing.

Boot

Shell

Wheels
The polyurethane wheels measure from 1½ to about 2¾ in. wide. They come in varying degrees of hardness to suit the different kinds of events.

Plate
The plate holds the 4 wheels.

Slider
The slider protects the plate. It allows the skater to slide instead of roll on surfaces such as stair railings.

Equipment

Lining

Shell

Wrist guards
The wrist guards have hard plastic inserts that help to prevent injury to the wrists and hands.

Elbow pads
The elbow pads are made of a combination of lightweight materials. They must stay in place without being attached too tightly.

Knee pads
The knee pads are made of materials that do not trap perspiration. The shell is made of hard plastic; the lining is foam.

In-line Skating

Street

In street competitions, the skater—also called the streeter—performs acrobatic figures on a course with obstacles and various structures such as the pyramid. Each competitor performs in two rounds of 60 or 90 seconds.

Pyramid
The pyramid is a box with ramps of different shapes and sizes. It is used for performing all kinds of figures in the street competition.

Misty flip
The misty flip is a difficult acrobatic move with a rotation in the air. The athlete skates up a ramp of the pyramid as quickly as possible. She extends her arms, spreads her legs, and turns her upper body to begin the rotation. She tucks her chin toward her chest, holds her thighs, and bends her legs. Continuing the rotation, she lets go of her legs and relaxes her arms. She lands facing the ramp. Her legs are slightly bent and her skates are in line with the ramp to maintain balance.

Soul grind
The skater approaches the stair railing at a speed that will allow her to jump onto the rail at a comfortable angle. She uses her arms and hands to help her balance on the railing. The front skate sits on the slider and the back skate sits on the back outside edge of the plate, making a T-shaped formation.

Half pipe

The half pipe is a wooden structure that looks like a tube cut in half lengthwise. Competitors perform aerial acrobatics in two rounds of 60 or 90 seconds. They are awarded points for the technical difficulty of their moves, the height of their jumps, and how smoothly they perform them.

Coping

540 flat spin
The athlete skates quickly up the side of the half pipe. After leaving the coping, she begins a diagonal rotation in the air, controlling her balance with one arm. During the first rotation, she holds one of her skates. When the first rotation is completed, she lets go of the skate. She performs another half turn before landing with her legs extended.

Roller Hockey

In-line roller hockey involves two competing teams facing each other on an indoor or outdoor rink with a dry floor. Teams consist of one goaltender and four other players (one winger, one center, and two defense players). Both teams try to score points by using sticks to hit a puck into their opponents' goals located at either end of the rink. Both men and women roller hockey players need to have endurance, speed, and excellent balance. Roller hockey is played in national championships in the United States.

The game

The rules of in-line roller hockey are similar to those for ice hockey. Players must leave the rink to serve penalty time when they commit faults. Physical contact is not allowed. Games are played in two periods of 22 minutes each. The team with the most goals at the end of the two periods wins the game.

In-line roller hockey rink

The rink is made of wood, cement, asphalt, or plastic. It may vary from about 132 ft to 200 ft long.

Equipment

In-line roller hockey skates
The boots on in-line skates sit close to the ground. This gives the athlete a lower center of gravity, which makes balancing on the skates easier. The boots are tilted to the front to make forward movement easier.

Wheels
The wheels are made of polyurethane. Inside the wheels are ball bearings, small metal balls that help the wheels turn quickly and smoothly. The wheels measure close to 3 in. wide.

Stick
The stick is made of wood and measures a maximum 5 ft in length.

Puck
The puck is made of hard rubber. It may also have bumps or ball bearings on its surface that help it slide across the rink more easily.

Goal judge (2)
Judges are stationed behind each of the 2 goals. They decide whether a goal counts or not.

Center
The center takes part in face-offs (putting the puck into play) and decides what offensive moves his team will perform.

Referee (2)
The referees enforce the rules and issue penalties to players who break them.

Players' and coaches' benches

Goaltender (2)
The goaltender is responsible for stopping the puck.

Winger
The winger's role is to score goals and to block the opposing team's winger.

Defense players
The defense player's main task is to prevent the opposing team from scoring goals.

Motor Sports

Automobile Racing
Formula 1
Formula 3000
Indy Car Racing
Motorcycling
Rallying and Off-road Rallying

Automobile Racing

Automobile racing is a sport in which drivers race cars that have been specially designed for high performance and speed. Races take place on oval tracks or road-racing courses of different shapes and lengths. Automobile racing tests the skills and endurance of the drivers and the power and handling of the vehicles. Racing drivers need to have good judgment, fast reflexes, perfect technique, and fearlessness. Although it is mainly men who race professionally, women also race at the amateur level.

Equipment

Driving suit
The driving suit is made of a special fabric that helps to protect the driver from serious burns. A fire can occur if the car is in an accident.

Gloves
The backs of the gloves must be made of at least 2 layers of fire-retardant fabric. Gloves must close at the wrist and cover the ends of the sleeves of the driver's suit.

Helmet
The helmet must cover the head and face completely. It is made of mixed materials such as Kevlar™ or carbon fiber, and weighs over 2½ lbs.

Earplugs
The earplugs reduce noise but still allow for radio contact between the driver and the pit crew. The pit crew is the group of mechanics whose job it is to repair and refuel the driver's car.

Shoes
The shoes must completely cover the feet and ankles. The soles of the shoes must be flame-resistant.

Driver
Driving a race car requires more endurance than physical strength. Drivers must be able to withstand heat, since the temperature inside a car can exceed 130° F. They also need to have excellent vision and coordination. Training consists of muscle strengthening in the neck, lower arms, abdominals, and legs. The training is designed to help the drivers control the steering wheel and operate the foot pedals with greater ease.

Automobile Racing

How a race car runs

How well a race car performs depends mainly on how smoothly its mechanical parts work together. Race cars require engines that turn at very high speeds to deliver power quickly. While a regular passenger car's engine may turn at speeds of 2,000 to 6,000 rpm (revolutions per minute), a race car engine may turn at 10,000 rpm and more. The weight of the car also helps to determine how fast it can go. A heavy car requires more power to propel it than a lighter car.

Officials

Automobile races held on closed courses are supervised by a team of officials who are responsible for ensuring events run smoothly. The race director oversees and starts the race. He can stop or interrupt the race, if necessary, and penalize drivers who have committed faults. Race stewards are responsible for applying all the rules. Timers record the times of each driver. Marshals give information to the drivers by waving flags.

Main signals and flags

 ## Stock-car Racing

The most popular form of automobile racing in the United States is stock-car racing. Stock cars may look like ordinary cars we see on the street but hide the fact that they have powerful racing engines under their hoods. Just slightly less sophisticated than one-seater race cars, stock cars can actually reach speeds of 200 mph. Major stock-car races include the Daytona 500 in Daytona Beach, Florida. The Daytona 500 is part of the Winston Cup series, a NASCAR (National Association for Stock Car Auto Racing) event.

White flag
The white flag signals that an ambulance, emergency vehicle, or slow-moving vehicle is on the track. In American racing series, the white flag shows that the race is in its final lap around the track.

Black flag with orange circle in the center
The black and orange flag, along with the car number, is waved at a driver to advise him that one of the parts on his car is a hazard for him or other competitors.

Black and white flag
The black and white flag is waved as a warning to a driver who has acted in an unsportsmanlike manner.

Blue flag
The blue flag is displayed to let a driver know that a faster car is preparing to pass. It warns the driver of the slower car not to block the faster car.

Yellow flag
The yellow flag is waved when there is danger. Drivers must slow down, and are not permitted to pass in the area where the yellow flag is being displayed.

Green flag
The green flag signals that there is no longer any warning. It is displayed after the yellow flag and lets drivers know that they can now pass.

Black flag
The black flag, along with the number of the car being signaled, is waved for the driver who has broken a particular rule. The driver must proceed to the service area, called the pits, to serve a penalty.

Yellow flag with red stripes
The yellow and red flag is displayed to show that there is a problem with the surface of the racetrack. The problem may be spilled oil, liquids, or other debris on the track.

Red flag
The red flag is displayed at the start and finish line. It signals that the race or practice session is being stopped.

Checkered flag
The checkered flag is waved at the winner of the race. It is also waved when a race or a practice session ends.

Formula 1

The most popular form of international automobile racing is Formula 1. The race is named after the Formula 1 (F1) car, one of several models in the Formula series of one-seater vehicles. Drivers compete in highly publicized events such as the Grand Prix and the Formula 1 World Championship. F1 races are held on city streets or on courses permanently built for F1 racing. Competitors must plan different strategies and adjust their style of driving to suit the type of course. On a course with many long straightaways, for example, drivers can reach high speeds and pass one another easily. Courses with tight curves require drivers to move into the best possible position before going into the curve, so that they can maintain their speed without losing control. On city street courses, there is little room for error, so competitors must drive extra carefully.

The Grand Prix

There are several Grand Prix races held in different parts of the world each year. Grand Prix races last three days. Drivers spend the first two days testing and adjusting their cars. They also drive several laps of the course to qualify for their starting positions. The third day, when the actual race takes place, drivers drive their cars one lap around the course to warm up their tires. This helps the tires to stick to the pavement better and helps to prevent skidding. After completing one lap, the cars take their places on the starting grid according to their starting positions. Five red lights come on one by one at 1-second intervals. The race starts when all five lights go out together.

Race course

The number of laps in a race varies according to the length of the circuit or course. A race on the Monza circuit, which is just over 3½ miles long, must run 53 laps to reach the standard Formula 1 race distance of 189 miles.

Chicane
The chicane is a twisting part of the circuit that breaks up a straightaway and forces drivers to slow down.

Curbs
Curbs are placed at the entrances and exits of turns. The curbs help the driver to see the turns ahead of time and also make it easier for the driver to see the edge of the track.

Gravel pits
The gravel pits help a skidding car slow down. They are especially effective for helping cars to stop spinning.

Tire barriers
Tire barriers help to absorb shock in a collision.

Formula 1

Roll bars
Roll bars help to protect the driver if the car flips over.

Wings
The wings create a downward force on the front and back of the car, helping the car to hold to the track.

Camera
The cameras allow the television audience to view the race from the driver's point of view.

Telemetry system
The telemetry system includes a transmitter that is mounted on one of the rearview mirrors. The transmitter sends information to the crew in the pits, who keep track of the car's main functions during the race.

Radio aerial
The radio aerial allows the driver and his team to communicate during a race.

Pitot tube
The pitot tube takes in air during the race. It is used to calculate the car's real speed, which is influenced by the speed of the wind.

Side fairings
The side fairings contain the car's radiators and electronic parts. They also channel fresh air to the engine.

Safety harness
The driver is securely strapped in by the safety harness. The harness consists of 2 shoulder straps, 2 belly straps, and 2 leg straps.

F1 cars
F1 cars are known for their incredible power and speed. They run at more than 800 horsepower and reach speeds of more than 200 mph. The average F1 car measures about 14 ft long and is less than 6 ft wide. The minimum allowable weight for a car with a driver in it is 1,322 lbs.

High-speed turn
The high-speed turn tests the car's stability and the driver's courage. Cars take the turn at over 100 mph.

Pole position
The pole position is the first-place position on the grid. It is given to the driver who recorded the fastest previous qualifying time.

4th row

3rd row

2nd row

1st row

Pit row
The pit row is located between the track and the pits. Drivers use the pit row for entering and exiting the pits.

The pits
Each driver and his team have their own pit. The pits are where cars are repaired, re-fueled, and have their tires changed.

Starting grid
The cars are arranged in 2 lines in a staggered formation on the starting grid of the track. The cars' positions are determined by their previous qualifying times, with the fastest cars starting in front.

Formula 1

Formula 1 World Championship

The Formula 1 World Championship features a series of 16 or 17 races held during a racing season. Twelve teams, each with 2 drivers, compete in the championship. The driver with the most points at the end of the season is the champion. There is also a Formula 1 championship for car manufacturers. The car maker that accumulates the most points, according to how well its vehicles and drivers perform, wins the championship at the end of the season. Points are awarded to the top 6 drivers on the following scale:

Formula 1 World Championship						
Finishing Position	1st	2nd	3rd	4th	5th	6th
Points	10	6	4	3	2	1

Rain tire

Slick tire

Tires

Tires are designed for different weather conditions. Smooth or slick tires are used in dry weather. Rain tires have deep treads that help push away large quantities of water from under the tires. In between are intermediate rain tires. Their treads are not as deep as the ones on the regular rain tires. Intermediate tires are used on damp tracks. Choosing the right tire is an important decision to make before the qualifying session. The type of tire being used on a car cannot be changed during the event.

Pit stop

During a race, cars may make one or two stops to refuel and have their tires changed. A good pit crew that works well together is able to refuel the car and change all four tires in less than eight seconds.

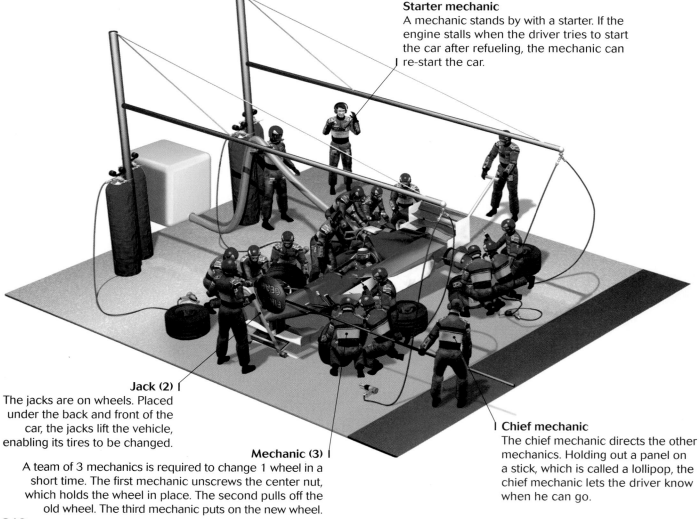

Starter mechanic
A mechanic stands by with a starter. If the engine stalls when the driver tries to start the car after refueling, the mechanic can re-start the car.

Jack (2)
The jacks are on wheels. Placed under the back and front of the car, the jacks lift the vehicle, enabling its tires to be changed.

Mechanic (3)
A team of 3 mechanics is required to change 1 wheel in a short time. The first mechanic unscrews the center nut, which holds the wheel in place. The second pulls off the old wheel. The third mechanic puts on the new wheel.

Chief mechanic
The chief mechanic directs the other mechanics. Holding out a panel on a stick, which is called a lollipop, the chief mechanic lets the driver know when he can go.

Formula 3000

The Formula 3000 championship is an event for single-seater cars on closed circuits. It is regarded as a training ground for Formula 1 racing. The Formula 3000 championship was designed to offer competition conditions similar to the Formula 1, but at a much lower cost. The international Formula 3000 championship takes place on circuits throughout Europe. With all drivers in technically identical cars, the difference between the fastest qualifying time and the 10th fastest time is rarely more than one second. A competitor's success relies mostly on his talents as a driver.

Formula 3000 drivers
The average Formula 3000 drivers are 20 years old. Their goal is usually to become F1 drivers or test-drivers for car manufacturers after 2 or 3 good seasons in Formula 3000.

The car
All Formula 3000 cars have identical equipment.

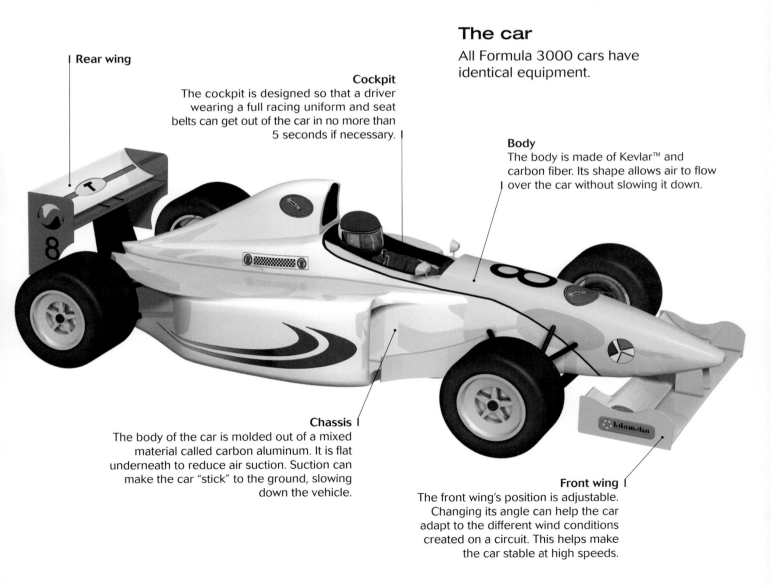

Rear wing

Cockpit
The cockpit is designed so that a driver wearing a full racing uniform and seat belts can get out of the car in no more than 5 seconds if necessary.

Body
The body is made of Kevlar™ and carbon fiber. Its shape allows air to flow over the car without slowing it down.

Chassis
The body of the car is molded out of a mixed material called carbon aluminum. It is flat underneath to reduce air suction. Suction can make the car "stick" to the ground, slowing down the vehicle.

Front wing
The front wing's position is adjustable. Changing its angle can help the car adapt to the different wind conditions created on a circuit. This helps make the car stable at high speeds.

Indy Car Racing

Indy Car Racing is a series of oval track events. It is named after the Indianapolis 500, one of the most famous automobile races. Events are held in the United States, Canada, Australia, Brazil, and Japan. Five car body manufacturers and four companies that build engines supply all the teams. The single-seater cars resemble Formula 1 cars but are heavier and sturdier. Although the cars may reach impressive speeds of 230 mph on straightaways, the sharp turns of the track force drivers to reduce their speed elsewhere. This makes Indy Car Racing races somewhat slower than Formula 1 races. Indy Car Racing is supervised by CART (Championship Auto Racing Teams) and IRL (Indy Racing League).

How a race is organized

On oval and superoval tracks, a rolling start is used. After getting a signal from the race director, the drivers head out onto the track to complete one or more warm-up laps. They must stay in their own grid positions. They follow the pace car, which maintains a constant speed. No car is allowed to move ahead until the green flag is displayed. At a road course event, the race director indicates beforehand whether the start will be a dry start or a wet start. In a dry start, drivers can choose the tires they are going to use. In a wet start, all drivers must start on rain tires. Unlike Formula 1 racing, pre-heating of tires is not permitted. In the CART series, drivers make many pit stops during a race to refuel and change tires. The first driver to cross the finish line when the checkered flag is displayed is the winner of the race.

The circuit

Indy Car Racing races are run over distances of 200, 300, 400, or 500 miles, on tracks called circuits. There are 3 types of circuits: ovals, superovals, and road courses. The ovals, or speedways, are asphalt or cement tracks measuring between 1⅔ and 2½ miles around. Ovals longer than 1 mile with steeply banked turns are called superovals, or superspeedways. Road courses, which measure between 1½ and 4 miles in length, may be either temporary tracks on city streets or specially designed permanent courses.

Cement retaining wall
Indy Car Racing tracks do not have safety run-off areas. The cement retaining wall prevents cars from crashing into the stands but is more dangerous for the drivers.

Pits
Tires and fuel tanks are stored in the pits. A maximum of 6 team members may work on a car.

Oval circuit

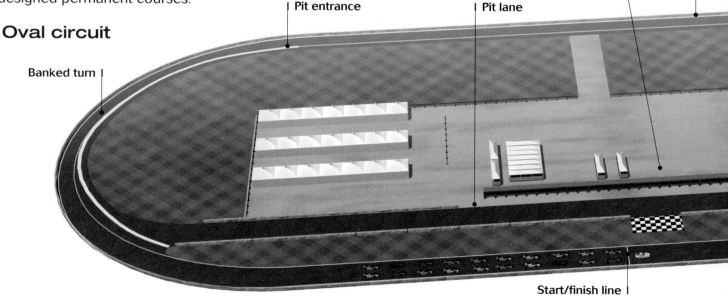

Pit entrance

Pit lane

Banked turn

Start/finish line
The cars are timed and the green and checkered flags are displayed at the start/finish line.

Indy Car Racing

The car

Indy Car Racing cars have adjustments made to them to suit the different circuits on which races are held. For example, the wings will be set one way for an event on a superoval track and another way for a race on an oval or for a road course.

Superoval cars
Smaller wings on the cars provide less downforce and allow for higher speeds.

Ovals and road course cars
Because top speed is not such an important factor as on the superovals, the wings are set to provide downforce. In this position, the wings create an air current that presses the car down on the track, helping to keep it stable.

Penalties

When a driver breaks a rule, the race director may impose different penalties, depending upon the seriousness of the infraction.

Lap penalty
This can occur if the driver illegally passes the pace car. The driver may have one or more laps deducted from the actual number of laps he completed.

Loss of position
Loss of position can occur if a driver passes under a yellow flag. The guilty driver may be moved down one or more positions in the finishing order. This penalty may be handed out during or after the race.

Penalty served in the pit lane ("stop and go")
A driver who goes over the speed limit in the pit lane (60 mph), runs over a piece of equipment (tire, hose, etc.), or commits an infraction under a green or yellow flag may be obliged to return to the pit lane, stop, and then go again when signaled by the race official. The driver may also be forced to rejoin the race at the back of the field.

Suspension
A driver can be suspended for performing a dangerous move. Officials may suspend a driver from more than one race for committing a serious infraction.

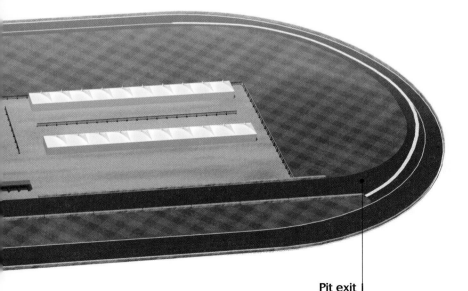

Pit exit

Pace car
The pace car sets the pace or speed for the rest of the cars before the race and during caution periods. During these periods, the cars must stay in their positions and not pass one another.

Motorcycling

Motorcycling is a sport in which drivers race two-wheeled vehicles on tracks or roads of varying lengths and conditions. Events include speed racing on flat tracks, motocrosses, and supercrosses, which take place on rugged dirt courses. There are also mixed on- and off-road races as well as long-distance races. Besides concentration and good driving skills, motorcycle riders need strength to balance and steer their heavy vehicles at high speeds without losing control. Although the sport is dominated by men, there are also women who participate in motorcycle racing at the amateur level.

Speed Grand Prix

Speed Grand Prix races are 20-to-30-minute races run on a closed circuit. In the Speed Grand Prix, riders first take some test runs to become familiar with the track, and then make adjustments to their motorcycles. Two one-hour qualifying races are held. These determine the riders' starting positions for the following day. The fastest riders will occupy the front positions. Before the race, the riders ride one or two warm-up laps in starting formation and then return to their positions. The course director signals the start, indicated by a red light followed by a green light. The first rider across the finish line at the end of the race is the winner.

Technique

Windshield

The start
The rider moves his weight to the front of the motorcycle to keep the front wheel from lifting as he speeds up. If the front wheel rises too high, he will have to slow down to regain control. He tucks his head behind the windshield to reduce wind resistance and gain speed.

Motorcycling

Motocross and Supercross

Motocross races are run on courses that feature natural terrain with hills, sharp drops, bumps, ruts, and other obstacles. Supercross events are run on artificial tracks, sometimes indoors. The track is made of earth or a mixture of sand and clay and features obstacles that lead to very high jumps. Twenty-five racers start side by side at the same time. The winner is the first rider across the finish line. World motocross and supercross championships involve 16 races each, with points awarded to the first 15 finishers. The world champion in each category is the rider with the most points at the end of the 16 races.

Group start
The riders stand with their engines running. The official holds up a card to show there are 30 seconds left before the start, and then another card to show when there are 5 seconds left. The start is signaled by the starting gate, which folds down. If a rider starts too soon and commits a false start, a red flag signals that all riders must return to the waiting area for a new start.

Equipment

Motocross helmet
All riders must wear helmets to protect their heads in case of a fall.

Protective goggles
The goggles are covered with several layers of plastic film. If the goggles get sprayed with dirt, the rider can quickly remove a layer and be able to see clearly again.

Gloves
The gloves are made of synthetic material. They are padded both inside and out to give drivers extra protection.

Tires
There are tires for 3 different types of terrain: soft, hard, and muddy.

Protective equipment
Riders may wear padding on their torsos, arms, elbows, knees, and backs to protect themselves in case of a fall.

Pants and shirt
The pants and shirt are light and made of synthetic fabric.

Motocross boots
The boots are made of leather and plastic.

Protective plate
The plate protects the engine from bumps and obstacles. Its design allows objects to slide underneath the motorcycle without getting caught on the engine.

Technique

Jump
On the ramp, the rider moves forward toward the handlebars before taking off. Once in the air, he moves backward and extends his arms. The rider needs to line up the motorcycle for a good landing. To do this, he can speed up, which lowers the back of the motorcycle, or he can brake, which lowers the front of the motorcycle. As he lands, the driver moves forward toward the handlebars to regain speed.

Rallying and Off-road Rallying

A rally is a race run on roads, often from city to city. Both men and women take part in rallies. Rallies are the longest of all automobile races. Each race is broken down into stages. In each stage, drivers go from one point to the next, following a fixed time schedule. Some stages are organized as races against the clock. Although the roads in a rally are often closed to regular traffic, drivers are still expected to obey the traffic rules.

Rally

The driver and co-driver share the duties. While one is driving, the other reads from the route card and calls out the different features along the course. The route card, which is provided by the organizer of the event, contains details about how the course looks. It includes turns, bumps, and dangerous parts. The drivers also get a control book, which tells them how long they should take to drive the distance between two checkpoints along the route. The route may cover a distance of a few miles or several thousand miles (in the case of off-road rallies). Scores are awarded by the officials when the teams present their control book at each checkpoint. Because the object of the race is to drive the route within a specified amount of time, drivers get penalties for arriving late or arriving too early. The driving team that accumulates the most points at the end of the rally season is declared the world champion.

Off-road Rally

An off-road rally is as much an adventure as a race. It takes place on roadless terrain, often in desert regions. The rally may span a distance of several thousand miles. Like the road rally, the off-road rally is broken down into stages and special timed sections. Technical and mechanical support crews follow the drivers in trucks, performing repairs along the way. Before each stage of the rally, the driving teams receive their route cards, which describe in detail the route to follow and show the places where they can get help or fuel. Rally teams may drive anywhere from 8 to 24 hours without stopping. To help them know where they are at all times, some teams use the GPS (Global Positioning System). Linked to a satellite, the GPS transmits information that indicates the team's exact position on Earth.

The Dakar
Run entirely in Africa, the rally stretches over 6,800 miles. The event consists of almost 1,900 miles of point-to-point stages that must be covered within certain time limits. The race also features over 4,000 miles of stages that are races against the clock.

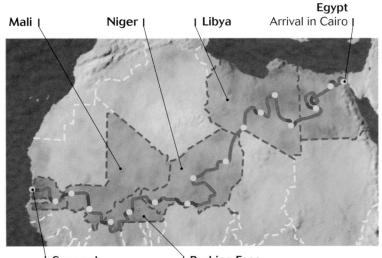

Multi Sports

Triathlon
Pentathlon
Orienteering

14

Triathlon

The triathlon is a three-event contest involving swimming, cycling, and running. The goal of the triathlon is very simple: the timer starts when the first phase (swimming) begins and it stops when the competitors cross the finish line of the last phase (running). The fastest athlete overall wins the competition. Triathletes practice to make the transition from one sport to the next as quickly as possible. They take only 8 to 10 seconds to go from swimming to cycling, or from cycling to running. Men and women triathletes work on improving their endurance for this difficult sport by perfecting their technique. Proper technique reduces tiredness and enables athletes to perform for long periods of time without using up all their energy.

Swimming
The freestyle swimming event usually takes place in open water. Although there is no required stroke, most athletes use the crawl because it is the fastest. Swimmers are allowed to stop and hold onto a floating buoy or an unmoving boat to rest, but may not use these to help them move forward.

Running
The last phase of the triathlon, the running event, draws on the athletes' last reserves of energy and endurance. Triathletes try to move as efficiently as possible. They run in an upright position, with their eyes focused ahead. To avoid getting worn out and to make breathing and leg movement easier, they keep their shoulders relaxed and their arms close to their bodies.

Cycling
The cycling event is usually a road race. Athletes must keep up a strong pedaling rhythm. They must also maintain a low position on the bike to reduce wind resistance. Cyclists can achieve an average speed of 28 mph during the race. They must carry their own tools and be able to repair their bicycles on the spot if needed.

Types of races				
Race	Swimming	Cycling	Running	Average duration
Classic/Olympic	1 mile (approx.)	25 miles	6 miles	under 2 hours
Sprint	½ mile	12½ miles	3 miles	1¼ hours
Half-triathlon	1 mile	56 miles	13 miles	4½ to 5 hours
Triathlon (Ironman)	2¼ miles	111 miles	26 miles	9 hours

The pentathlon is the only Olympic event that combines five different sports: shooting, fencing, swimming, riding (horseback), and running. Men and women compete separately in this one-day test of mental and physical endurance. Athletes start off with 1,000 pentathlon points in each event. They can then gain or lose additional points based on their performances. Athletes can make up for low scores in some events by excelling in others. The total number of points earned in each of the five events are added up and then converted into a final score.

* Did you know?

The unusual combination of sports in the pentathlon was inspired by the adventure of a French officer in Napoleon's army some 200 years ago. The soldier had to cross enemy lines and overcome many obstacles on his way to deliver a message for his troops.

Fencing

The weapon used in the fencing event is the epée, a type of sword. Each competitor has a chance to fence against each of the other competitors. Matches last a maximum of 1 minute and end at the first touch of the epée on the opponent's body. Fencers gain extra points for winning more than 7 out of 10 matches and lose points for winning fewer than 7 out of 10. A match with no touch is counted as a defeat for both athletes.

Shooting

The athlete shoots at a target approximately 33 ft away. The target is marked with circles worth 1 to 10 points. The athlete gains extra points for scoring more than 172 shooting points within 20 shots, but loses points for scoring less than 172 points in 20 shots.

Swimming

The 200 m freestyle is a test of speed. Men earn an extra point for every tenth of a second less than 2:30 minutes they take to swim the race. Each tenth of a second over 2:30 minutes costs them one extra point. The women's race has the same point system based on swimming the race in 2:40 minutes.

Riding

The course is approximately 1,300 ft long and features 12 obstacles for the horse and rider. The obstacles include at least one double and triple combination. Knocking down a pole on an obstacle costs a competitor 30 points. If a horse misses or refuses to jump an obstacle, 40 points are deducted. Each second over the time allowed for riding the course costs 3 points. If there is a tie between competitors, the rider with the fastest overall time is the winner of the event.

Running

The running phase consists of a 3,000 m cross-country race. The athlete who is leading in points after the first 4 events starts first. The rest of the competitors follow in order according to the number of points they have already earned. The athlete who crosses the finish line first wins the competition.

Orienteering

Orienteering is a sport in which athletes run, ski, or bicycle over an unfamiliar cross-country course using only a map or compass to find their way. Athletes must pass each of several checkpoints during the course of the race. Orienteering is practiced in several forms: in relays, on mountain bikes, on cross-country skis, and in long-distance races that may last several days. Distances in professional competitions vary from about 6 to 12 miles for men and about 4 to 9 miles for women. Competitors may take approximately 75 to 90 minutes to complete a course.

The competition

The athletes are taken to the starting point, where they each pick up a map of the region. One at a time, they set out on the course, leaving at timed intervals. The competitors must arrive at the checkpoints, called control sites, in a certain order. The control sites are marked on the map. Each site has equipment that enables the participants to prove that they have passed that point. They may take any route they choose to get to each control site. The winner is the athlete who finishes the course in the shortest time.

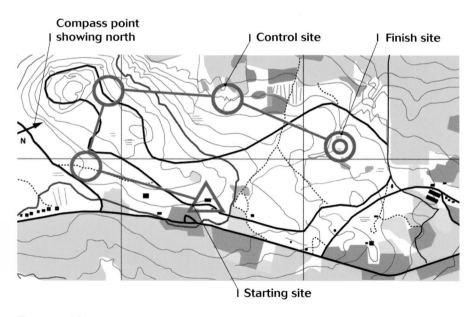

Compass point showing north | Control site | Finish site

Starting site

Topographic map
The topographic map is a basic part of the competition. It has special symbols on it that indicate what type of terrain lies in the area: mountains, water, forests, and other vegetation. Vegetation such as thick brush or swamp, which may be harder to travel through, is marked in colors that correspond to its level of difficulty. Areas marked in white are the most difficult.

Equipment

Shoes

Clothing
Orienteers wear clothing made of tough fabric to withstand the rough woodland terrain. The fabric must breathe, allowing heat and sweat to escape. Athletes also wear special lightweight, waterproof shoes. They have metal and rubber cleats on the soles to help the orienteers run and climb without slipping.

Compass
The compass is as important a piece of equipment as the map. With its magnetic needle that always points to the north, the compass helps orienteers find and maintain their direction in the wilderness. The most popular compasses are the thumb compass and the baseplate compass.

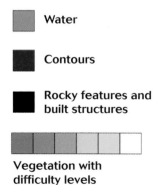

Water

Contours

Rocky features and built structures

Vegetation with difficulty levels

Glossary

aquatic (adj)
Taking place in water, such as swimming and water polo.

combat sports (n)
Fighting sports, like boxing, wrestling, and martial arts.

defense (n)
A team protecting its goal from the opponents; protecting a goal from attack.

deflect (v)
To make something change direction by hitting it, such as a soccer player deflecting a ball by hitting it with his head.

endurance (n)
The ability to perform difficult or painful actions for long periods of time without giving up.

equestrian (adj)
Sports relating to horseback riding.

fault (n)
A mistake or an incorrect action that goes against the rules of a sport.

intercept (v)
To stop or change the direction of a moving object from its planned course. In football, for example, a player may intercept the ball as it is passed between two players of the opposing team.

maneuver (n)
An action made up of a series of skillful and sometimes acrobatic moves, such as the 5/0 grind maneuver in skateboarding.

martial arts (n)
Fighting and self-defense sports, mainly of Asian origin, in which the hands and feet are used as weapons. Judo and karate are examples of martial arts.

multidisciplinary sports (n)
Sports that combine several different kinds of athletic events. A triathlon, for example, made up of swimming, cycling, and running, is a multidisciplinary sport.

nautical (adj)
Relating to sailing or other forms of water travel, such as kayaking and surfing.

offense (n)
An attacking team; attacking or trying to score a goal.

routine (n)
A planned series of movements that are always performed the same way, such as a gymnastic routine.

stamina (n)
The ability to perform actions that involve a lot of physical or mental effort for a long period of time.

synchronized (adj)
Performed, often to music, by two or more athletes at the same time, such as synchronized swimming.

synthetic (adj)
Manufactured by a chemical process using manufactured rather than natural materials; a product made to imitate a natural material, such as synthetic rubber.

tactic (n)
An action or series of actions planned by the athlete to gain an advantage. In boxing, for example, tiring out the opponent by evading his punches is a tactic.

technique (n)
The combination of skills used by an athlete to perform a particular sport.

Key to abbreviations

(n) = noun
(v) = verb
(adj) = adjective

Index

bold = main entry

1,500 meter	22, 34
10,000 meter	22
100 meter	20
200 meter	21, 34
4 x 100 meter relay	23
4 x 400 meter relay	23
400 meter	21, 34
5,000 meter	22
800 meter	22, 34

A

accuracy sports, precision and	95
acro (freestyle skiing)	122
aerials (freestyle skiing)	124
aerodynamics	37
alpine skiing	118
America's Cup	84
aquatic sports	57
Ali, Muhammad	15
archery	96
artistic gymnastics	48
Australian Open	171
Australian-rules football	148
automobile racing	206
axel	110

B

backstroke	60
badminton	174
balance beam	51
ball sports	131
Barracuda	64
Baryshnikov technique	27
baseball	132
basketball	152
beach volleyball	168
bicycle motocross	40
biking, mountain	44
Blair, Bonnie	15
bmx	40
bobsledding	117
bowling	98
boxing	196
boxing, Olympic	197
boxing, professional	197
breaststroke	61
British Open	100
butterfly	61

C

canoeing	78
canter	86
CART	212
catamaran	83
Championship Auto Racing Teams	212
circuit race (road racing)	36
classic race (road racing)	36
collection	88
Comaneci, Nadia	15, 49
combat sports	181
combined eventing	92
compass	220
coxswain	76
crawl	60

cricket	140
cross-country	33
cross-country (mountain biking)	44
cross-country (skiing)	127
curling	97
cycling	35, 218

D

Dakar	216
Daytona 500	207
decathlon	34
Diamidov	52
dirt competition (bmx)	41
discus	25, 34
dislocation	53
diving	68
double mini-trampoline	56
downhill (alpine skiing)	120
downhill (mountain biking)	46
dressage	88
Dunhill World Cup	100

E

equestrian sports	85
Europe 1-star	82
eventing, combined	92

F

fencing	190, 219
FIBA	152
field hockey	142
figure skating	108
figures (waterskiing)	75
flatland (bmx)	42
flatwater racing (canoeing and kayaking)	78
flour	49, 53
football	156
football, Australian-rules	148
Formula 1	208
Formula 3000	211
free routine (synchronized swimming)	63
freestyle (cross-country skiing)	127
freestyle (sailboarding)	80
freestyle skiing	122
freestyle (swimming)	60
freestyle wrestling	193
French Open	171
front walkover	64

G

gaits (horse)	86
giant slalom (alpine skiing)	121
giant slalom (snowboarding)	130
Giro	36
Global Positioning System	82
golf	99
GPS	82
Grand Prix	208
Greco-Roman wrestling	193
gymnastics	47
gymnastics, artistic	48
gymnastics, rhythmic	54

H

half pipe (bmx)	42
half pipe (in-line skating)	203
half-pipe (skateboarding)	200
half-pipe (snowboarding)	129
hammer	25
handball	149
handball, team	150
Harlem Globetrotters	155
Heian Godan (karate)	184
heptathlon	34
high jump	28, 34
hiking out	84
hockey	104
hockey, field	142
hockey, roller	204
horizontal bar	53
horse	86
hurdles	24, 34

I

ice and snow sports	103
ice-dancing	109
Indianapolis 500	212
Indy Car Racing	212
Indy Racing League	212
in-line roller hockey	204
in-line skating	202
International America's Cup Class	84
International Basketball Federation	152
International Rugby Board	160
inverted cross	52
IOC	14
ippon	186
IRB	160
IRL	212

J

javelin	26, 34
jibe	81
Jordan, Michael	15
judo	185
judogi	186
jump, high	28
jump, long	30
jump, triple	30
jumping	90
jumping, ski	126
jumping (waterskiing)	75

K

karate	182
kata demonstrations	182
kayaking	78
koka	186
kyoruki	189

L

lacrosse	138
Lewis, Carl	15
long jump	30, 34
long-distance (sailboarding)	80

long-track (speed skating) 114
luge **116**
lutz 110

M

Madison race (track racing) 38
marathon **32**
match sprint (track racing) 39
McGill, Mike 129
McTwist 129
medley (swimming) 62
mini-trampoline, double 56
moguls (freestyle skiing) 123
monohull 83
motocross 215
motor sports 205
motorcycling **214**
mountain biking **44**
multi sports 217

N

NASCAR 207
National Association for Stock
  Car Auto Racing 207
National Basketball Association 152
nautical sports 71
NBA 152
netball **164**

O

O'Brien technique 27
ocean races (sailing) 82
ocean surfing **72**
off-road rally 216
Olympic boxing 197
Olympic course (sailboarding) 80
Olympic course (sailing) 82
Olympic Games 14
Olympic sprint (track racing) 38
orienteering **220**

P

parallel bars 52
passage 89
peloton 37
pentathlon **219**
piaffe 89
pit stop 210
pitches, (baseball) 135
platform 65
pole vault **29**, 34
polo **93**
pommel horse 53
precision and accuracy sports 95
professional boxing 197
pursuit (track racing) 38

R

racewalking **31**
racing, automobile 206
racing, road 36
racing, track 38
racquetball **180**
rally 216

rallying **216**
regattas (sailing) 82
relay (swimming) 62
relay, 4 x 100 meter 23
relay, 4 x 400 meter 23
relays **23**
rhythmic gymnastics **54**
riding 219
rings 52
road racing **36**
roller hockey **204**
rollerblading 202
routine (artistic gymnastics) 49
routine (synchronized
  swimming) 63
rowing **76**
Rufolva 51
rugby **160**
Rugby Union 160
Rugby World Cup 161
running 218, 219
RWC 161
Ryder Cup 100

S

sailboarding **80**
sailing **82**
salto 49
Schuschunova 49
schuss 120
shiai 182
shooting 219
short-track (speed skating) 112
shot put **27**, 34
Six Nations Tournament 161
skateboarding **200**
skating, figure 108
skating, speed 112
skeleton **117**
ski jumping **126**
skiing, alpine 118
skiing, freestyle 122
slalom (alpine skiing) 121
slalom (sailboarding) 80
slalom (waterskiing) 74
snow sports, ice and 103
snowboarding **128**
soccer **144**
softball **136**
Speed Grand Prix 214
speed skating **112**
speed skiing **125**
Spitz, Mark 15
spirals 111
sports on wheels 199
squash **178**
stage race (road racing) 36
steeplechase 24
stock-car racing 207
street (bmx) 43
street (in-line skating) 203
street (skateboarding) 200
super giant slalom 120
supercross 215
Super-G 120
surfing, ocean 72
swimming 58, 218, 219
synchronized swimming **63**

T

table tennis **176**
tack 87
tae kwon do **188**
tameshi wari
  demonstrations 182
Tchatchev splits 50
team handball **150**
technical routine (synchronized
  swimming) 63
tennis **170**
tennis, table 176
Thomas flair 53
time trial (road racing) 36
time trial (track racing) 39
toe loop 110
topographic map 220
Tour de France 36
Tour of Italy 36
track and field 17
track race (bmx) 41
track racing **38**
trampoline **56**
trapeze 84
triathlon **218**
trimaran 83
triple jump **30**
trot 86
Tsukahara 51

UV

U.S. Open (golf) 100
uneven parallel bars 50
US Open (tennis) 171
vault (artistic gymnastics) 50, 51
vault, pole 29
volleyball **166**
volleyball, beach 168

W

wakeboard 75
walk (horse) 86
water polo **66**
waterskiing **74**
wave (sailboarding) 80
waza-ari 186
whitewater slalom
  (canoeing and kayaking) 79
Wimbledon 171
windsurfing 80
Winston Cup series 207
WNBA 152
Women's National Basketball
  Association 152
Women's World Cup (soccer) 145
World Cup (soccer) 145
wrestling **193**
wrestling, freestyle 193
wrestling, Greco-Roman 193

XYZ

yuko 186
Yurchenko 50

Acknowledgments

Alpine Skiing
Christian Femy, Vincent Lévesque

American and Canadian Football
Jacques Dussault, Jacques Moreau

Archery
Gabriela Cosovan, Gilbert Saint-Laurent

Artistic Gymnastics
Emmanuel Jacquinot

Australian Rules Football
Bruce Parker

Badminton
Gaëtan Jean

Baseball
Marc Griffin, André Lachance

Basketball
Philippe Nasr

BMX
Michel Lecourt, Pierre Thibault,
Dylan Jagger Vanier

Bobsledding
Ermanno Gardella, Owen A. Neale,
Pascal Richard, Jean Riendeau, Sarah Storey,
Katja Waller

Bowling
Robert Langlois

Boxing
Kenneth Piché

Canoe-kayak: Flatwater Racing
Mark Granger

Canoe-kayak: Whitewater
Tim French, Jonathan Tremblay

Cross-country Skiing
Stephane Barrette

Curling
Benoit Cyr

Diving
Donald Dion, Donald Normand

Equestrian Sports
Marie-Josée Delisle, Daniel Dubé,
Marcelle L'Heureux

Fencing
Danek Nowosielski, Claudia Viereck

Field Hockey
Josette Babineau, Chantale Berridge,
Suzanne Nicholson

Figure Skating
Diane Choquet, Deanne Graham,
Professional Skating Association.

Formula 1, Formula Indy, and Formula 3000
René Fagnan

Freestyle Skiing
Luc Belhumeur

Golf
Louis Lavoie, Sylvain Leblanc

Greco-Roman and Freestyle Wrestling
Dominique Choquette

Handball
Danny Bell

Handball (Team)
Denis Dubreuil

Ice Hockey
Chris Clow, Gaétan Ménard

Judo
Patrick Vesin

Karate
Ronald Auclair, Chanh Chau Tran

Kickboxing and Full Contact
Patrick Giroux

Lacrosse
Pierre Filion

Luge
Sandy Caligiore, Birgit Valentin, Katja Waller

Marathon
Daniel Furlong, Mark Selig

Modern Pentathlon
Denise Fekete

Motorcycling
Buddy Ford, Bertrand Gahel

Mountain Biking
Michel Leblanc

Netball
Marina Leigertwood

Ocean Surfing
Maurice Muise

Orienteering
Marie-Catherine Bruno

Polo
Regan Dellazizzo, Elizabeth Hallé

Race Walking
Roger Burrows, Octavio Castellini,
François Pap

Racquetball
Josée Grand'Maitre

Rallying
Yves Barbe, Patrick Mannoury

Rhythmic Gymnastics
Daniela Arendasova

Roller Hockey
Dave Easter, Eric LaTerreur, Bernard Seguy,
Carlos Graça

Rowing
Vincent Vandamme

Rugby
Jean-Michel Rabanel

Sailboarding
Stephane Ouellet

Sailing
Suzanne Cadieux, Simon Forbes,
Meredith Gray, Jérôme Pels, Roch Pilon,
Heinz Staudt, Marc Wilson

Skateboarding
Patrick Arsenault, Jean-François Brault

Skeleton
Ryan Davenport, Mark Kaye,
Jean Riendeau

Ski Jumping
Andrew Rhéaume

Snowboarding
Jean-Louis Donaldson, Rémi Laliberté

Squash
Yvon Provençal

Soccer
André Gagnon

Softball
Gisèle Vezina

Speed Skating
Ginette Bourassa, Robert Bourassa,
Susie Gibbon, Isabelle Laferrière,
Serge Lemieux, Sean Maw, Stuart Pass,
Pierre Sammut

Swimming
Claude Warren

Synchronized Swimming
Diane Lachapelle

Table Tennis
Rodrigue Bédard, Pierre Desjardins

Tae Kwon Do
Michel Jobin

Tennis
Louis Cayer, Eugene Lapierre,
Frederic Ledoux

Track and Field
Louis Brault, Linda Coupal,
Serge Jeudy, Daniel Mercier,
Michel Portmann, Serge Thibodeau

Track Cycling and Road Racing
Louis Barbeau

Trampoline
Alain Duchesne

Triathlon
Roger Perreault

Volleyball
Alain D'Amboise

Water Polo
Paul-David Bernard

Water Skiing
Francis Millaire, Philippe-André Tellier

Photo credits